Internationalizing the
History of Psychology

Internationalizing the History of Psychology

EDITED BY

Adrian C. Brock

New York University Press

NEW YORK AND LONDON

NEW YORK UNIVERSITY PRESS
New York and London
www.nyupress.org

Library of Congress Cataloging-in-Publication Data
Internationalizing the history of psychology / [edited by] Adrian C. Brock.
        p.   cm.
Includes bibliographical references and index.
ISBN-13: 978-0-8147-9944-4 (cloth : alk. paper)
ISBN-10: 0-8147-9944-2 (cloth : alk. paper)
1. Psychology—History.   I. Brock, Adrian C.
            BF81.I575   2006
    150.9—dc22   2006008219

New York University Press books are printed on acid-free paper,
and their binding materials are chosen for strength and durability.

Manufactured in the United States of America

10 9 8 7 6 5 4 3 2 1

Contents

Acknowledgments

I thank my former Ph.D. supervisor, Kurt Danziger, for encouraging my interest in international affairs when I was a graduate student in the history and theory psychology program at York University in Toronto, Canada. Although he is not credited as an editor of this book, he was always on hand to offer advice. I thank the various authors for their stimulating contributions. Thanks are also due to Jennifer Hammer of New York University Press for the professionalism with which she supervised the work.

Introduction

Adrian C. Brock

Difference between U.S. History and World History

The title of this section is meant to be tongue in cheek, but it does have a serious purpose. Many psychologists acquire their knowledge of the history of psychology from one or more of the glossy American textbooks on the subject. This is especially true of the vast majority of psychologists who do not go on to become specialists in the area. The textbooks not only are read and studied by Americans but also are widely used in other English-speaking countries, such as Canada, Ireland, the United Kingdom, South Africa, and Australia. The works are also very often translated into other languages, such as Spanish, for use in non-English-speaking countries. The ramifications of this topic, therefore, go well beyond the United States.

The reason American textbooks are so widely used is due partly to the sheer size of the population of the United States and partly to the sheer size of its psychology "industry." Another factor may be that history of psychology is widely taught in the United States, whereas it is not a priority in many other countries. For example, the university in Manchester, England, where I did my undergraduate degree, offered only a brief sketch of the history of psychology, which was provided as part of an introduction to the subject in the first year. The same was true of the university in Dublin, Ireland, where I currently teach, until I arrived. All these factors taken together mean the potential market for history of psychology textbooks in other countries is so small that it is not economically viable to produce their own. American textbooks tend to be used instead.

What kind of a view of the history of psychology can be found in these texts? There is certainly a great deal on the history of psychology in the

United States, as one might expect. That can be expected not only because the textbooks are American but also because American psychology has been influential throughout the world. We therefore find accounts of American "pioneers" like William James, G. Stanley Hall, and James McKeen Cattell. We also find accounts of behaviorists like John B. Watson and B. F. Skinner, as well as humanistic psychologists like Carl Rogers and Abraham Maslow. Even the approaches to psychology that European refugees brought to the United States, mainly psychoanalysis and Gestalt psychology, are given their due.

Some of the Europeans whose early work shaped the course of psychology are covered as well. Thus we have, for example, accounts of the work of Gustav Fechner and Wilhelm Wundt in Germany; the work of Charles Darwin and Francis Galton in England; and the work of Jean-Martin Charcot and Alfred Binet in France. Even the work of Ivan Pavlov in Russia is covered. It may look as if the history of psychology is already a very international field. Why, then, would anyone suggest that it is in need of internationalization?

If we scratch the surface of this comfortable picture, all is not what it seems. The European figures in these textbooks all have one thing in common: their work had an influence in the United States. Thus Wundt is included because he had American students, and some of the Gestalt psychologists are included because they emigrated to the United States. However, figures such as Felix Krüger and Willy Hellpach, who were important in the German context but who had no American connections, are not. Krüger was a former of student of Wundt who eventually became Wundt's successor at Leipzig University in 1917. He was one of the most important psychologists in Germany between the wars. Hellpach was a central figure in the establishment of social and cross-cultural psychology in Germany and even stood as a presidential candidate in the elections of that country in 1925. Neither is typically mentioned in the American texts.[1]

Another example is Karl Bühler, who was the head of the Vienna Psychological Institute between the wars and one of the most important psychologists of the time. He was so important that when William McDougall left Harvard University to take up a position at Duke University in 1927, Bühler was offered his chair. He decided to turn the offer down. It was an unfortunate decision, for when Bühler eventually came to the United States as a refugee from the Nazis at the end of the 1930s, he had little success. He was unable to obtain a permanent position at a major American university and died in relative obscurity in Los Angeles in 1963 (Brock,

1994). Because he had little success in the United States, Bühler is rarely, if ever, mentioned in American texts.

This selectivity even operates with the different aspects of a psychologist's work. Thus Kurt Lewin's work in the United States is well known, but his work in Germany prior to his emigration is not (Danziger, 1990).

There is nothing unique about German psychologists in this regard. For example, only two British psychologists have ever had the distinction of being knighted: Sir Frederic Bartlett and Sir Cyril Burt. Neither is typically mentioned in the American texts.

This brings us to the first rule of inclusion/exclusion in the history of psychology:

> Rule #1: If your work did not have a major impact on American psychology, however influential it might have been elsewhere, it does not count.

One could argue in response to this assertion that the most important people in the history of psychology are those whose work had an international impact and that this impact would have been felt in the United States.

There are several problems with this argument, but one of them is that the same situation does not apply in reverse; namely, the American psychologists who are included in these histories did not always have a major impact overseas. Referring to recent attempts to write the history of psychology from a European perspective, Danziger writes:

> Major themes in the American context, like behaviorism, are relegated to minor footnotes, and other themes, unknown to American psychologists, become highly significant. Important developments for American psychology, like the cognitive revolution, turn out to be non-events from a European perspective, because of the existence of a local cognitivist tradition that never managed to cross the Atlantic. (1994, pp. 476–477)

Many American psychologists assume that behaviorism was equally influential throughout the world and thus speak of a "cognitive revolution" in the 1960s. This will only work if one's horizons extend no further than the United States because behaviorism had a very limited impact overseas. European psychologists like Piaget, Vygotsky, Bartlett, and the Gestalt psychologists did not abandon the study of "mind." This difference explains why the work of Piaget and Vygotsky from the 1920s and 1930s was belatedly "discovered" by American psychologists in the 1960s after the influence of behaviorism began to wane. Similarly, attempts were made to export humanistic psychology to other countries but with equally limited success.

This brings us the second rule of inclusion/exclusion in the history of psychology:

> Rule #2: If your work had a major impact on American psychology, even though its influence was limited or nonexistent elsewhere, it is an important part of the history of psychology.

All this is leading in one direction: the content of these textbooks is not the history of psychology at all. It is the history of American psychology. European psychologists are included if, and only if, they had an influence in the United States. This is why there is a preponderance of European figures, like Wundt and Freud, in the early part of the history of psychology when American psychology was relatively undeveloped. It is impossible to write a history of American psychology without reference to them. This is not the case once American psychology has become established. The European psychologists who are included from later years are mainly refugees who came to the United States. These include psychoanalytic theorists, like Fromm, Horney, and Erikson, and the Gestalt psychologists.

Let me stress here that there is nothing wrong with writing a history of psychology in the United States (e.g., Popplestone and McPherson, 1999), just as there is nothing wrong with writing a history of psychology in Argentina (Rossi, 1994), India (Sinha, 1986), or the Netherlands (Dehue, 1995). That is not the issue at stake. The important point here is that no one would ever confuse the history of psychology in Argentina, India, or the Netherlands with the history of psychology as such, and yet this has happened with the history of psychology in the United States. American textbooks are usually local histories masquerading as universal histories.

This situation may go some way toward explaining the third rule of inclusion/exclusion in the history of psychology:

> Rule #3: Asia, Africa, Latin America, and Oceania do not exist.

If we accept that what is taken to be the history of psychology is actually the history of American psychology, the exclusion of these countries makes eminent sense. As previously mentioned, Europe is included in

American histories of psychology because this is where psychology first appeared in the second half of the nineteenth century and it was the leader of the field until the dawn of the twentieth century. Moreover, there were several European refugees from the 1930s who had a major impact on American psychology. It is therefore impossible to provide an adequate account of the history of American psychology without any reference to Europe.

This is not the case with Asia, Africa, Latin America, and Oceania, where psychology was less influential or developed relatively late. It is therefore quite possible to write a history of American psychology without any reference to these parts of the world. While it true that these regions have traditionally been importers, rather than exporters, of psychological knowledge, it does not mean that nothing of interest to historians of psychology happened there. This situation can become a kind of self-fulfilling prophecy. We know nothing about the history of psychology in these countries and therefore assume that there is nothing to know, or at least nothing of any significance. Having made that assumption, we will never know if the assumption is correct.

How This Situation Came About

Foreigners are often surprised at how little Americans in general know about the rest of the world. Explanations that are sometimes used include the size of the United States and the fact that it has oceans on both sides. Although it has traditionally been a country of immigrants, it has also pursued the policy of the "melting pot." Less charitable observers have resorted to terms like "arrogant." Many Americans find the latter offensive and understandably so. However, even the more charitable explanations fail to convince.

The basic problem with these explanations is that they cannot account for the historical changes that have taken place in relations between the United States and the rest of the world. This is as true of the history of American psychology as it is of American politics. It is well known that Europe was the center of psychology during the early years of its existence. This was a time when many Americans obtained German Ph.D.'s. Becoming fluent in German in order to obtain their Ph.D.'s appears to have been no hardship. Even then the United States was a big country, and it had oceans on both sides. Intercontinental travel was also more difficult than it is now. In addition to the younger Americans who studied in Europe, there were older figures, like James and Hall, who traveled to Europe to keep themselves abreast of developments there (Danziger, chapter 11 in this volume).

In the first decade of the twentieth century, American psychology grew to the point where it overshadowed European psychology in size, and it was less common for Americans to study in Europe, even before the outbreak of World War I. The United States has continued to be the most important center for psychology ever since. However, the story of historical variation does not stop there as the importance of American psychology in relation to the rest of the world has continued to vary ever since (e.g., Gielen and Pagan, 1994; Hogan, 1995; Rosenzweig, 1999).

The situation in the 1920s was like a marathon race where American psychology was in the lead, but the chasing pack was not very far behind. As marathon runners tend to do in such situations, American psychology had to constantly look over its shoulders to see what the others were doing. Hogan and Vaccaro (chapter 7 in this volume) paint a very interesting picture of American psychology in this period. American psychologists were much more familiar with foreign languages than they are today, and American journals tended to have more international editorial boards. When the International Congress of Psychology came to the United States in 1929, the American Psychological Association (APA) canceled its annual meeting so that its members could attend the International Congress instead. This is the only year in which APA has not held an annual meeting since it was founded in 1892.

This situation had changed dramatically by the end of World War II. Much of Europe lay in ruins, especially Germany, which had the strongest tradition of psychology in Europe before the war. German psychology also had to contend with the suspicion that it might in some way be connected to Nazism. At the same time, psychology had yet to be established in many countries outside Europe. American psychology reigned supreme: to use the metaphor of the marathon runner, there was now a huge gap between it and the chasing pack.

This situation did not, and could not, last forever. European psychology not only got back on its feet in the postwar years but also began to expand. For example, psychology existed in the United Kingdom only in particular places, such as Cambridge and London. Even Oxford did not have a psychology department. Most British universities began to establish psychology departments after the war. There were even European countries, such as Ireland and Spain, where psychology hardly existed. These, too, experienced significant growth, as did many countries outside Europe. The various chapters in Sexton and Hogan (1992) provide more details of this growth.

American psychology continued to grow during these years as well, but the potential for growth was obviously much less than it was in a country where psychology scarcely existed or did not exist at all. The end result is that the percentage of psychologists in the world who live and work in the United States, and the proportion of psychological research emanating from the United States, has continued to decline. The international situation in psychology is slowly moving back to the situation of the 1920s; that is, the marathon runner is still in the lead, but the chasing pack is beginning to catch up.

There has been a corresponding change in American psychology in recent years. A division for "International Psychology" (Division 52) was established within the APA in the mid-1990s, and *American Psychologist* has undertaken to devote more space to international affairs (Fowler, 1996).[2] There has also been a spate of publications on international psychology, of which the well-known book by Sexton and Hogan (1992), *International Psychology*, is but one. The present work should be seen in the context of these developments. There was probably no time in the history of psychology when American psychologists could afford to ignore developments overseas, but such ignorance is now an even riskier strategy than it once was.

The history of psychology has a unique role in this move toward "internationalization." History is often a controversial subject because our views of the present help to shape our views of the past, just as our views of the past help to shape our views of the present. Thus if we confuse the history of American psychology with the history of psychology itself, we are less likely to take an international view of the field. A more international history of psychology is, therefore, an essential basis for a more international psychology.

What Is to Be Done?

I have some sympathy for textbook authors who might have read my critique. So the history of psychology is really the history of American psychology. Do we now start producing textbooks of 5,000 instead of 500 pages in order to put this situation right? That is clearly no solution. It may also be difficult to decide which aspects of the history of American psychology should be left out in order to make way for a more international history. A further problem involves identifying the information that has been left out. It is not as if everyone knows what this information is and has deliberately decided to omit it. The information is simply not known, and it will take a great deal of original research before it becomes known. Whether or not this research is likely to be done is discussed below.

For the moment, I focus on the pedagogical aspects of the situation. The history of psychology is very unusual as far as specialities within psychology go. It is unusual in that the pedagogical aspects of the subject dwarf original research in size. Indeed, history of psychology existed as a pedgagogical branch of psychology long before it occurred to anyone to do any original research (Brock, 1998).

The basis of my own solution to these problems can be found at the start of Kurt Danziger's chapter in this book. Danziger points out that history is inevitably selective. One human life is not long enough to cover everything that has happened in the history of psychology, let alone one university course or one text. Selections must inevitably be made, even if we are not aware of the selection or the criteria that have been used. The best we can hope for is to be aware that selection occurs and to make our selections wisely.

I was made aware of this problem at the start of my career, and so I have never made an attempt to be comprehensive in my courses. Currently, I teach two history of psychology courses. One is to the first-year undergraduates who have come straight from high school and, in most cases, have no prior knowledge of psychology. Here I give them some intellectual biographies, using Fancher's *Pioneers of Psychology* and similar work (Fancher, 1996). I am more than happy if they come away from the course with some knowledge of who people like Pavlov, Skinner, and Piaget were and what they did. Note that there is no attempt at comprehensiveness here. Selections have been made and not only in relation to the figures who are covered. The decision to build the course around intellectual biographies involves selection of a kind since this is only one way of organizing historical information. This point is often forgotten by American historians of psychology whose work tends to be focused on individuals. I do it at this level only because it makes the material easier for the students to understand.

Perhaps more interesting is the final year undergraduate course that I teach. Here I do not use any pedagogical literature at all. The students are usually ready for "grown-up" literature at this stage. I therefore choose a selection of books on the history of psychology that I regard as some of the best contemporary literature in the field, and we study these books in depth. Here there is no attempt at comprehensiveness whatsoever. I would rather expose my students to the ideas of writers like Danziger (1997), Hacking (1995), and Rose (1999) than fill them with useless "facts." I am sure that the students prefer this situation as well.

International Research

Much of the literature on international psychology consists of descriptive accounts of psychology in a particular country (e.g., Gilgen and Gilgen, 1987; Sexton and Hogan, 1992). Such works have their uses, but they are hardly representative of what historians of psychology do. Perhaps the subtitle of the present work should have been "against comprehensiveness," because no attempt at comprehensiveness was made in this work, either. I did try to make sure that there was at least some work on Asia, some work on Africa, and some work on Latin America, but that was with a view to diversity rather than comprehensiveness. These chapters are simply examples of the kind of historical work that can be written from an international perspective. This point has to be stressed because there is so much literature of the "encyclopedic" kind that some people cannot conceive of any other kind.

The general pattern in this "encyclopedic" work is to have each chapter devoted to a particular country and to get someone in that country to write the chapter. Similarly, most historians of psychology write about the history of psychology in their own countries. The programs of APA's Division 26 (History of Psychology) and Cheiron (International Society of Behavioral and Social Sciences) contain a very high percentage of papers on the history of psychology in the United States. The same is true of North American journals like *History of Psychology* and *Journal of the History of the Behavioral Sciences*. I should add here that there is no conspiracy to prevent international research from being presented at conferences or published. I have always had a positive response when I have approached conference program chairs or journal editors with suggestions for work of this kind. However, no program chair or journal editor can include international work if no such work is received.

Europeans are no different in this regard. The European equivalent of Cheiron, ESHHS (European Society for the History of the Human Sciences) generally has papers on the history of psychology in Europe on its program, usually papers on the European country that the speaker comes from. Some of the authors in this book have also written about their own countries. The main difference here is that the countries in question (e.g., Argentina, India, South Africa, and Turkey) are very different from the countries that are usually discussed.

People may want to write on psychology in their own countries for a variety of reasons. They may feel that they know more about their own country than anywhere else. They may be interested in using archival material and need to be close to particular archives in order to do that. They may also have political agendas, such as trying to encourage their colleagues to adopt a more indigenous approach. However, I suspect that, in at least some cases, it is due to a lack of imagination.

There is no reason anyone should be confined to doing research on their own country. I am British, and I have never done any work on British psychology in my life. My early work was on the history of psychology in Germany and Austria (e.g., Brock, 1991; 1992; 1994), and I am currently interested in the history of psychology in Cuba (Brock, chapter 8 in this volume). That may be unusual, but it is far from unique. Christiane Hartnack, for example, has done research on psychoanalysis in India (Hartnack, 2001), while one of the contributors to this book, Geoffrey Blowers, is a specialist on the history of psychology in China (Blowers, 2001; chapter 5 in this volume). Why not? As long as one has the necessary linguistic skills and can cover any travel expenses, there is no reason why the work should be inferior to that of a native. Indeed, bringing the perspective of an "outsider" to the situation may be an advantage in itself (Shapin and Schaffer, 1986).

This point is particularly important because there are few specialists on the history of psychology outside Western Europe and the United States. It is not even a priority in these relatively wealthy parts of the world. It is less of a priority in countries with more pressing social concerns. Thus, as long as we continue with this assumption that people can only write about their own countries, we will continue to have a history of psychology that is mainly focused on Western Europe and the United States.

Another way in which this book differs from the more encyclopedic accounts is that the chapters are not specifically focused on countries but on theories of psychology that have broader applicability. Thus Johann

Louw (chapter 1 in this volume) contrasts his own work with work on "psychology in country x," even though his chapter focuses on South Africa. What is the distinction that is being made? Louw's chapter is not really about South Africa. It is about the phenomenon of "psychologization." He discusses a thesis that was originally made in relation to Western Europe and North America and shows how it can be applied to the South African context. Similarly, my own chapter is not really about the history of psychology in Cuba. It is about an influential thesis that psychology and liberal democracy are particularly compatible, and I use evidence drawn from the Cuban context to suggest that there is no basis to this view. Thus the chapters in this book are not merely descriptive accounts of psychology around the world. They use evidence drawn from unusual contexts in order to draw conclusions about psychology in general.

A genuinely international history of psychology will place a great deal of emphasis on comparison since it is only through comparison that we can hope to find out what psychology in different countries has in common and what makes it unique. Although there are no explicitly comparative studies in this volume, an examination of psychology outside its traditional heartland of Western Europe and North America inevitably involves comparison with those places. It is very similar to anthropological work. Thus the classic studies in anthropology, such as Bronislaw Malinowski's work on the sexual lives of the Trobriand Islanders and Margaret Mead's work on coming of age in Samoa, were only partly about the societies they described (Malinowski, 1932; Mead, 1943). The results were also thought to have implications for the societies from which the anthropologists came. Similarly, the more recent work of Catherine Lutz on the emotions of Pacific islanders has implications for our own view of the emotions and their presumed universality (Lutz, 1988).

There is no reason why an international history should be focused on specific countries at all. Thus Irmingard Staeuble (chapter 10 in this volume) discusses the rise of international organizations like the International Union of Psychological Science. Danziger (chapter 11 in this volume) and Fathali Mogahddam and Naomi Lee (chapter 9 in this volume) are similarly concerned with relations between countries rather than solely with the countries themselves. It is this focus on international relations that makes their work genuinely international. Work on "psychology in country x" is by definition national, not international. We should be wary of replacing one kind of parochialism with another.

All of the above means that it would be inadequate to attempt to justify the internationalization of the history of psychology on purely empiricist grounds: that is, in terms of "inclusion" or righting the wrongs of the past. An international history of psychology can offer much more than this. It can help to shed new light on existing topics of interest, such as the spread of "psychologization," the politics of psychology, the importance of the social context, and what the proper subject of the history of psychology should be (Richards, 1987; Smith, 1988). Perhaps even more importantly, it can raise new issues that are of little relevance to Western Europe and North America and are consequently not major topics of interest at the present time. These issues include cultural imperialism, psychology and the project of modernity, and the relationship between indigenization and universalism in psychology (Danziger, 1994). More will be said about these matters in the postscript to the book. For the moment, I would like to explain how the various decisions were made.

Approach of This Book

The demographics of the contributors are interesting. Only four of the contributors (Ardila, Blowers, Gulerce, and Louw) live outside Western Europe and North America. However, another four contributors are residents of North America but are originally from Asia, Africa, or Latin America (Danziger, Moghaddam, Paranjpe, and Taiana). This point is particularly interesting because it is much more difficult to ignore people when they are on the "inside" than when they are on the "outside." As Western societies, and their psychology, become more multicultural, these kind of issues are more likely to come to the fore.

Last but hopefully not least, these authors are supplemented by five contributors (Brock, Hogan, Lee, Staeuble, and Vaccaro) whose roots are firmly in Western Europe or North America but who, for idiosyncratic reasons of their own, have become interested in international affairs. In my own case, I have lived in nine countries on four different continents and traveled in over seventy others. If that does not lead to an international outlook, then nothing will.

While I am happy to acknowledge that a person's background will influence their views, I was less interested in the background of the contributors than the quality of the work that they were likely to produce. It was important to me that the contributors were acknowledged specialists in history or theory of psychology, and that their work in these areas was well known in either Western Europe or North America, or both. This meant that historians of psychology in these parts of the world would be much more likely to take their work seriously.

The contributors were not asked to conform to any preexisting model. Once potential authors had been identified, they were allowed to write on any topic they wanted, as long as it was compatible with the aims of the book. If the authors had been asked to conform to a preexisting model, such as having one chapter per country that was written by an author in that country, as one anonymous reviewer of the proposal wanted me to do, a great deal of creativity would have been lost. Fortunately, the psychology editor at New York University Press, Jennifer Hammer, understood my objections to that suggestion, and I am grateful to her for her support.

Perhaps I should conclude by reminding the reader once again that there is no attempt at comprehensiveness here. No one book can provide a comprehensive account of the history of psychology. There are some books that pretend to do this, but selectivity of some kind always occurs, even if the selectivity and the logic behind the selection are not consciously recognized or known. It will take a lot more than one book on the history of psychology to overturn the parochialism that currently exists. In concluding this introduction, I am reminded of Winston Churchill's famous words: "This is not the end. It is not even the beginning of the end. But it is, perhaps, the end of the beginning."[3]

NOTES

1. Information about these figures can be found on the Internet.

2. This editorial was the preface to a special issue devoted to international affairs (e.g., Mays et al., 1996).

3. Speech given at the Lord Mayor's Luncheon, London, November 10, 1942. (See http://www.winstonchurchill.org, retrieved February 24, 2006.)

REFERENCES

Blowers, G. (2001). To be a big shot or be shot: Zing-Yang Kuo's other career. *History of Psychology*, 4, 367–387.

Brock, A. (1991). Was macht den psychologischen Expertenstatus aus? Eine Auseinandersetzung zwischen Wundt und Stumpf [What is psychological expertise?

A controversy between Wundt and Stumpf]. *Psychologie und Geschichte*, 2, 109–114.

Brock, A. (1992). Was Wundt a "Nazi"? Völkerpsychologie, racism and anti-Semitism. *Theory and Psychology*, 2, 205–223.

Brock, A. (1994). Whatever happened to Karl Bühler? *Canadian Psychology*, 35, 319–329.

Brock, A. (1998). Pedagogy and research. *Psychologist*, 11, 169–171.

Danziger, K. (1990). *Constructing the subject: Historical origins of psychological research*. New York: Cambridge University Press.

Danziger, K. (1994). Does the history of psychology have a future? *Theory and Psychology*, 4, 467–484.

Danziger, K. (1997). *Naming the mind: How psychology found its language*. London: Sage.

Dehue, T. (1995). *Changing the rules: Psychology in the Netherlands, 1900–1985*. New York: Cambridge University Press.

Fancher, R. (1996). *Pioneers of psychology* (3rd ed.). New York: Norton.

Fowler, R. D. (1996). 1996 Editorial: 50th Anniversary Issue of *American Psychologist*. *American Psychologist*, 51(1), 5–7.

Gielen, U. P., and Pagan, M. (1994). International psychology and American mainstream psychology. *International Psychologist*, 34(1), 15–19 and 34(2), 5.

Gilgen, A. R., and Gilgen, C. K. (Eds.) (1987). *International handbook of psychology*. New York: Greenwood.

Hacking, I. (1995). *Rewriting the soul: Multiple personality and the sciences of memory*. Princeton: Princeton University Press.

Hartnack, C. (1991). *Psychoanalysis in colonial India*. New Delhi: Oxford University Press.

Hogan, J. D. (1995). International psychology in the next century: Comment and speculation from a U.S. perspective. *World Psychology*, 1, 9–25.

Lutz, C. (1988). *Unnatural emotions*. Chicago: University of Chicago Press.

Malinowski, B. (1932). *The sexual life of savages on North-Western Melanesia* (3rd ed.). London: Routledge and Kegan Paul.

Mays, V. M., Rubin, J., Sabourin, M., and Walker, L. (1996). Moving toward a global psychology: Changing theories and practice to meet the needs of a changing world. *American Psychologist*, 51, 485–487.

Mead, M. (1943). *Coming of age in Samoa*. Harmondsworth: Penguin.

Popplestone, J. A., and McPherson, M. W. (1999). *An illustrated history of American psychology*. Akron, Ohio: University of Akron Press.

Richards, G. (1987). Of what is history of psychology a history? *British Journal for the History of Science*, 20, 201–211.

Rose, N. (1999). *Governing the soul: The shaping of the private self* (2nd ed.). London: Routledge.

Rosenzweig, M. (1999). Continuity and change in the development of psychology around the world. *American Psychologist,* 54, 252–259.

Rossi, L. (1994). *La psicología en Argentina: Capítulos olvidados de una historia reciente* [Psychology in Argentina: Forgotten chapters of a recent history]. Buenos Aires: Teckne.

Sexton, V. S., and Hogan, J. D. (Eds.) (1992). *International psychology: Views from around the world.* Lincoln: University of Nebraska Press.

Shapin, S., and Schaffer, S. (1986). *Leviathan and the air pump: Hobbes, Boyle and the experimental life.* Princeton: Princeton University Press.

Sinha, D. (1986). *Psychology in a third world country: The Indian experience.* New Delhi: Sage.

Smith, R. (1988). Does the history of psychology have a subject? *History of the Human Sciences,* 1, 147–177.

Chapter 1

Constructing Subjectivity in Unexpected Places

Johann Louw

I started my academic career twenty-five years ago, in a new, small university in a remote area of South Africa. I had just completed a postgraduate degree in the Netherlands, and I was overwhelmed with a feeling of isolation and being far away from it all—in more than one sense. Over the years parts of this sense of being stuck far from the center remained; after all, I lived not only on the southern tip of Africa, but it was also apartheid South Africa. It surely felt like a huge drawback to be a psychologist-academic so far from what I perceived (together with most psychologists in the world) as "the center": Europe and North America.

But fifteen years or so ago I lost that sense of being on the periphery of things in at least one regard: in my academic life as a psychologist. As I grew older, and as different things in Psychology[1] started to interest me, I came to realize that, even if it were true, this was a strength, rather than a drawback.

What brought about this change in perception; that to live and work in Africa as a psychologist might, in fact, be an advantage rather than a handicap? In short, it came about through my interest in the history of psychology. During the 1980s I continued my studies toward a Ph.D. in the Netherlands, focusing on aspects of the history of South African psychology. Gradually I came to realize that the study of psychology itself is one of the most rewarding and enlightening things a psychologist can do. In particular, it was the relationship between the discipline, its subject matter, and the social reality beyond the discipline, which struck me as a fundamental aspect of the discipline and its relation to the kinds of person we have become.

I arrived at an interest in these matters via the history of Psychology. It was not history per se that interested me; it was what could be done with history as a way of making sense of the discipline, its subject matter, and its social foundations. It was only later that I realized what I was interested in was a history of the present, in Michel Foucault's (1975) terminology. Or, as Roger Smith wrote in a well-known paper, a "'present-centred' history in the sense that it constructs a past in order to expose the conditions making possible our present, a present which otherwise appears as a given or 'natural' reality" (1988, p. 150).

When Psychology emerged as an independent discipline in Western Europe (and the United States) in the second half of the nineteenth century, it did so against the backdrop of social and cultural processes that have been in place for centuries (Jansz 2004 provides a good summary of these processes). In these societies, human beings increasingly saw themselves as autonomous individuals with a unique internal mental state. Psychology's emergence as a discipline intersected with a certain kind of subjectivity, already in place by the second half of the nineteenth century. Indeed, it could be argued that these were the "conditions of possibility" for Psychology—that it could come into existence because of receptivity for subjective, individual states in these societies.

The historical development of these kinds of subject of course preceded the emergence of academic and professional Psychology, and the discipline can claim no real contribution to this process. However, the situation changed quite dramatically in the twentieth century. The historical expansion of Psychology in Western Europe and the United States, especially after World War II, had an impact on society, as expressed in the increasing numbers of university departments, students, fields of practice, professionals, et cetera. But Psychology achieved more than simply an extension of its academic and professional numbers, along with its field of expertise. During the twentieth century, it became a powerful part of the cultural and historical processes that we characterized as individualization and the development of inwardness. It contributed in a major way to the formation of the "psychological subject," in which individual human beings interpret themselves and others as having a unique subjective, internal mental state, with important truths about ourselves contained in the structures or forms of the interior world.

Through the work of historians like Kurt Danziger, Graham Richards, Nikolas Rose, Ian Hacking, and others, we know how Psychology's practices, vocabulary, techniques, and knowledge are thoroughly implicated in the formation of new kinds of persons, of different "subjects." Indeed, the "turn inward" intensified once Psychology emerged and flourished in the twentieth century. Roger Smith portrayed the pervasive construction of the psychological subject, as "the internalization of belief in psychological knowledge, so that it acquired a taken-for-granted quality, altered everyone's subjective world and recreated experience and expectations about what it is to be a person" (1997, 575).

It is this literature, and approach to subjectification, that I believe have much to offer to the discussion about internationalizing the history of Psychology. When the discipline migrates to countries outside its historical heartland, countries that do not share the cultural and historical processes mentioned above, a lack of fit between the discipline and its sociohistorical context is introduced. As a result, the discipline is often criticized in terms of a lack of responsiveness to different cultures or for its cultural one-sidedness. These critiques are often phrased in terms of "Eurocentric" (e.g., Bulhan 1985; Howitt and Owusu-Bempah 1994), "Westocentric" (Holdstock 2000), "individuocentrism" (Holdstock 2000), "irrelevance" (Berger and Lazarus 1987), and "ethnocentrism" (e.g., Marsella 1998). Various remedies are then suggested to rectify the situation, framed as the opposite of these terms: the discipline must be made more practically relevant, community-orientated, socially responsive, Afrocentric, and so on.

But this debate misses the historical processes involved when Psychological knowledge is employed to achieve positive goals in virtually all countries where Psychological expertise is valued. Although these processes often operate on a large scale, and affect many people, they often go unnoticed—maybe because they are so much part of our everyday lives. I would argue that they provide a line of inquiry that is particularly fruitful if we want to understand what happens to Psychology in societies outside the heartland of the discipline, when psychological practices and techniques are employed at different sites and in a variety of institutions. Nikolas Rose (1990) has shown, for European and American Psychology, how subjects are created through the micropowers of the clinical interview, the psychological test, and the epidemiological survey, in institutions like the school classroom, the military parade ground, the factory, and the mental hospital. It is on such a microlevel that the individual gets in touch with subjectifying practices, or, as Rose put it: "The subject is less the outcome of cultural history than of a history of what Foucault terms 'techniques of the self'" (2000, 152).

Although the focus in the chapter is on microprocesses, there is a larger background against which they play themselves out. Rose's starting point is the link between liberal societies and psychology: "The history of psychology in liberal societies joins up with the history of liberal government" (Rose 1996b, 12). In liberal democracies citizens are defined as individuals with rights and freedoms, and the values of individuality, freedom, and choice are greatly emphasized. Thus a powerful individualizing force already exists at a constitutional level—in post-apartheid South Africa, for example, chapter 2 of the Constitution contains a Bill of Rights, which states: "This Bill of Rights is a cornerstone of democracy in South Africa. It enshrines the rights of all people in our country and affirms the democratic values of human dignity, equality and freedom" (quoted from the 1996 South African Constitution, to be found at http://www.gov.za/constitution/1996). In the regulation (or government) of social and economic life, the rights of free and equal citizens must be protected, while positive objectives such as health promotion, disease prevention, and labor productivity have to be pursued. Rose (1990; 1996b) has argued that Psychology is attractive to all modern (or modernizing) societies, as a result of its promise to achieve socially desirable objectives through the disciplining of human differences, among other things.

In the rest of the chapter I examine two institutions (or sites) in contemporary South Africa, where techniques and practices of a liberal democracy are employed that invite citizens to be certain kinds of people. I believe these are particularly useful in investigating how the psychological subject is constructed in "nonpsychologized" communities. South Africa shares with other developing countries what Fathali Moghaddam (1993) referred to as a "dualism" in society. It consists of a modern industrial sector overlaid by the traditional society of a "Third World country," with fundamental cultural rifts between the two sectors. Although the modern/traditional is not as sharply drawn as might be suggested here, Psychology is of course much closer to the modern than to the traditional sector, I show that there are subjectifying factors at work in both sites that bring members of the traditional sector much closer to Psychology than one would expect, and that they do so almost imperceptibly. These are the recently completed hearings of the Truth and Reconciliation Commission and an HIV/AIDS prevention program.

Commission Hearings

A major objective of the Truth and Reconciliation Commission (TRC) was to restore "the human and civil dignity of such victims by granting them an opportunity to relate their own accounts of the violations of which they are the victims" (Promotion of National Unity and Reconciliation Act, No. 34 of 1995; see http://www.polity.org.za). Its Human Rights Violations Committee encouraged (for example, by means of radio and newspaper advertisements and posters) victims of such violations to approach the TRC to relate what happened to them. The victims' accounting of events became known as "telling their stories" and was the key mechanism in the hearings on human rights abuses. Fiona Ross (2003) drew on earlier work to portray story-telling as the capacity to narrate life events, as it relates to the self, to a wider audience.[2]

An intriguing part of this for the purposes of this chapter is that story-telling was constituted as an authentically African mode of communication (Ross, 2003). In the words of Archbishop Tutu:

> Storytelling is central, not only to many religious practices in this country but also to the African tradition of which we are a part. Ellen Kuzwayo is quoted . . . as saying: "Africa is a place of storytelling. We need more stories, never mind how painful the exercise may be. . . . Stories help us to understand, to forgive and to see things through someone else's eyes." (Tutu 1996, 7)

There is a substantial international literature that reflects the belief that testimony heals (Agger and Jensen 1990, for example). This belief was translated quite directly in the practices of story-telling of the TRC. Commissioners frequently spoke of the healing powers of story-telling—more attractive than psychotherapy for them, because it is situated within an African cultural tradition. Although the report acknowledges that "not all storytelling heals. Not everyone wanted to tell his or her story," on the whole, the commission believed that it was beneficial to do so (TRC 1998, Vol. 5, 352; also Vol. 2, 112). Ross (2003) speaks of biomedical and psychological metaphors used by the commission to describe its work in terms of "healing."

Two illustrations from these testimonies will have to suffice to indicate that what was originally narrated here reflected a subjectivity that was quite far removed from the Western psychologized individual.

First, Ross worked with women from Zwelethemba, an African township outside Worcester, a town in the wine- and fruit-growing region of the Western Cape Province, about an hour's drive from Cape Town (and elsewhere in South Africa). It struck her that these women came to provide testimony of what had happened to their husbands and their children, and not so much about what happened to them. A commissioner had this to say: "Women are articulate about describing their men's experiences but are hesitant to talk about themselves. . . . The pain expressed has been the pain of others, not of themselves" (Ross 2000, 29).

The harm inflicted on others nevertheless changed these women, but even then they described their lives in terms of physical health changes. Ross (2000, 60) quoted unpublished research reports that indicated that women talked about psychosomatic and psychological problems they experienced. The women interviewed in Ross's study mostly reported the psychosomatic consequences of their experiences: high and low blood pressure, diabetes, stress, and dizziness. In Vol. 5, p. 141, of their report, the commission says: "There is also evidence that people exposed to trauma, even indirectly, are more likely to develop stress-related illnesses such as heart disease and high blood pressure."

Similar findings were reported in a study conducted in the same Zwelethemba Township from where Ross drew her interviewees (Skinner 1998, 184–187). These researchers were more specific in describing the medical and psychological symptoms among the 45 people they studied. They found:

- At least 22 percent reported headaches, "physical weakness," and "other body pain."
- Some 51 percent reported feeling "sad or down," and 40 percent said they cried easily. One-third of the respondents said they were unable to "feel emotions"; 33 percent also reported feelings of anxiety, fear or worry.
- About 55 percent said they tried to keep busy so that they did not think about the "trauma"—but it is not clear who uses this word.
- At least 13 percent reported drinking or taking drugs, although the majority of them said that they "seldom" did so.

Skinner's study concluded that the profile of respondents indicated the presence of post-traumatic stress disorder. But these clearly were the conclusions of the researchers; not one of the interviewees in the study used these terms, or even the term "trauma."

In addition, in many of the verbatim quotes in the report, it is clear how these African survivors of violence spoke of external events rather than an interior life (often despite invitations from the commissioners). Indeed, Ross gives evidence of how detention and arrest were experienced, and were dealt with by young people:

> Many in Zwelethemba considered contact with prison cells to be defiling. Detention was believed to expose young people to (symbolic) pollution and on their release, some young people . . . were ritually cleansed *(ukuhlanjwa)* in an attempt to remove the effects of contact with evil and to protect against a repetition of detention. Not all families subscribed to the ritual but even those who did not subscribe to notions of ritual pollution felt defiled by their contact with prison. (2000, 143)

In our terms we could say that these young people had experienced a loss of personal agency but framed it as caused by an intruding spirit and in need of a cleansing ritual. Individual agency is experienced as diminished, but framed in a very nonpsychological way.

When the work of the TRC was done, and their five-volume report handed in, these story-telling practices did not come to an end. The Institute for the Healing of Memories, for example, runs weekend workshops in an encounter group format for South Africans of all social, racial, and political affiliations based on the premise that telling one's experiences of the apartheid years can lead to a process of healing. The Cape Town–based Trauma Centre for Victims of Violence and Torture is another nongovernmental organization that offers trauma debriefing and counseling to victims of political and criminal violence. One of the groups it assists is the Khulumani (Western Cape) Support Group, a victim support and advocacy group in Cape Town. Khulumani is composed of victims of apartheid-era political violence, and they too engage with this therapeutic mode of story-telling. Trauma Centre counselors facilitate the story-telling sessions of Khulumani.

What stories do people tell at these sessions, and how do they tell them? The stories are most often about persecution at the hands of the police and the loss of loved ones, either through violence in their communities or while in police custody. Christopher Colvin (2002) states that these stories are "tight" in their construction, reduced to the essential elements needed to make the point—what happened, to whom, where, and when. There is little exploration of why these things might have happened or of what life is like in the present. The facilitators are the ones who offer some very quick comments about what might be going on psychologically with those telling or listening to these stories. Colvin says that these comments are not designed to be interpretations of stories or analyses of individual storytellers—rather, they are supposed to be general commentaries on the overall nature of psychological trauma and recovery.

Caution has to be exercised when considering the effect of the TRC as an institutionalized truth-telling exercise. This was a fairly limited exercise in terms of numbers of people reached, and the commission lasted for only a few years. Nevertheless, it dominated the South African social discourse in the time that it operated. Its hearings were broadcast live on radio and television (later reduced to weekly or daily summaries), newspapers carried daily summaries, and for those with such access, the commission had an active Website. Thus one could claim that the commission reached quite a broad audience, both nationally and internationally. The number of people testifying before the Human Rights Violations Committee was significant as well: 21,298 statements were received by December 1997, and seventy-six hearings were held in 1996 and 1997 (Ross 2003).

What can one conclude from these brief descriptions of the TRC process? First, story-telling, as practiced in the TRC hearings and in its aftermath, contains powerful possibilities for being the mechanism to bring about new subjectivities. It is identified within a traditional, African, rural experience to give it cultural legitimacy (keep in mind that the vast majority of testifiers were African). At the same time, however, the telling of one's own story, and the suggestions given by others (commissioners and counselors), smuggle in an invitation to join a different discourse. This is the discourse of telling the truth about oneself—to problematize a particular (violent) kind of experience and to consider its aftermath for one's own life. "Rendering the self into thought" (Rose 1996c, 121) forges a link between "self" and "story" and potentially produces the kind of authentic self that psychologists understand. The assumption that testimonial statements of this kind generate an authentic self is at least worthy of consideration. Ross (2003, 330) says that "the testimonial form became a means of fashioning the self in relation to changing social circumstances, a model through which people could engage in the work of considering experience, reshaping their understandings and seeking acknowledgement."

Second, telling one's story is meant to accomplish therapeutic release for the narrator. This is a particularly powerful incentive to make the practice of story-telling a psychological practice, even if it is only in its consequences. In a cultural context unacquainted with psychotherapeutic processes, Colvin (2002) argues that the monthly meetings of the post-TRC support groups have created a "therapeutic space" for people attending them. Here they learn not only a new vocabulary (of "trauma," for example) but also new possibilities for action, for expressing distress. Suffering becomes psychologized, and story-telling becomes a component of psychotherapeutic treatment. After all, therapists argue that telling stories about traumatic events is the only route to psychological repair. And the consequences are almost immediate: Colvin (2002, 1) speaks of South Africa since the TRC being "infused with an attention to trauma."

Psychological categories are culturally embedded and represent ways in which members of a particular culture make sense of human life. In testimony before the TRC, these survivors did not have these categories available, or did not make use of them much. But they were continuously being invited to join a psychotherapeutic discourse. Psychotherapeutic professionals provided the vocabularies that assisted in this re-constituting of subjectivity. For example, "symptoms related to post-traumatic stress syndrome . . . often appeared afterward" (Graybill 2002, 84) among those who testified at the TRC. Other psychological symptoms and signs included self-blame, anger, and social and interpersonal problems. Research also showed that significant numbers of survivors of human rights violations have shown high rates of substance abuse and psychiatric symptoms such as depression, post-traumatic stress, and other anxiety disorders despite their experience of testimony at the TRC (Kaminer, Stein, Mbanga, and Zungu-Dirwayi 2000).

The psychotherapeutic atmosphere of the hearings was heightened by the presence of persons appointed by the commission to brief and debrief testifiers. All the debriefers had some form of psychological training and could often be seen on the television broadcasts assisting the testifier. In addition, the services of a trained psychologist were made available to the commission and its personnel to ensure their emotional and psychological health. Even journalists were given psychological counseling to deal with "secondary traumatization."

However, at present we have no evidence, apart from these somewhat sketchy and speculative accounts, of how members of "nonpsychologized". communities reacted to the attempts to frame their problems and experiences in psychological terms. What we have are the efforts of the psy experts to conceptualize experiences in this way. But so far we have little evidence of whether people who testified understood themselves differently as human beings after the hearings. My argument is that the TRC hearings had the potential to create new kinds of subjectivity, and that there are very interesting empirical investigations to be done in this regard.

Peer Education and HIV/AIDS Prevention

The HIV/AIDS pandemic, and the way it affects developing countries, provide another example of a less obvious site for the subjectification of citizens. It is estimated that in 2003, 40 million people lived with HIV/AIDS worldwide, and that 95 percent of those lived in the developing world. Sub-Saharan Africa remains the worst affected, as an estimated 26.6 million people were living with HIV in 2003. (These figures were extracted from reports by UNAIDS and the World Health Organization; see http://www.aidsinsite.co.za). In South Africa, HIV prevalence among pregnant women receiving antenatal care was placed at 27.9 percent (Department of Health 2003).

The response to the pandemic has targeted almost every institution of South African society. Schools and universities launched special prevention programs, and sex education curricula are standard in schools. Many employers initiated workplace programs to educate workers about HIV. National and provincial governments, and nongovernmental organizations, run programs to reach those who may still fall outside the net of these preventative programs. I believe that in these all-pervasive programs, microprocesses recruit individuals as subjects to work on themselves as a strategy to prevent the spread of HIV/AIDS.

Any number of illustrations is possible here, ranging from knowledge-based programs and assertiveness training courses to LoveLife, a national HIV prevention program with a strong media component (see http://www.LoveLife.org.za).[3] Rather than focus on one of these, I have chosen an HIV prevention program that, on the face of it, is not easily characterized as an example of constructing individual subjects. The description of the program is drawn largely from Catherine Campbell (2003), who described two peer education programs in a gold-mining region near Johannesburg, one delivered to commercial sex workers and the other to school learners. It was delivered in a township that has a population of 150,000 black African people, mostly living in small formal houses, informal shacks made of corrugated iron, or mine hostels, with high levels of unemployment (40 percent). Serious concern existed about HIV/AIDS in the community, as 68 percent of sex workers in the area of interest were HIV positive. In this area, and with this population, a community-led participatory HIV-prevention program was regarded as the intervention that stood the best chance of success. The approach that informed the program was critical of seeing health-related behaviors in terms of properties of the individual, and it argued for a contextual approach that would be more collectivist in its orientation. Peer education was chosen as the delivery mechanism, as it was regarded as an approach that switches the locus of behavior change from the individual to the peer group.[4]

Although the focus is on two instances of peer education in a local context, they are not atypical of what happens in AIDS education. Indeed, peer education is commonly used as a strategy of HIV prevention worldwide (UNAIDS 1999). It is based on the assumption that health messages have greater credibility if they come from someone who is similar to the receiver in terms of age, gender, ethnicity, and other characteristics. At one level, peer education is informational in nature, and its activities are designed to raise awareness or increase knowledge in recipients. At another level, however, it is much more than this; it is also about oneself. Jeffrey Kelly (2004, 144) captured the general expectation that these are "messages that directly target and are meant to influence the norms, attitudes, perceived personal risk, behaviour change intentions, and self-efficacy of others." In other words, peer education (or peer support, as some prefer to call such interventions) is about changing psychological factors like perceptions about norms of one's sexual partner, attitudes, behavior intentions, perceived personal risk, self-efficacy perceptions, skills to resist peer pressure, and relationship variables.

The subgroup of approximately 2,000 commercial sex workers in Campbell's (2003) study lived in a shack settlement that was part of the larger community, where the living conditions were even more basic (windowless shacks with no running water or sanitation) than in the surrounding area. A number of sex workers were identified and trained as peer educators, to recognize and understand HIV symptoms and to understand the relationship between sexually transmitted infections and HIV (Campbell and Mzaidume 2001). In addition, they were given free condoms to distribute to their peers. The training also aimed at promoting discipline and self-respect, as it strongly encouraged punctuality, personal hygiene, dressing appropriately for meetings, and so on (Campbell 2003).

At the local high school, twenty school learners volunteered to be peer educators (Campbell and MacPhail 2002). They, too, were trained in participatory HIV-prevention methods, which included techniques such as role plays, games, dramas, and the use of music. The training, and the program, stressed the importance of communication: "Teenagers are more likely to practise safe sex if they have the opportunity to communicate openly about sex—with sexual partners, peers, and parents or other significant adults" (Campbell 2003, 138). By talking about their conduct in a group setting, led by peers, group norms about sexual behavior are expected to emerge. Once identified, the discussions would enable young people to question these norms and to develop an understanding of sexuality as a socially negotiated phenomenon. They are expected to develop a critical consciousness (from Paolo Freire) that will enhance their ability to act and to gain control over aspects of their lives. Campbell identified two consequences of this practice: the first is a renegotiation of sexual and social identities, and the second is a sense of empowerment to implement health-enhancing "ways of being."

The aims of the two peer education programs were to increase women's sense of control over their health, provide opportunities for the collective renegotiation of social and sexual identities, and encourage a supportive community context. It was argued that women would feel "empowered" if they could exercise control over their sexual health and would experience "ownership" of the problem—that it was their own responsibility and not that of some faceless government department. Renegotiating social identities would involve, for example, constructing "new sexual norms and values which are less damaging to their sexual health" and using "peer education settings as a forum for sharing ideas about ways in which they might assert themselves in their relationships" (Campbell 2004, 342).

These aims reveal that subjectifying processes are at work, even in marginalized communities, in a program that "recruited" participants via collective action. Although political mobilization and collective action were stressed in the program, it is clear that the participants—peer educators and peers alike—were required to work on themselves in particular ways. To be successful, peer education must do more than simply educate, train, or persuade; it must change the way people experience themselves and the world. In their newfound capacities to resist peer pressure, to be self-efficacious, empowered, and so on, people are invited to rationalize ordinary aspects of their lives (e.g., to communicate or to negotiate) into psychological tasks. Peer education becomes a technical device or procedure to reconfigure aspects of one's life or of oneself.

There is no evidence from Campbell's studies that participating in peer education efforts, either as educators or as recipients of the intervention, actually resulted in the kinds of change that I am suggesting here (after all, this was not the purpose of her research). Writers like Steve Parkin and Neal McKeganey (2000), however, have summarized evidence that peer educators exhibited an increase in knowledge of HIV/AIDS, raised self-esteem, heightened self-confidence, improved communication skills, and improved leadership abilities. Thus, at least for the peer educators themselves, there is evidence that they were changed as a result of participating in such activities.

The two peer education programs clearly were based on a community level of intervention, trying to "get local people collectively to 'take ownership' of the problem, engaging in collective action to increase the likelihood that people will act in health-enhancing ways" (Campbell 2003, 3). Let it be clear that the rationale for delivering the program, and the possible effectiveness in terms of achieving the outcomes they were looking for, are not in dispute here at all (although the behavioral outcomes of the project were very disappointing). The point is that by taking participants who are not psychological subjects through a set of collectively based educational practices inscribes an identity in ways that parallel individualizing practices.[5]

Conclusion

What then is the advantage of doing the history of Psychology at "the periphery," as I indicated in the opening paragraphs? It certainly is not in "the history of Psychology in country x," although there is a place for such accounts as well. Instead, the history of Psychology presents powerful opportunities for psychologists in non-Western and developing countries to analyze and understand the present position of the discipline in their countries—one that is different from analyses in terms of its Eurocentrism, Westocentrism, ethnocentrism, et cetera. At the same time, such histories will assist us in understanding how Psychology "makes up" people not just in the past but on an ongoing basis. In other words, "an extremely thoughtful presentism" (Smith 1988, 151) presents us with opportunities to analyze the different forms that the relationship between

Psychology, its subject matter, and the social reality within which it is practiced can take on.

My preference for a broadly Foucauldian approach, as interpreted by Nikolas Rose, should be obvious by now. In South Africa, such a Foucauldian history of Psychology resonates most strongly within a small but significant group of critical psychologists (see the textbook published by Hook 2004, for an extensive example).

From these authors, and the ones mentioned earlier in the chapter, we know that the history of Psychology is not just about the history of the discipline but is also about the history of its subject matter. The two histories are reflexively intertwined (Richards 1996, 4). As a result, Psychology does not study transhistorical "human nature," but it makes up or co-constructs its subject matter as it carries on with its business.

The discipline does this less with its ideas, theories, and ideologies than with its practices, those mundane microprocesses that operate right in front of our eyes but are so often overlooked in the critical debates about Psychology and its relation to society. Following Rose, I have argued that this is where we have to look if we want to understand the history of Psychology in its international context. In particular, practices cross cultural and national boundaries easily, as democratizing (or developing) societies are faced with the challenge of governing the free, autonomous individual who is the citizen-subject of such societies. Psychology becomes an attractive discipline in a country with a constitution like South Africa's, because of its administrative usefulness in "governing the self." Kevin Durrheim and Don Foster (1999), for example, demonstrated how psychological expertise on crowd psychology is used under South Africa's current liberal-democratic constitution to manage crowd activity. Thus despite concern about cosmology, ideology, cultural imperialism, indigenous knowledge, and the like, the administrative requirements of modern societies encourage the use of psychological tests, clinical interviews, personnel selection techniques, regimes of child rearing, managing the workplace, and other practices as techniques to manage the psychological subject.

Strictly speaking, the practices at the two loci of subjectification discussed in this chapter are not uniquely Psychological practices. Nevertheless, I believe they are already saturated with Psychological knowledge, vocabulary, and categories. Story-telling is truth-telling about one's own experiences, and peer education is a technique for behavior and community change. As such, they encompass in different ways the three forms of relating to the self that Rose (1996a) has identified: know yourself, master yourself, and care for yourself. Psychology provides the guidelines on the road to self-knowledge and bestows upon us the techniques for examining and evaluating the self. It is an essential resource as we work on ourselves as free, autonomous subjects in liberal democracies. A democratic South African society, irrespective of whether the citizen comes from the modern industrial or the traditional sector depends on its citizens being politically able selves (Cruikshank 1993). They must be skilled in a number of personal capacities, have information about themselves, be informed about the world around them, and steer their careers and lives—in short, recognize and act on their own subjectivity. Cruikshank's notion of the "technologies of citizenship" that is required to generate politically able selves is particularly apt here: "These technologies . . . emerge from the social sciences, pressure groups, social work discourses, therapeutic social service programs, and so on. Their common goal, nevertheless is to get the citizen to act as his or her own master" (1993, 340).

The most important conclusion to be drawn from the discussion is that the construction of human subjectivities in countries like South Africa will take place in many sites and via many practices, some of them coming from Psychology, some of them from elsewhere. As a result, I believe it will be almost impossible to predict exactly where and how these constructions will come about. There certainly will be homogenizing forces at work, and the creation of constitutional democracies, plus the way they problematize certain aspects of personhood, is likely to be such a force. But there will be diversifying forces as well, provided by the contexts within which individuals define and describe themselves. The history of Psychology in its international perspective provides a window on the multiplicity of ways of being and of understanding ourselves, as well as the numerous sources available to us. Michael Dean called this the challenging task of developing a "critical ontology of ourselves" (1996, 210).

As a result of these numerous and different possibilities, we can fully expect the concepts of personhood, of subjectivity, to become more disparate in all parts of the world. As Danziger states:

> Keeping in mind that these procedures are not idiosyncratic but socially institutionalized, it follows that in societies with significantly different "technologies of the self" people will tend to experience and understand themselves in different ways. As these technologies change historically, there will be corresponding changes in the way individuals relate to themselves. (1997, 151)

NOTES

1. I follow a distinction made by Graham Richards (1996), between "psychology" with a lowercase "p" when referring to its subject matter and "Psychology" for the discipline itself.

2. I am indebted to two colleagues, Christopher Colvin of the University of Virginia and Fiona Ross of the University of Cape Town, for the primary research they have done.

3. Lindy Wilbraham (2004) conducted an analysis of the LoveLife program that shows a close affinity to the arguments made in the present chapter.

4. Rose has pointed out that subjectification operates through collective processes as well as through individualization: "That is to say that the kinds of relations envisaged, the kinds of dispositions and habits inculcated, the very inscription of governmentality into the body and the effects of the governed, was differentiated in collective ways" (2000, 153).

5. Contrast this for example with P. Kiguwa's (2004) description of virginity testing procedures to curb the spread of HIV/AIDS in Swaziland. In September 2001 the Swaziland government issued a five-year sex ban for young women to combat HIV/AIDS. It followed an announcement by the Swazi king to revive a local chastity rite as a way to combat AIDS, a rite policed by traditional Swazi chiefs. Young women who participated in the sex ban were to wear blue and yellow tassles to mark their participation in this "gender script." This is a far cry from the "psychological" intervention described above (although, it must be said, "howls of protest" followed this proposal; p. 300).

REFERENCES

Agger, Inge, and S. B. Jensen. 1990. Testimony as ritual and evidence in psychotherapy for political refugees. *Journal of Traumatic Stress* 3: 115–130.

Berger, Shirley, and Sandy Lazarus. 1987. The views of community organisers on the relevance of psychological practice in South Africa. *Psychology in Society* 7: 6–23.

Bulhan, Hussein. 1985. *Frantz Fanon and the psychology of oppression.* New York: Plenum Press.

Campbell, Catherine. 2003. *"Letting them die": Why HIV/AIDS intervention programmes fail.* Oxford: James Currey.

Campbell, Catherine. 2004. The role of collective action in the prevention of HIV/AIDS in South Africa. In *Critical psychology,* ed. Derek Hook. Cape Town: University of Cape Town Press.

Campbell, Catherine, and Catherine MacPhail. 2002. Peer education, gender and the development of critical consciousness: Participatory HIV prevention by South African youth. *Social Science and Medicine* 55: 331–345.

Campbell, Catherine, and Yodwa Mzaidume. 2001. Grassroots participation, peer education, and HIV prevention by sex workers in South Africa. *American Journal of Public Health* 91: 1978–1987.

Colvin, Christopher. 2002. Limiting memory: The roots and routes of storytelling in post-apartheid, post-TRC South Africa. Paper presented at the Conference on Narrative, Trauma, and Memory, Cape Town, South Africa.

Cruikshank, Barbara. 1993. Revolutions within: Self-government and self-esteem. *Economy and Society* 22: 327–344.

Danziger, Kurt. 1997. The historical formation of selves. In *Self and identity,* ed. Richard D. Ashmore and Lee Jussim. New York: Oxford University Press.

Dean, Michael. 1996. Foucault, government and the enfolding of authority. In *Foucault and political reason,* ed. Andrew Barry, Thomas Osborne, and Nikolas Rose. London: University College London Press.

Department of Health. 2003. *Report: National HIV and syphilis antenatal seroprevalence survey in South Africa.* Pretoria: Department of Health, Directorate Health Systems Research.

Durrheim, Kevin, and Don Foster. 1999. Technologies of social control: Crowd management in liberal democracy. *Economy and Society* 28: 56–74

Foucault, Michel. 1975. *The birth of the clinic.* New York: Random House.

Graybill, Lyn. 2002. *Truth and reconciliation in South Africa.* Boulder, CO: Lynne Riener Publishers.

Holdstock, T. Len. 2000. *Re-examining psychology: Critical perspectives and African insights.* London: Routledge.

Hook, Derek, ed. 2004. *Critical psychology.* Cape Town: University of Cape Town Press.

Howitt, Dennis, and J. Owusu-Bempah. 1994. *The racism of psychology: Time for change.* Hemel Hempstead: Harvester Wheatsheaf.

Jansz, Jeroen. 2004. Psychology and society: An overview. In *A social history of psychology,* ed. Jeroen Jansz and Peter van Drunen. Oxford: Blackwell.

Kaminer, Debrah, Dan Stein, Irene Mbanga, and Nompumelelo Zungu-Dirwayi. 2000. Forgiveness: Toward an integration of theoretical models. *Psychiatry: Interpersonal and biological processes* 63: 344–357.

Kelly, Jeffrey A. 2004. Popular opinion leaders and HIV prevention peer education: Resolving discrepant findings, and implications for the development of effective community programmes. *AIDS Care,* 16: 139–150.

Kiguwa, P. 2004. Feminist critical psychology in South Africa. In *Critical psychology,* ed. Derek Hook. Cape Town: University of Cape Town Press.

Marsella, Anthony J. 1998. Toward a "global-community psychology." *American Psychologist* 53: 1282–1291.

Moghaddam, Fathali. 1993. Traditional and modern psychologies in competing cultural systems: Lessons from Iran 1978–1981. In *Indigenous psychologies: Research and experience in cultural context*, ed. Uichol Kim and John W. Berry. Newbury Park: Sage.

Parkin, Steve, and Neil McKeganey. 2000. The rise and rise of peer education approaches. *Drugs: education, prevention and policy* 7: 293–310.

Richards, Graham. 1996. *Putting Psychology in its place*. London: Routledge.

Rose, Nikolas. 1990. *Governing the soul*. London: Routledge.

Rose, Nikolas. 1996a. Identity, genealogy, history. In *Questions of identity*, ed. Stuart Hall and Peter du Gay. London: Sage.

Rose, Nikolas. 1996b. *Inventing our selves: Psychology, power, and personhood*. Cambridge: Cambridge University Press.

Rose, Nikolas. 1996c. Power and subjectivity: Critical history and psychology. In *Historical dimensions of psychological discourse*, ed. Carl F. Graumann and Kenneth J. Gergen. Cambridge: Cambridge University Press.

Rose, Nikolas. 2000. Governing liberty. In *Governing modern societies*, ed. Richard Ericson and Nico Stehr. Toronto: University of Toronto Press.

Ross, Fiona. 2000. Bearing witness: Women and the South African Truth and Reconciliation Commission. Ph.D. diss., University of Cape Town, South Africa.

Ross, Fiona. 2003. On having voice and being heard: Some after-effects of testifying before the South African Truth and Reconciliation Commission. *Anthropological Theory* 3: 325–341.

Skinner, Donald. 1998. *Apartheid's violent legacy*. Cape Town: Trauma Centre for Victims of Violence and Torture.

Smith, Roger. 1988. Does the history of psychology have a subject? *History of the Human Sciences* 1: 147–177.

Smith, Roger. 1997. *The Fontana history of the human sciences*. London: Fontana Press.

Truth and Reconciliation Commission. 1998. *Truth and Reconciliation Commission of South Africa Report*, Vols. 1–5. Cape Town: Juta.

Tutu, Desmond. (1996). Foreword to *To remember and to heal: Theological and psychological perspectives on truth and reconciliation*, ed. Russel Botman and Robin Petersen. Cape Town: Human and Rousseau.

UNAIDS. 1999. *Peer education and HIV/AIDS: Concepts, uses and challenges*. Geneva: UNAIDS.

Wilbraham, Lindy. 2004. Discursive practice: Analysing a Lovelines text on sex communication for parents. In *Critical psychology*, ed. Derek Hook. Cape Town: University of Cape Town Press.

Chapter 2

Transatlantic Migration of the Disciplines of the Mind

Examination of the Reception of Wundt's and Freud's Theories in Argentina

Cecilia Taiana

The intellectual relationships between Argentina and Germany and between Argentina and France are examined through the particular case of the arrival of the theories of Wilhelm Wundt and Sigmund Freud in Argentina in the first half of the twentieth century. An analysis of the under-representation of Wundt's theories in Argentina's experimental psychology and the struggle for the emergence and ascendancy of psychoanalytical discourse demonstrates independently that preexisting discourses in the disciplines of the mind (neurology, psychiatry, and psychology) provided the conditions of possibility for a complex history of resistance to, and acceptance of, Wundt's and Freud's theories in this period.[1] The author poses the question: What characterized the Argentinean reception of these theories? Both theories arrived via France, imprinted with the long shadow of Théodule Ribot in the case of Wundt and of Pierre Janet in the case of Freud.

Theories, like people, seem to migrate from place to place, with intermediate, transforming stops where different strands weave an idiosyncratic reception pattern rooted in the history of a place. A critical survey of the transatlantic migration of psychological theories and their reception in Argentina raises the broader issues of the nature of the cultural and social roots of local interpretations induced by the circulation of theories across national fields of scientific inquiry. Transatlantic mutations of European theories developed in relation to an Argentinean national field and to the historicity of its categories of interpretation, both of which underwent transformations themselves. It is argued that national intellectual fields mediate in the foreign trade of theories.

History is best understood as a field of multiple-force relations; it cannot be reduced to a single principle of explanation. The histories of psychoanalysis and experimental psychology in Argentina are no exception; they emerged out of a multiplicity of relations, national as well as international, cultural as well as scientific.[2] These contextual relations, which present themselves as a general arrangement of knowledge within an epoch, operated as a conceptual paradigm or discursive framework. The working assumption, in this investigation of the emergence of psychoanalysis and experimental psychology in Argentina, is that conceptual paradigms decide what counts as knowledge at any given moment and are, therefore, decisive in admitting into evidence or rejecting new data and theories.[3] A particular conceptual paradigm, or discourse, "facilitates certain things and hinders others, allows one to see certain things while blinding one to others."[4] A given discourse makes sense of new data by fitting them into the preexisting chain, adding something to the chain without fundamentally altering it. This chapter documents the scientific paradigms shaping the field that Wundt's and Freud's theories entered.

Cultural Filter: Metaphor for the Reception of Theories

Using the particular case of the reception of Wundt's and Freud's theories in Argentina in the first half of the twentieth century, I trace the formation of a cultural filter in Argentinean scientific thinking, which developed within a network of both local and imported knowledge, a space determined not only by its relationships with the social institutions in which it emerged, but also, and most importantly, by the other knowledges with which it merged or that it, sometimes, resisted.[5]

Psychoanalysis and experimental psychology in Argentina were products of European and local traditions—-borrowed, but also resisted. The notion of cultural filter put forward here as a metaphor to understand the history of psychoanalysis and experimental psychology in Argentina is based on the function of a filtration process, in that it both allows passage and retains. What are the particles retained in the process, withheld upon arrival? What are the particles allowed through that prosper and sediment? A filter or process of filtration is the reception mechanism and belongs to the conceptual paradigm in place. It can be said, then, that the filter is the culturally specific paradigm operating in a given place and a given time. This important mechanism at play in the process of the migration of ideas articulated an idiosyncratic reception pattern rooted in the history of Argentina.

Following its independence from Spain (1816), Argentina maintained close cultural and scientific ties with Europe, including Germany, Italy, and Spain, but with France in particular. France and French culture provided the "mirror" into which the Argentinean secular and republican intelligentsia gazed to confirm its identity and destiny. It could be argued that in the 1930s, when Argentina entered a long period of intermittent dictatorships, this identity was shattered. However, the shredded pieces of that republican French mirror were preserved in the form of "subjugated knowledge," bringing France back as a preferred ideal, time and again, for the remainder of the twentieth century. This phantasmatic or imaginary identity guided Argentineans' intellectual choices throughout the century and became a form of cultural filter for transatlantic migrating discourses in the disciplines of the mind.[6]

Foucault uses the concept of "subjugated knowledge" to describe "the historical contents that have been buried and disguised . . . knowledge that has been disqualified . . . or insufficiently elaborated." He links the study of subjugated knowledge to genealogical research—that is, the study of "*historical knowledge of struggles*" (italics in the original).[7] The metaphor of a cultural filter advances our understanding of the historical knowledge of struggles in Argentina.

The metaphor of a filter as a culturally specific paradigm operating in a given place and a given time occurred to me after reading numerous primary and secondary sources in Argentinean archives.[8] I noticed a number of patterns and repetitions and decided to formulate a set of questions that otherwise have gone unremarked or unnoticed. These questions point to the importance of "bodies," "language," "translations," "authorship, debates, and citations," "academic politics and alliances." Accordingly, I asked the following questions:

- Who went where and when between Argentina and Europe?
- Did the scholars receiving the theories have the ability to read Wundt's and Freud's original language of publication?
- How were Wundt's and Freud's theories appraised and communicated to students?
- Who wrote what when, and who cited whom when?

- What were the internal politics shaping the field of academic neurology, psychiatry, and psychology at the University of Buenos Aires (UBA)?

The answers to these questions reveal the idiosyncrasies of the scholarly space in which Wundt's and Freud's writings became inserted. I will look at each author in turn, since the purpose of this chapter is not to examine or compare their theories but, rather, to compare the transatlantic migration of these theories at the point of production and at their destination.

Transatlantic Migration of Wundt's Theories

Psychology as an independent discipline did not exist in Argentina during the nineteenth century. Psychological knowledge was taught as part of moral science (ethics) in the faculty of law. In hospitals, patient care was provided by neurologists, psychiatrists, or members of Catholic religious orders. At the end of the nineteenth century, psychological knowledge began to create its own space within the institutional settings of hospitals and the university.

A disciple of Wundt, Prof. Felix Krüger was a visiting professor in the UBA psychology program in 1906–7. His stay was marked by intense theoretical debates with the head of the experimental psychology program, Prof. Horacio Piñero, and his colleagues. Krüger left Argentina in what seems to have been a "huff" and returned to Germany to later occupy Wundt's chair at Leipzig University (1917–45). The lines of the theoretical debate between Piñero and Krüger trace the emergence of various discourses in the sciences of the mind at this historical moment.

It is not enough to describe this conflict at the UBA as arising from a clash between empiricists and anti-empiricists. Such blanket terms mask the secret that these explanations have "no essence or that their essence was fabricated in a piecemeal fashion from alien forms."[9] The task is to find out why and how Krüger's ideas encountered an epistemological resistance. Why did the conditions of possibility for the emergence of such psychological discourse not exist in Argentina?

The answers to these questions weave a pattern that points to at least four relevant themes: (1) the recognition of the critical role of France as a cultural filter, combined with an absence of personal visits to Leipzig by

Argentinean scholars; (2) an established preexisting discourse in experimental psychology tied to a physiological understanding of psychology guided by an associationist theory; (3) specific conceptual struggles in the experimental psychology program resulting from this understanding; and, finally, (4) a brief comparison with the United States that reveals a different transatlantic migration process. Only the first and the third of these themes are discussed in this chapter.

Paris versus Leipzig

In 1903, addressing L'Institut Général Psychologique of the Société de Psychologie in Paris, Piñero described the traditions he initiated in experimental psychology at the UBA as a combination of Wilhelm Wundt's teachings and Théodule Ribot's clinical approach to the study of psychopathology.[10] However, there is no evidence that Argentineans visited Zürich or Leipzig or that Wundt's books were translated early in the century, other than *Grundriss,* the introductory book mentioned in Krüger's letters.[11] These self-declared disciplinary boundaries are therefore problematic, and the genealogy of this so-called combination is questionable.

France and French scholars were the preferred authoritative source for Argentinean experimental psychologists. In his speech, Piñero referred to the influence of Ribot in Argentina as "extraordinary": "[The works] of Prof. Ribot have had an extraordinary influence on our young intellectuals. . . . So, gentlemen, during the past ten years or so, we have been changing our whole educational system, due to his influence."[12] Going on to describe the influence of Wundt in Argentina and comparing it to his influence in the United States, Piñero stated that "the Wundt School of Psychology has also influenced our studies, but I must say that it has not had the enormous success that it encountered in North America."[13]

In Piñero's lecture there is evidence of misrecognition of the genealogy of Ribot's ideas; the ancestry of his theories remained masked. Piñero did not understand Ribot as a great synthesizer and disseminator of English associationism and German experimentalism—the best description of his work and influence—but rather as an originator of "new" theories, presumably entirely new ones. The academic model that Piñero and colleagues considered ideal for teaching empirical psychology at the UBA was the model proposed by Ribot—in other words, an experimental psychology filtered through the French model and removed from the Wundtian experimental psychology that Krüger wanted to teach.

A few years later, Gardner Murphy, a historian of psychology, would make a very different appraisal of Ribot's contributions:

A dominant figure, alert to all the newer British and German trends and fully expressive of the medical and psychiatric approach of French psychology, was Ribot. He represented the fusion of two streams, psychiatric practice and mechanistic theory . . . he made brain physiology and brain disease the basis of personality and its disorders. . . . Ribot interpreted British and German psychology to his countrymen and carried on the great tradition in medical psychology.[14]

In their recent biography of Ribot, Serge Nicolas and David J. Murray concurred that one of Ribot's important contributions was to inform the emerging field of French scientific psychology about the more advanced works produced in England, Germany, and even the United States.[15] The authors also agreed that the beginnings of scientific psychology in France were slow and laborious.[16] The "grand" Ribot, under whom almost all dominant French and Argentinean psychologists at the beginning of the century had studied, tried to acquaint French readers with English and German scientific psychology; nevertheless, he continued to define psychology according to the French tradition, in medical terms with mechanistic associationist psychology providing his primary hypothesis.[17]

The filter of Ribot gave rise to an experimental psychology in Argentina that was quite different from the one evolving in Germany and in the United States, where Wundt's ideas were also profoundly transformed and Ribot's were virtually ignored. Psychology in Argentina remained tied to physiology and did not exclude clinical psychology; that is, a clinical practice focused on an organic, somatic, psychopathology, closely linked to French medical psychology and generally divorced from the debates in theoretical psychology that dominated German experimental psychology in Krüger's time.[18]

Epistemological Resistance: The Place of Physiology in Psychology and the Notion of Psychic Totality

At first glance, this limited familiarity with German psychological and philosophical theoretical debates seems to be predicated on the absence of good and numerous translations of Wundt's works. In 1906, only the *Grundriss* had been translated and, in the words of Krüger, "very poorly."[19]

However, lack of awareness of Wundt's many works was not the whole explanation, because Krüger also encountered epistemological resistance to Wundt's ideas among his colleagues.[20] What counted as knowledge within the experimental field at the time in Argentina were physiological investigations of pathological conditions undertaken within a framework of associationist and evolutionary theories. For Argentinean psychologists at the turn of the twentieth century, these theories constituted the disciplinary boundaries of modern psychology and, therefore, what counted as knowledge excluded all notions of consciousness as an object of study. On this last point, Kurt Danziger commented that "although Wundt fully accepted that psychology had to start with observable mental life and had to avoid explanations in terms of mental faculties, he regarded the mechanistic alternative represented by traditional associationism as a temptation to be avoided."[21]

Krüger was a disciple of Wundt, who had argued both against British associationism and German "faculty psychology" and had proudly wrestled psychology as a field of study away from the physiologists. In the words of G. Stanley Hall, Wundt's major contributions are as follows: "By his development of the doctrine of apperception [Wundt] took psychology forever beyond the old associationism which had ceased to be fruitful. He also established the independence of psychology from physiology."[22] Within Germany, the concept of apperception had received a great deal of attention in the philosophical debates on the underlying unity of the mind.[23] Krüger's letters reveal that the place of physiology in psychology and the concept of apperception seemed to have been at the center of his conflict with Piñero. If apperception was resisted as an experimental concept, then the study of voluntary attention as a means of manipulating the apperception process experimentally was filtered out of the Argentinean understanding of Wundt's theories. In her book *Psicología en Argentina*, Liliana Rossi stated that Krüger "introduced for the first time the notion of psychic totality centered in the experience of the individual, a view considerably different from pure analytic experimentalism [of physiological psychology]."[24] Krüger's ideas did not find acceptance among the academics of the time in Argentina; according to Rossi, he "did not find an echo; his position was considered tenuous, weak, and excessively close to philosophical sources" by Piñero and colleagues.[25] In the words of Hugo Vezzetti, a historian of psychology in Argentina, "the terrain [in Argentina] was not favorable to Krüger's ideas, and he found himself in an academic milieu dominated by the ideas of a deterministic positivism."[26]

Wundt's thought developed in relation to a particular field, both a German national field, which itself was undergoing continual transformation, and a European field, with its competing philosophical traditions, all of which made up the context in which Wundt's intellectual project took root.[27] By the time Krüger came to Argentina in 1906, its methods were disputed and considered inadequate to analyze complex reactions. In addition, theories of volitional activity and emotions were moving in "new directions, far afield from the Wundtian models."[28]

Krüger undoubtedly knew about Wundt's opponents in psychology and philosophy. He arrived in Argentina already aware of the fact that some psychologists were diverging from the Wundtian course; he possibly recognized in the Argentinean opposition to his ideas some of the same theoretical arguments. By 1906–7 there were already many competing interpretations of psychology in Germany, even of experimental psychology. Wundt's approach was losing the support of the majority of German psychologists, some of whom were adopting French or British approaches, as were the Argentineans.[29] Krüger's efforts to gain recognition for his claims about mental functions such as apperception did not prosper. What counted as truth in psychology did not change, shift, or mutate to include Krüger's and Wundt's theories.

In summary, many factors contributed to the stunted emergence of Wundtian theories of psychology in Argentina. Their reception was also hampered by Argentinean psychologists' overall lack of familiarity with the German strands of theoretical psychology. There are no documented personal contacts with any German centers of experimental psychology during the last two decades of the nineteenth century, few Argentinean scholars read German or English, and Spanish translations of the German texts were few and poor. All these factors interacted to make it difficult for Argentinean scholars to get a firm grasp of the theoretical framework put forward by Wundt. The Wundt they received prior to the arrival of Krüger was filtered, as were so many of the theories arriving from Europe to Argentina, through France.

Transatlantic Migration of Freud's Theories

Archival evidence from the turn of the twentieth century clearly demonstrates that Argentinean neurologists, psychiatrists, and psychologists interested in psychopathology were reading the same authors and attending the same conferences that, for example, their American colleagues were. However, psychoanalysis took four decades to formally appear in Argentina (1942), while, in the United States, the first formal association was created in 1911.

During the first half of the twentieth century, psychoanalytical discourse in Argentina did not find a receptive niche among any of the disciplines of the mind. In psychology, at the time of the arrival of Freud's theories, what counted as knowledge was the physiological study of the brain.[30] In the same period, neurology and psychiatry were dominated by nineteenth-century theories of degeneracy and somatic explanations of insanity imported from Germany and France. This organicist approach, also referred to as the German *Somatiker* tradition, attributed mental diseases to physical causes and to brain conditions, as opposed to the French *Psychiker* tradition, which experienced a revival in France around 1880 and emphasized the emotional and functional causes of such diseases.[31] Although Freud never doubted the physiological nature of the psychic process, he believed that, "The psychic is, therefore, a process parallel to the physiological, a 'dependent concomitant.'"[32] In Argentina, organicist theories of degeneracy and insanity continued to be argued, published, and taught by university professors in neurology, psychiatry, and psychology as late as the 1940s.[33]

It is a fundamental assumption of all critical histories of psychoanalysis that psychoanalysis emerged from the struggle between certain conceptual paradigms, which were gradually overthrown to give way to new ones; such is the case of the *Somatiker* and *Psychiker* paradigms in the disciplines of the mind. In Argentina, the dilatory factors in the emergence of Freud's theories are associated with a deeply established *Somatiker* paradigm, which operated as a resistant episteme to the *Psychiker* understanding of the mind-body relationship proposed by Freud.[34]

However, it is not enough to describe the discourse wars as arising from a clash between *Somatiker* and *Psychiker* understandings of the mind–body relationship. The task is to find out why and how Freud's ideas encountered an epistemological resistance. Although Freud's name was cited by Argentinean authors at the turn of the twentieth century, his ideas did not find an institutional niche among the disciplines of the mind until the second half of the twentieth century. Which factors could be considered as dilatory factors in the emergence of Freud's theories in Argentina? Why did the conditions of possibility for the emergence of psychoanalytical discourse not exist in Argentina? From the answers to these questions, four themes are clearly identified.

Argentina's idiosyncratic reception process of Freud's theories requires the recognition of the critical role of France as a cultural filter; this theme, named "Paris versus Nancy," emphasizes the importance of personal contacts in the migration of ideas. The second theme traces the importance of foreign—that is, other than Spanish—language proficiency and the availability of original sources that operated as cultural filters and agents of discourse formation. The third theme analyzes the institutional and political context created by the emergence of psychoanalytical discourse in Argentina, and a fourth, a comparative analysis with the United States, attests to an asynchronous parallel process of reception. Only the first and third of these themes are discussed in this chapter.[35]

Paris versus Nancy

At the end of the nineteenth century, the theorists who provided the best arguments to counter the prevalent somatic paradigm on the causes of insanity were in Paris. A few Argentinean neurologists, psychiatrists, and psychologists visited Paris regularly and cited French authors in the area of psychopathology, in particular Charcot and Janet.[36] But early in the twentieth century, while American and other scholars extended their visits to include Nancy and Vienna, Argentineans did not.[37] The quiescent dominance of the somatic/hereditary/degenerative discourses on insanity among Argentinean neurologists, psychiatrists, and psychologists was also marked by the monoculture of French authors preferred by Argentinean scientists of the mind in the pre-Freudian period.

The Argentinean neurologists, psychiatrists, and psychologists interested in Freud relied heavily on French secondary sources; what French authors quoted from or wrote about Freud was generally uncritically accepted. Angel T. Sosa y Sanchez, a medical student writing his thesis on dreams and psychoanalysis in 1920, stated:

> Argentine physicians, in their majority, with a few exceptions among psychiatrists and specialists in legal medicine, ignore absolutely the existence of psychoanalysis, and if anyone knows about it he knows it through a French book written by Regis and Hesnard in 1914, that is, fourteen years later than the Viennese neurologist wrote his book titled the *Interpretation of Dreams*.[38]

Sosa y Sanchez commented on the merit of this publication:

> The book of Regis and Hesnard is the most complete piece of work that has been written in France on psychoanalysis; however, it is a biased book intended to partially illustrate, and to prove above all, that everything that the psychoanalytic theory had to say had been said before [by French authors]. This means that whoever reads this book acquires an imperfect knowledge of its significance.[39]

Furthermore, the Argentineans favored Paris over other centers in France to pursue their studies. There was "an embittered struggle" between Jean-Martin Charcot in Paris and Hippolyte Bernheim in Nancy.[40] The school of Nancy accepted Charcot's explanations but advanced his psychic arguments even further. Taking issue with Charcot, Bernheim argued that "it was absurd to suppose that hypnosis was a rarity, induced only in hysterics. Hypnosis was nothing but sleep caused by suggestion, and every normal person was suggestible."[41] Janet, who is cited extensively by Argentinean authors well into the 1930s, sided with the school of Paris and distanced himself from the assumptions of the school of Nancy.[42] Freud, on the other hand, visited Nancy and developed an interest in Bernheim's theories on suggestion and hypnosis. He agreed with him that the mechanism of hysterical symptoms is psychic and not physical but contradicted Bernheim by claiming that this mechanism is not one of simple suggestion.

The importance of the school of Nancy in the Freudian project cannot be overestimated. Performing as a stepping stone, Freud's attempt to resolve the Salpêtrière–Nancy controversy reinforced the direction of Freud's research and helped him to move gradually from physiological to psychological explanations. Freud's own evolving theories took a long time to achieve independence from the thinking of Charcot, Janet, and Bernheim. In time, Freud distanced his emerging understanding of hysterical symptoms from both schools by identifying and developing the concept of resistance and by paying attention to the role of memory and meaning and their dynamic relation to the symptoms in the psychic apparatus through the creative process of *Nachträglichkeit*—that is, the constructive and reconstructive nature of memory in what is called by today's neurologists the process of "retranscription." Oliver Sacks comments that "at the higher level, Freud regarded memory and motive as inseparable. Recollection could have no force, no meaning, unless it was allied with motive."[43]

There is no clear evidence that any Argentineans visited Bernheim at Nancy. This significant finding provides one of the reasons for the delayed arrival of Freudian theories to Argentina. An analysis of the articles published by Argentinean physicians interested in Freud reveals that the important debate taking place between the school of Paris and the school of Nancy in the late nineteenth century was underrepresented in the Argentinean scholarly literature. This omission is also indicative of the presence of fragmented and incomplete theoretical debates that led to the misrecognition of the importance of Freud's theoretical innovations. The debate between Janet and Bernheim is understated in the Argentinean literature, and when it is specifically discussed, as in the case of José Ingenieros, Janet is favored: "It can be seen that his [Janet's] method of psychological analysis is more fertile than the 'psycho-analysis' of Freud."[44]

For the most part, Argentineans acquired their understanding of Freudian theories from French sources, in particular from Janet's characterization of psychoanalysis. Spanish translations of Janet's works reached Argentina sooner than did the translations of Freud's publications before World War I. Janet continued to teach in Paris at the Collège de France and opposed Freud's new interpretation of the unconscious and its dynamic processes. At the beginning of 1896, Freud sketched his new classification of neuroses and emphasized his divergence from Janet.[45]

The Argentineans, with their long traditions of Parisian education, continued to center their study visits in Paris, missing the newer developments in Freud's theories and understanding Freud's ideas as an unimportant variation of Janet's theories. In short, the Argentinean authors underestimated the importance of the differences between Freud and Bernheim on issues of suggestion; between Freud and Charcot on issues of heredity; and between Freud and Janet on issues of heredity, repression, and therapeutics. Freud's writings came to Argentina via France. A French cultural mediation to his texts had been applied before their arrival in Argentina, where further cultural filtration occurred. This cultural filtering of theories is an important condition of possibility for the emergence of psychoanalytical knowledge in Argentina.

Epistemological Resistance: Freud's Theories as an Anti-Fascist Refuge

During the period under study (1900–50), psychoanalysis played a relatively minor role in psychiatric hospitals and university programs. The training of students at the undergraduate and graduate levels was entirely in the hands of non-Freudian neurologists and psychiatrists and, therefore, psychoanalysis was not able to make deep inroads into institutional psychiatric treatment of psychoneuroses or psychosis. In the case of psychology, Freud was minimally taught among many other authors, and the university curriculum in the program of psychology did not include psychoanalytical clinical training until the 1960s.

After World War I, the continuing French monoculture in the reading of Freud in Argentina introduced a further and very different transforming step, when a small number of neurologists, psychiatrists, and psychologists interested in psychotherapy filtered Freud's ideas through the interpretations of French Marxist thinkers. Attempts to harmonize Freud's theories with Marxist theories became an important theoretical preoccupation of many of the scholars interested in Freud in the 1920s and 1930s. It is a relatively unknown fact that, with very few exceptions, most of the authors who cited Freud in Argentina until 1935 were Marxist-Socialists.[46] During the first four decades of the twentieth century, at least three of them were expelled or discharged from their hospitals and university, and in many cases they became voluntary exiles in Europe or in neighboring countries in South America.[47]

The efforts made by Argentineans early in the twentieth century to integrate the ideas of Freud and Marx were, in large measure, dependent on the French-Soviet connection and its critique of psychoanalysis. In this sense, it could be argued that the early medical and literary authors put Freud's theories through a double filter, that of the French-Marxist interpreters. This double filtering of Freud's ideas had important consequences when the transmission of Freud's theories to Argentina was interrupted, and in most cases abandoned, when the continuity between psychoanalysis and Marxist discourse exploded and fractured in Europe in the 1930s. In Argentina, the opposition to psychoanalysis from the Left followed the local Communist Party line, a line that responded to the Soviet Union under Stalin and increasingly spoke of the evil of psychoanalysis as a bourgeois ideology.[48] This critique resulted in a sea change in Argentina against Freud's theories during the second half of the 1930s; the Argentinean Marxist-Socialist neurologists, psychiatrists, and psychologists who had supported Freud's theories turned against him and, in some cases, became rabid enemies of psychoanalysis.[49]

The first scholars early in the twentieth century (1900–30) to enunciate Freud's theories in Argentina were politically affiliated with the Left, with strong political loyalties outside their institutional frame. In the 1940s, they were replaced as agents of transmission by the founders of the Argentinean Psychoanalytical Association (APA), who were anti-fascist but not Marxist, referred to as the "Pioneers" in the literature. They began to transmit Freud's theories through an Anglo-Saxon cultural filter in the decade of the 1940s and beyond.[50]

Argentinean psychoanalysts in the early Freudian period developed as the Europeans did: segregated from official medicine. Psychoanalytical practice in Argentina grew outside hospitals and universities, creating a parallel institutional field centered on the APA.[51] This initial noninstitutional development in Argentina requires an analysis of the conditions that made it impossible for psychoanalysis to grow inside established institutions, such as hospitals and universities, and to prosper in the 1940s and beyond as an outside institution strongly linked to international—mostly Anglo-Saxon—scientific culture, particularly during World War II and the postwar period.

Against the absolute and perfect "masculinity" of fascism, Freud's theories offered Argentinean intellectuals a space of retreat, a place to enter the epistemology of the "wounded mind." The position of psychoanalysis as an outsider to the dominant discourse at the time of its emergence in Argentina at the end of the 1930s is not, therefore, related only to the dominance of the *Somatiker* discourse in universities and hospitals; it is also related to a new discursive formation resulting from the interlocking of psychoanalytic discourse and anti-fascist sentiment in Argentina. This new discursive formation united a group of anti-fascist intellectuals, artists, and scientists in the decades of the 1930s and 1940s. It provided a place of refuge from an increasingly national fascist environment and the possibility of an identity aligned with the anti-fascist struggles unfolding in European countries and the United Kingdom.[52] From this subversive position, Argentinean intellectuals and scientists fought both the institutional resistance to psychoanalytic discourse and pro-fascist military governments in the 1930s and 1940s. Adding greater demarcation to their preferences—scientific as well as political—the Pioneers introduced Freud's ideas in the 1940s through the Anglo-Saxon filter rather than the earlier French filter. To be interested in Freud at the end of the 1930s and during the 1940s was to be anti-fascist, anti-government, anti-military, and pro-Anglo-Saxon; in short, anti-establishment. The only place to grow was outside established institutions.

In the 1930s, fascism drove many Jewish psychiatrists from Central

Europe to North and South America. The number of refugee analysts from Europe was not large.[53] Their impact in Argentina was important but not major. Marie Langer, who arrived in Argentina in 1942, was the only refugee fully trained in psychoanalysis. Heinrich Racker, who arrived shortly thereafter, completed his psychoanalytical training with Langer in Argentina. However, the contribution of Argentinean-born neurologists, psychiatrists, and psychologists of Jewish ancestry to the emergence of psychoanalysis was vital to its establishment.

Conclusions

An analysis of the struggle for the emergence and ascendancy of psychoanalytical discourse and the underrepresentation of Wundt's theories in Argentina's experimental psychology demonstrates independently that preexisting discourses in the disciplines of the mind (neurology, psychiatry, and psychology) provided the conditions of possibility for a complex history of resistance to, and acceptance of, Wundt's and Freud's theories in this period.

The main purpose of this chapter has been to elaborate on the concept of cultural filter as a way of analyzing the transatlantic migration of the disciplines of the mind. The aforementioned analysis is necessarily abbreviated, and the themes found in this investigation represent only a distillation of the main findings of a larger analysis that allows us to generate a new way of questioning the evidence.

It has been argued that the Argentinean intellectual field mediated the foreign trade of theories in the disciplines of the mind at the turn of the twentieth century. This means that the interpretations that academics make at the destination are linked to the local roots of discursive struggles and traditions. The historicity of their categories of perception and interpretations operates as the condition of possibility for emerging psychological knowledge.

The understanding of a cultural filter as a specific conceptual paradigm operating in a given place and a given time consists primarily in the refinement of a set of questions that guide a genealogical exploration of patterns, repetitions, and disperse events. According to Foucault, the study of the genealogy of a given discourse, in our case psychoanalytical and experimental, "does not pretend to go back in time to restore an unbroken continuity that operates beyond the dispersion of forgotten things." On the contrary: "To follow the complex course of descent is to maintain passing events in their proper dispersion; it is to identify the accidents, the minute deviations—or conversely, the complete reversals—the errors, the false appraisals, and the faulty calculations that gave birth to those things that continue to exist."[54] Psychology in Argentina remained tied to physiology and did not exclude clinical psychology—that is, a clinical practice focused on an organic, somatic psychopathology, closely linked to French medical psychology and generally divorced from the debates in theoretical psychology that dominated German experimental psychology in Wundt's time.

A marked discontinuity was emerging between a certain accepted way of talking, describing, discussing, and documenting evidence in the domain called experimental psychology at the UBA and the notion and discursive implications of the Wundtian concept of apperception and psychic totality. In Argentina, Krüger's theoretical discourse was considered dangerously philosophical, meaning scholastic, when in fact he was critical of both associationism and scholasticism. Krüger tried, but failed, to create in Argentina a theoretical psychology distinct from physiological and philosophical psychology.

In Argentina, this prior discursive framework in the disciplines of the mind also created considerable resistance to the arriving *Psychiker* paradigm proposed by Freud's explanations of the mind–body relationship. As a firmly established pre-Freudian order that was pervasive and slow to innovate, the somatic paradigm, it is argued, delayed the entrance of Freud's theories and other *Psychiker* explanations of mental pathology.

Neurologists, psychiatrists, and psychologists interested in Freud's work did not reach positions of authority within the institutional settings of universities and hospitals, and, therefore, they were unable to shape their respective disciplines during this period. As a result, psychoanalytical discourse emerged, changed, shifted, and mutated in relation to, but also divorced from, national institutions such as hospitals and universities. The preexisting discursive framework did not offer a common field of study; therefore, psychoanalysts ultimately created a parallel institutional niche, the lifeblood of which was the International Psychoanalytical Association.

Wundt's and Freud's theories were filtered, as were many theories arriving from Europe to Argentina, through France. The cultural filter of France belonged to the cultural filter of Argentina, which, in turn, was part of the Argentinean search for a lost, but desired, shattered French identity.

Criticized by many and used by few, Wundt's and Freud's theories never gained discursive continuity with established neurological, psychiatric, or psychological theories prevalent in hospitals and universities in Argentina during the first part of the twentieth century.

NOTES

1. I use the term "disciplines of the mind" to include neurology, psychiatry, psychology, and psychoanalysis since all these disciplines are interconnected; the history of one cannot be understood without knowledge of the others. For the definition of "discipline" as distinct from "science," I refer the reader to Timothy Lenoir. He defines "discipline" as "the infrastructure of science embodied above all in university departments, professional societies, textbooks, and lab manuals." Timothy Lenoir, "The Discipline of Nature and the Nature of Disciplines," in *Knowledges: Historical and Critical Studies in Disciplinarity*, ed. Ellen Messer-Davidow, David R. Sherway, and David J. Sylvan (Charlottesville: University Press of Virginia, 1993) 72, 77–8.

2. On this struggle Michel Foucault elaborated: "Emergence is thus the entry of forces; it is their eruption, the leap from the wings to center stage. . . . Emergence designates a place of confrontation, but not as a closed field offering the spectacle of a struggle among equals. Rather, as Nietzsche demonstrates in his analysis of good and evil, it is a 'non-place,' a pure distance, which indicates that the adversaries do not belong to a common space. Consequently, no one is responsible for an emergence; no one can glory in it, since it always occurs in the interstice." Michel Foucault, "Nietzsche, Genealogy, History" in *Foucault Reader*, ed. Paul Rabinow (New York: Pantheon, 1984), 84–5. This essay first appeared in *Hommage à Jean Hyppolite* (Paris: Presses Universitaires de France, 1971), 145–72.

3. This investigation is informed by the Kuhnian concept of paradigm, Michel Foucault's related concept of the episteme, and one of Jacques Lacan's four discourses—that is, the university discourse. In a postscript, written in 1969, to the 1962 edition of *The Structure of Scientific Revolutions*, Thomas Kuhn clarified the two "different senses" in which he uses the concept of paradigm. The first sense he considered to be sociological in nature and the second philosophical (175). Kuhn's philosophical sense of paradigm comes very close to Foucault's notion of *episteme* when he argues that the student of science discovers "a way to see his problem as *like* [italics in the original] a problem he has already encountered. Having seen the resemblance, grasped the analogy between two or more distinct problems, he can interrelate symbols and attach them to nature in the ways that have proved effective before" (189). Thomas Kuhn, *The Structure of Scientific Revolutions* (Chicago: University of Chicago Press, 1962)

Foucault refers to this discursive space as the *episteme*. An *episteme*, for Foucault, "is the conditions of possibility of empirical sciences at a given time—the contextual relations that present themselves as a general arrangement of knowledge within a given epoch." Michel Foucault, *The Order of Things: An Archaeology of the Human Sciences* (New York: Random House, 1970), xxii; 157–8. See also Michel Foucault, *Power/Knowledge: Selected Interviews and Other Writings 1972– 1977*, ed. Colin Gordon (New York: Pantheon, 1980), 197.

Jacques Lacan identifies four different kinds of discourses: the Master's discourse, the University discourse, the Hysteric's discourse, and the Analyst's discourse. See Bruce Fink, *The Lacanian Subject: Between Language and Jouissance* (New Jersey: Princeton University Press, 1995) 130–6.

4. Fink, *Lacanian Subject*, 130.

5. Two separate investigations provided me with the case history for this inquiry into the transatlantic migration of the theories in the disciplines of the mind. One is my doctoral dissertation: Cecilia Taiana, "The Emergence of Psychoanalysis in Argentina: An Examination of the Pre-Freudian and Early Freudian Periods" (Ph.D. diss., Carleton University, 2002). More recently, in Cecilia Taiana, "Conceptual Resistance in the Disciplines of the Mind: The Leipzig–Buenos Aires Connection at the Turn of the Twentieth Century," *History of Psychology* 8(4), 338– 340, I examined the genealogy of the theoretical debate taking place during the visiting professorship of Felix Krüger, a disciple of Wilhelm Wundt, at the UBA experimental psychology program in 1906–7. In both investigations, I found certain commonalties and repetitions that point to a pattern worth exploring.

6. Foucault, *Power/Knowledge*, 81–2; 82. Also see Barbara Gabriel, "The Wounds of Memory: Mavis Gallant's "Baum, Gabriel (1935–), National Trauma, and Postwar French Cinema," in *Essays in Canadian Writing, Special Issue: Cultural Memory and Social Identity*, no. 80 (Fall 2003), in particular Section III, Collective Memory Acts, 199–200 and footnotes 4, 6.

7. Foucault, *Power/Knowledge*, 84–5.

8. Mainly the archives of the faculty of medicine and the faculty of philosophy of the University of Buenos Aires, the Argentinean Scientific Society, and the Argentinean Psychoanalytical Association, among others.

9. Foucault, "Nietzsche, Genealogy, History," 78. See also Loïc Wacquant, who studied the transatlantic reception and interpretation of Pierre Bourdieu's theories in the United States: Loïc Wacquant, "Bourdieu in America: Notes on the Transatlantic Importation of Social Theory," in *Bourdieu: Critical Perspectives*, ed. Craig Calhoun, Edward LiPuma, and Moishe Postone (Chicago: University of Chicago Press, 1993).

10. Horacio Piñero was a member of the International Institute of Psychology founded by Pierre Janet in 1901. He traveled to Paris in 1903 and presented a paper on experimental psychology in Argentina. His lecture was published in French in Argentina on two occasions: "La psychologie expérimentale dans la République Argentine. Communication faite à L'Institut Général Psychologique sur la

demande de la Société de Psychologie de Paris. Instituto de Filosofía, Sección de Psicología" [Experimental psychology in the Republic of Argentina. Paper presented at the Institut Général Psychologique under the sponsorship of the Société de Psychologie de Paris. Institute of Philosophy, Psychology Section], *Revista de la Sociedad Médica Argentina* 11 (1903): 303–25; and thirteen years later as part of a University of Buenos Aires publication, *Trabajos de psicología: Normal y patológica 1 (1905–1910)* [Research in normal and pathological psychology I (1905–1910)] (Buenos Aires: Compañia Sud-Americana de Billetes de Buenos Aires, 1916). Lecture from pp. 264–88.

11. See Eleonore Wundt, ed., *Wilhelm Wundt Werk: Ein Verzeichnis seiner sämtlichen Schriften* [The work of Wilhelm Wundt: a list of his complete writings] (Munich: C. H. Beck, 1927), 67.

12. Piñero, *Trabajos de Psicología*, 279.

13. Ibid., 280.

14. Gardner Murphy, *Historical Introduction to Modern Psychology*, rev. ed. (New York: Harcourt, 1949), 170, 211, and 435. See also Théodule A. Ribot, *La psychologie allemande contemporaine, école expérimentale* [Contemporary German psychology: The experimental school] (Paris: G. Bailliere, 1879), and Théodule A. Ribot, *La psychologie anglaise contemporaine, école expérimentale* [Contemporary English psychology: The experimental school] (Paris: G. Bailliere, 1881).

15. Serge Nicolas and David. J. Murray, "Le fondateur de la psychologie 'scientifique' française: Théodule Ribot (1839–1916)" [The founder of French "scientific" psychology: Théodule Ribot (1839–1916)], *Psychologie et histoire* 1 (2000): 13.

16. Ibid., 22. "Les débuts de la psychologie scientifique en France furent lents et laborieux" (The beginnings of scientific psychology in France were slow and laborious).

17. Murphy, *Historical Introduction*, 35.

18. These debates in Germany, though more philosophical, still paralleled the Krüger versus Piñero debate. For example, Wundt versus Stumpf, or Wundt versus Külpe, or Dilthey versus Ebbinghaus. See David K. Robinson, "Wilhelm Wundt and the Establishment of Experimental Psychology, 1875–1914: The Context of a New Field of Scientific Research" (Ph.D. diss., University of California, Berkeley, 1987), chaps. 7–8. Also, Mitchell G. Ash, *Gestalt Psychology in German Culture 1890–1967: Holism and the Quest for Objectivity* (Cambridge: Cambridge University Press), chaps. 1 and 2.

19. Krüger letter to Wundt, November 16, 1906, Archives of Wilhelm Wundt, University of Leipzig, Germany.

20. Kurt Danziger sharpens and clarifies the difference between Bain and Wundt in his chapter, "Wundt and the Temptations of Psychology," in *Wilhelm Wundt in History: The Making of a Scientific Psychology*, ed. Robert W. Rieber and David K. Robinson (New York: Kluwer Academic/Plenum Press, 2001), 69–94.

21. Ibid., 79.

22. G. Stanley Hall, as cited by Robert Rieber in his chapter "Wundt and the Americans: From Flirtation to Abandonment," in *Wilhelm Wundt in History: The Making of a Scientific Psychology*, ed. Robert W. Rieber and David K. Robinson (New York: Kluwer Academic/Plenum Press, 2001), 145.

23. Wundt had adopted this concept from Herbart but took it further away from an associationist notion of "forces of attraction among mental contents" to signify an "act of consciousness as a whole." Danziger, "Wundt and the Temptations of Psychology," 76–7.

24. Liliana Rossi, *La psicología en Argentina: Capítulos olvidados de una historia reciente* [Psychology in Argentina: Forgotten chapters of a recent history] (Buenos Aires: Teckne, 1994), 12.

25. Ibid.

26. Hugo Vezzetti, ed., *El nacimiento de la psicología en la Argentina: Pensamiento psicológico y positivismo* [The birth of psychology in Argentina: Psychological thought and positivism] (Buenos Aires: Puntosur Editores, 1988).

27. "The reaction-time experiment was arguably the most integral part of the research program in the first decade [1875–1885] of the Leipzig institute, when that institution was the unchallenged leader in the field." David K. Robinson, "Reaction-Time Experiments," in *Wilhelm Wundt in History: The Making of a Scientific Psychology*, ed. Robert W. Rieber and David K. Robinson (New York: Kluwer Academic/Plenum Press, 2001), 193.

28. Ibid., 195.

29. For greater detail on the theoretical debates in Germany at the beginning of the twentieth century, see Robinson, "Reaction-Time Experiments," 184. Also Kurt Danziger, *Constructing the Subject: Historical Origins of Psychological Research* (Cambridge: Cambridge University Press, 1990), and Ash, *Gestalt Psychology in German Culture*.

30. In the words of Prof. Felix Krüger: "Psychology [in Argentina] is equated with physiology of the brain." Letter from Felix Krüger to Wilhelm Wundt, 11 June 1907. Archives of Wilhelm Wundt.

31. Henri Ellenberger, *The Discovery of the Unconscious: The History and Evolution of Dynamic Psychiatry* (New York: Basic Books, 1970). Ellenberger documents that *Psychiker* explanations of insanity declined in 1840 but reemerged with Charcot's theories in the 1880s (284).

32. Sigmund Freud, *On Aphasia*, transl. E. Tengel (London: Imago Press, 1953), 55.

33. Francisco De Veyga, *Degeneración y degenerados* [Degeneration and degenerates], as cited by Osvaldo Ludet in *Historia de la psiquiatría argentina* (Buenos Aires: Ediciones Troquel, 1971), 130.

34. The assumption behind this statement is that discourses emerge, change,

shift, and mutate in relation to a wider field of the *episteme* that is always historical. For a discussion on the *Somatiker* and *Psychiker* paradigms in psychiatry, see
Ellenberger, *Discovery of the Unconscious*, 284–91.

35. All these themes are discussed in detail in Cecilia Taiana, "The Emergence
of Freud's Theories in Argentina: Towards a Comparison with the U.S.," *Canadian
Journal of Psychoanalysis*, forthcoming 2006.

36. Jorge Balán, *Cúentame tu vida: Una biografía colectiva del psicoanálisis
argentino* [Tell me your life: A collective biography of Argentine psychoanalysis]
(Buenos Aires: Planeta, 1991); *Primeras Jornadas de Historia: Historia de la crisis y
de los cambios en psicoanálisis*, APA, 20–21 de Mayo, 1994 [Transcripts of presentations to an academic session organized by the Department of History of Psychoanalysis at the APA, 20–21 May, 1994]; Hugo Vezzetti, *Aventuras de Freud en el país
de los argentinos* [Adventures of Freud in the country of the Argentines] (Buenos
Aires: Paidos, 1996).

37. "Freud and innumerable Americans, Morton Prince among them, studied
hypnotic therapeutics at Nancy." Nathan Hale, *Freud and the Americans: The Beginnings of Psychoanalysis in the United States, 1876–1971* (New York: Oxford University Press, 1971), 125. Also John Burnham, *Psychoanalysis and American Medicine: 1894–1918* (New York: International Universities Press, 1967); Gail Hornstein,
"The Return of the Repressed: Psychology's Problematic Relations with Psychoanalysis, 1909–1960," *American Psychological Association* 57(2): 254–63.

38. A. T. Sosa y Sanchez, *Los sueños y el psicoanálisis* [Dreams and psychoanaly-
sis] thesis no. 3782 (Facultad de Medicina, Universidad de Buenos Aires, 1920).

39. Ibid., 7–8.

40. Ellenberger, *Discovery of the Unconscious*, 87.

41. Ibid. 759. "Bernheim defended the Nancy position, namely, that anyone
could be hypnotized." See also in Ellenberger, the section "The Decline of the Salpêtrière School," 762.

Citing Pierre Janet, *Psychological Healing* (New York: Macmillan, 1925), 173,
Hale, in Freud and the Americans, writes referring to Bernheim's theory: "Bernheim defined suggestion vaguely as the influence 'exercised by an idea that has
been suggested and has been accepted by the brain'" (125).

42. See also Ellenberger, *Discovery of the Unconscious*. In chapter 6, endnote 40,
he wrote: "Janet gave his impressions on Argentina in the *Journal des Nations
Americaines: Argentine*, Nouvelle Serie, I, No.7, June 18, 1933, 411." See Pierre Janet,
"Discusión del rol de la emoción en la génesis de los estados neuropáticos," *La
Semana Médica* (1912): 553–7. (Original text published in 1909).

43. Oliver Sacks, "The Other Road: Freud as Neurologist," in Sigmund Freud,
Conflict and Culture: Essays on His Life, Work, and Legacy, ed. Michael S. Roth
(New York: Vintage Books, 1998), 231.

44. J. Ingenieros, *Histeria y sugestión: Estudios de psicología clínica* [Hysteria

and suggestion: Studies in clinical psychology], 5th ed. (Buenos Aires: Talleres Gráficos de L. J. Rosso y Cia, 1919), 43.

45. After the death of Charcot (1893), Janet was displaced from La Salpêtrière by Charcot's disciples Joseph Babinski, Fulgence Raymond, and Georges Dumas. His lectures at the Collège de France were attended by colleagues and foreign visitors but few students. In his new position, Janet did not have access to clinical settings to continue developing his theories. From then on, his publications began to explore philosophical, cultural, and religious issues. Ellenberger, *Discovery of the Unconscious*, 779, 793

46. For example, Jorge Thenon, Aníbal Ponce, Gregorio Bermann, Emilio Pizarro Crespo, and José Ingenieros. Balán, *Cúentame tu vida*, 60, and Vezzetti, *Aventuras de Freud en el país de los argentinos*, 145, 150.

47. Jorge Thenon, Aníbal Ponce, and Gregorio Bermann were expelled or discharged. Gregorio Bermann, José Ingenieros, and Emilio Pizzaro Crespo were voluntary exiles.

48. A. Cucurullo, A. H. Faimberg, and L. Wender, "La psychanalyse en Argentine," [Psychoanalysis in Argentina], in *Histoire de la psychanalyse* [History of psychoanalysis], Vol. 2, ed. Roland Jaccard (Paris: Hachette, 1982), 399. See also Taiana, "Emergence of Freud's Theories in Argentina," chap. 4, section 4.2, "The Groundbreakers: A French Reading of Freud."

49. Jorge Thenon, "J. Thenon visto por Thenon" [J. Thenon seen by Thenon], *Acta Psiquiatrica y Psicología de América Latina* 15(4) (1969): 381–5.

50. The founders of the Argentinean Psychoanalytical Association were Angel Garma, Céles Cárcamo, Arnaldo Rascovsky, Enrique Pichon Rivière, Guillermo Ferrari Hardoy, and Marie Langer.

51. By the end of the 1950s and the beginning of the 1960s psychoanalysis gained for the first time a firm hold on the medical and psychiatric university curricula. Balán, *Cúentame tu vida*, 113.

52. This place of refuge from dictatorship was again offered to Argentineans by Lacanian psychoanalysis in the last dictatorship period (1976–83). See Cecilia Taiana, "The Armor of Words: The Case of Lacanian Psychoanalysis in the Last Argentinean Dictatorship (1976–83)," in progress.

53. Of the 250 psychiatrists who came to the United States, not more than 50 were analysts. Yet many were very well known: Franz Alexander, Sandor Rado, and Otto Fenichel from Berlin; and Herman Ninberg, Felix Deutsch, Paul Federn, Heinz Hartmann, Ernst Kris, Paul Schilder, Else Pappenheim, Rudolph Loewenstein, René Spitz, and Robert Waelder from Vienna. The émigré analysts made a major impact on American psychiatry and psychoanalysis. Edward Shorter, *A History of Psychiatry: From the Era of the Asylum to the Age of Prozac* (New York: Wiley, 1997), 166–7.

54. Foucault, *Power/Knowledge*, 84–5.

Chapter 3

From Tradition through Colonialism to Globalization
Reflections on the History of Psychology in India

Anand C. Paranjpe

The history of psychology in India, as in the case of its history in the Western world, stretches back to ancient times. Contemporary Indian psychologists generally tend to ignore the contributions of the pre-modern period. Trained in modern Western psychology, they tend to share their Western counterparts' enthusiasm for "scientific" psychology, as well as a Whig approach to history that views later developments as superior to earlier ones (Leahey, 1987). In India as in the West, pre-modern psychology is often deemed to be philosophy. However, in India when compared to the Western world, there is an additional factor that has added to the psychologists' disdain for ancient insights of their own tradition. This factor involves the effects of colonial rule under which everything Indian was considered inferior to its Western counterpart. Given the widespread lack of awareness of psychological contributions of pre-modern India, I first describe in brief some of their salient features before turning to a still briefer account of psychology in India in modern times. Toward the end of this essay I discuss how and why the pre-modern insights were ignored in both colonial and postcolonial times, and I indicate the significance of the recent resurgence of interest in pre-modern insights in the context of internationalization and globalization.

Psychology in Ancient and Medieval India

Significant contributions to psychological thinking in India can be traced back to the early Upanishads, philosophical texts that were composed sometime between 1500 to 600 years BCE. About a dozen of the most ancient among these texts (Hume, 1931; Radhakrishnan, 1994) are seminal. They set the tone for an uninterrupted intellectual tradition. Over the centuries, many schools of thought that tried to interpret and systematize the Upanishadic and pre-Upanishadic ideas developed. Side by side several rebels and dissenters, such as the Buddhists, Jains, and the materialist Lokayatas, developed their own schools of thought. During the course of this development psychology did not form a separate discipline, but psychological concepts and methods were integral parts of philosophical, religious, artistic, and spiritual pursuits. The psychological contributions of this pre-modern period have been charted by a number of modern scholars (J. Sinha, 1958; 1961; Ramachandra Rao, 1962; Safaya, 1976). A selective overview of some of the important ideas from the literature of these times is given below. Before beginning that overview, it is necessary to note the history of intercontinental exchange of ideas in the ancient times.

Halbfass (1988) has charted the exchange of ideas between India and Europe through the ages. He notes some prominent instances of ideas that traveled from India to Europe that have implications for the history of psychology in India and Europe. He notes, for instance, that Philostratus, one of Pythagoras's junior contemporaries, presents Pythagoras (582– c. 507 BCE) as a recipient and transmitter of Egyptian, and ultimately Indian, wisdom (p. 9). Pythagoras's ideas about the distinction between the soul and the body and his belief in the transmission of the soul across life cycles are mentioned as indicative of the Indian influence.

The next most significant landmark is Plotinus (c. 205–270 CE), whose contacts with the East were affirmed by his disciple and biographer Porphyry. Plotinus's focus on contemplation, his description of his own ecstatic or mystical states, and his adoption of a monistic philosophy have been traced to the Upanishads. There is considerable amount of recent scholarship on this East-West connection (Harris, 1982). The influence of Plotinus and other neo-Platonic philosophers on St. Augustine is well known. The thin but continuing thread of the inward look for truth in the Western tradition from St. Augustine (354–430) in the fourth century to Husserl (1859–1938) in the twentieth century constitutes a lasting parallel between Indian and Western approaches to psychology. What we now call "internationalization" is, after all, not a new phenomenon; its roots go back to a longer history of intercontinental movement of people and ideas. Given the widespread amnesia about Indian contributions to psychology from the pre-modern period, I present a selective sketch of the same in the following section.

Distinctive Contributions of Psychology in Pre-modern India

Psychology of Consciousness

One of the most ancient texts called the *Māṇḍūkya* Upanishad (Radhakrishnan, 1994, pp. 695–705) refers to the four states of consciousness: namely, wakeful, dream, deep sleep, and another simply called the Fourth State. Another Upanishad called the *Bṛhadāraṇyaka* (4.3.33)[1] describes such a state as immensely blissful in nature and suggests deep contemplation as a way to attain it. It is said to be a nonintentional state of awareness devoid of content and devoid of subject/object split. The experience of such a state has been highly valued for millennia because of at least two reasons. First, because it is said to be a zillion times[2] more intense than the highest happiness a strong and healthy person may be able to attain with the help of the greatest amount of wealth and power. Second, because the experience of the Fourth State is said to reveal the true, unchanging self that underlies continually changing images of the self, and thereby end the chase of a still better version of one's self. This idea needs more explanation, which is attempted below.

Discovery of an Unchanging True Self in the Fourth State of Consciousness

It is commonplace that human beings develop views about oneself that demand continual revision in light of the unfolding of history and life history. It is equally true that, despite the continually changing images of virtually every aspect of oneself, most of us for the most part of life get an unmistakable feeling of having been the same person. The inherent contradiction of being the same person despite incessant change involves the "problem of identity." This problem is a complex philosophical puzzle, as well as an existential conundrum that some of the greatest minds of the world have tried to solve without reaching a universally satisfactory solution. Thinkers of the Indian tradition have suggested a psychological solution to this problem, claiming that an unchanging basis underlying continually changing images of the self is directly experienced in the Fourth

State of consciousness. The chase after an increasingly pleasing image of the self, which is common to most people, is said to be futile, regardless of any amount of success in any endeavor. This is because human expectations—or "pretensions" as William James (1983, p. 296) called them—always tend to exceed even the greatest levels of success. Alternatively, experience of the Fourth State is said to help discover an inner source of inexhaustible bliss that is independent of all external conditions.

Nature of Self: Its Affirmation and Denial

As noted above, the Upanishads strongly affirmed the existence of a true and unchanging self. Gautama Buddha, who rebelled against several religious practices of the Vedic tradition to which the Upanishads belong, proposed a dialectically opposing doctrine of the no-self (*anattā*). Over the millennia, Buddha's followers developed a number of philosophical systems that often differed radically from one another, but almost all of them followed the doctrine of no-self. At the same time, many differing schools of thought in the Upanishadic tradition proposed equally sophisticated arguments affirming the self. As shown by Paranjpe (1998b), the dialectics of the Upanishadic affirmation versus Buddhist denial of self in the Indian tradition has interesting parallels with the affirmation of self from Kant to Erikson versus denial of self from Hume to Skinner in the history of Western psychology. In the Indian tradition, however, despite the irreconcilably opposing claims for and against the self, there is virtually consensual opinion about the desirability of the attainment of higher states of consciousness through various techniques of meditation. "Yoga" is a generic term for a wide variety of techniques designed to alter one's consciousness. In the remainder of this section, I briefly describe the essential features of four major types of Yoga: namely, Patañjali's Dhyāna-Yoga, and the Jñāna-, Karma-, and Bhakti-Yogas. The reason for choosing these four is that they focus on, respectively, consciousness, cognition, volition, and emotion—psychological phenomena that have been viewed as central issues for psychology in the West, as well as in India.

Stream of Consciousness and Its Control in the Dhyāna-Yoga of Patañjali

The focus of Patañjali's famous aphorisms (Woods, 1972) is on the "mind-river" (*citta nadī*), or the stream of consciousness as William James called it. Patañjali suggests that the "self," as we commonly understand it, commonly remains identified with the passing thought of the moment and thereby keeps on changing as long as the stream is allowed to flow. Unlike the protagonist of Sartre's (1964) novel *Nausea*, who finds himself helplessly drifting with the ongoing flow of the stream of consciousness (pp. 99–100), Patañjali claims that, with the relentless effort in the prescribed direction, it is indeed possible to bring the stream of consciousness to a virtual halt. When this task is accomplished, self-realization is attained as the unchanging backdrop underlying changing images of the self is revealed in the experience of a state called the *Samādhi*.

Cognition and the Path of Knowledge: Jñāna-Yoga

Almost all schools of Indian thought—the Upanishadic, Buddhist, Jaina, and so on—have developed complex theories of cognition and epistemology. Of these schools, a prominent one called the Advaita (meaning nondualist) Vedānta emphasizes the constructive aspects of cognition. It suggests that there is an unmistakable element of cognitive construction in human processes of getting to know the world. It insists that the world, as we know it, is largely a matter of cognitive construction (Paranjpe, 1998a). Individuals continue to construct and continually reconstruct their images of the self within a shared world view of the community. The Advaita Vedānta system postulates a single, ubiquitous, and unchanging principle of reality underlying the flux of the universe and claims that this reality provides the unchanging backdrop that underlies the continually changing images of the self. Following the *Bṛhadāraṇyaka* Upanishad mentioned earlier, it has developed a rigorous method of critical self-examination as a way to recognize that all images of the self (or self-concepts) are ultimately changeable, no matter how serviceable they are in carrying out one's business in the practical world. Through relentless self-examination, it is claimed, one is able to clearly distinguish the changing images of the self from the unchanging nature of the true self and then directly experience it in the Fourth State of consciousness. A person who has thus experienced the true self can remain stably anchored in it and carry on in daily life without riding high on an ego fluffed with success or feeling depressed with failure. An unshakable inner calm—a highly desirable state—is thus attained.

Volition and the Path of Action: Karma-Yoga

One of the fundamental assumptions that is almost universally shared in the schools of Indian thought is the Law of Karma, which states that all actions, indeed all events in the universe, are inevitably followed by their legitimate and inevitable consequences. As pointed out by Potter (1980), this assumption is similar to the law of causality in the natural sciences in assuring that the universe is a cosmos and not a chaos, except that according to the Law of Karma, lawfulness extends beyond the physical world to the mental and moral worlds as well. As in the Bible, it is assumed that as you sow, so shall you reap. As one action leads to its appropriate consequences, whether in the form of reward or punishment, new experiences occur eliciting new responses, and the individual gets "bound down," so to speak, to an unending chain of cause and effect. Within such a conceptual framework, the *Bhagavad-Gītā*, a highly popular text of great antiquity, suggests a way for getting oneself unbound from the karmic chain.

The way out suggested by the *Gītā* (as the *Bhagavad-Gītā* is briefly referred to) follows from a rational analysis of the many factors that shape the outcome of an action—namely, (a) the context of action, (b) the agent, (c) the various means or instruments available to the agent, (d) the specific activities undertaken, and finally (e) "fate," or chance. Although the agent is but one of these many factors determining the outcome, people often tend to take credit for success and blame outside factors for failure. Such a tendency has been commonly noted in the literature on attribution theory, and Greenwald (1980) has coined the term "beneffectance" to refer to it. The *Gītā* prescribes that one should monitor this tendency and learn to be rational in judging one's contributions to success and failure. It also asks us not to hanker for rewards, because hankering leads to high levels of ego-involvement and constant oscillation between euphoria and despair with success and failure. By following the *Gītā*'s prescription, a person can learn to put one's ego in its place, as it were, and eventually abide in the unchanging self rather than riding high and low with success and failure. Obviously, retaining inner peace and calm in the face of the ups and downs in life is considered a valuable existential gain.

Emotion and the Path of Devotion: Bhakti-Yoga

Although psychology in India is dominated by the spiritual quest, other mundane interests have also helped shape psychological thought. A prime example of this is approaches to emotion that developed in the context of dramatics. Bharata's *Nāṭyaśāstra* (Bharatamuni, 1956), a major treatise on drama and aesthetics, identifies eight major and thirty-three minor emotions, providing detailed analysis of their causal determinants, contextual elicitors, and bodily expressions (Paranjpe, 1998a, for interpretation in the context of contemporary psychology). Bharata distinguishes major emotions such as love and fear from minor ones, arguing that the former are common to animals and humans and that they are more durable ones when compared with the relatively transitory "minor" emotions such as shame. He not only realized the commonality of emotions in the animal world but also noted that the expressions of emotions were guided by both animal instincts and social conventions. Bharata distinguishes emotions from aesthetic sentiments that are experienced in the process of relishing the portrayal of emotions in works of art, particularly drama. Many scholars who followed Bharata's lead pointed out that aesthetic sentiments —called the *rasas*—are socially shared, and placed them in social reality rather than exclusively in the physical reality or bodily tissues. The placing of aesthetic sentiments in the social reality strikes a chord with the recently emerging social constructionist view of emotions (Harré, 1986).

An important observation of the *rasa* theory is that the aesthetic sentiments aroused in the appreciation of art affords the distancing of the ego from its mundane concerns, thereby offering an enjoyable transformation of not only the pleasurable emotions such as love and mirth but also of unpleasant emotions like fear and even disgust. In the late fifteenth century Rūpa Gosvāmī (1981) brought the concept of *rasa* from its relatively "secular" context of art to help explain the nature of religious devotion. Sometime in the early Christian era, a great "mythological" work on the life of Krishna called the *Bhāgavata Purāṇa* (see *Śrīmad Bhāgavatam*) tried to explain the self-transforming effects of religious devotion through the intensification of emotions—of not only love but even single-minded hatred—directed to a deity. Gosvāmī and his nephew Jīva developed a systematic theory of religious devotion explaining, first, the self-transforming effect of approaching the deity, Krishna, in a variety of role relationships such as child, friend, master, lover, and so on, and, second, the relevance of the use of song, dance, drama, and other forms of art in creating an intense experience of devotion *(bhakti)* as an all-encompassing sentiment, or *rasa*. The Gosvāmīs argued that through the intensification of emotion by means of role play and with the use of various art forms, a devotee can immerse herself or himself in an intense experience of devotional *rasa* that involves an all-pervading divine love embellished by a variety of ancillary aesthetic sentiments. Such experience, they claim, far exceeds the uplifting function of the experience of art. While the experience and appreciation of works of art only temporarily relieves the aesthete from mundane concerns of the ego, the experience of devotional *rasa* dissolves the ego by totally immersing the devotee in the experience of divine love.

Psychology in India during the Colonial Period

The British East India Company established its political dominance in India by the late eighteenth century. The company's educational policies were discussed in the British Parliament well before the Indian subcontinent was formally accessioned to Queen Victoria's Empire in 1857. As early as in 1835, Thomas Macaulay (1972), a member of the British Parliament, convinced his colleagues that the company must adopt exclusively European ideas in education within its territories. He denigrated traditional knowledge by saying such things as "information . . . collected from all the books written in the Sanskrit language is less valuable than what may be found in the most paltry abridgements used at preparatory schools in England" (p. 241). It is under an exclusively Westernized educational system guided by Macaulay's ideas that the universities in the British Raj always functioned. The colonial educational system did not—and could not—bring the Indian intellectual tradition to a complete stop; works in Sanskrit have continued to be published till this day. However, traditional scholarship was systematically marginalized under the colonial rule, and the trend continued as colonial mentality persisted for decades after independence.

It is within the totally Westernized educational system that the first psychology laboratory was started in 1905 at the University of Calcutta. Narendra Nath Sengupta, the first chairman of the department of experimental psychology was trained under Hugo Münsterberg at Harvard. This was the beginning of the transplantation of modern Western psychology onto Indian soil. Sengupta's successor, Girindra Sekhar Bose, learned psychoanalytical concepts from Freud's books and became one of the few psychoanalysts officially accredited on the basis of self-analysis. He founded the Indian Psychoanalytical Society in 1922. The life and work of Bose forms an important chapter in the history of India during the colonial period (Nandy, 1998). Christiane Hartnack (2001) has published a comprehensive history of psychoanalysis in colonial India. As pointed out by her, despite vigorous activity in psychoanalytical society centered mainly in Calcutta, the psychoanalytical movement gradually faded away.

During the four decades that elapsed between the founding of the first psychological laboratory in 1905 and the end of colonial rule in 1947, Western psychology was steadily but firmly transferred to the Indian subcontinent through a long line of scholars trained abroad. The two main areas of research were experimental and psychometrics. In 1924 M. V. Gopalaswami started a laboratory in Mysore after being trained under Spearman at London University. He gave an impetus to work in psychometry, as well as experimental psychology. The *Indian Journal of Psychology* was started in 1926. By 1947 there were only three universities offering graduate programs in psychology. Durganand Sinha's historical overview of publications in this colonial period points out that Indian psychology "remained tied to the apron-strings of the West" (1986, p. 36). It would be hardly surprising if the flow of ideas during the colonial period was from powerful West to the subjugated East, but it is worth noting the flow of ideas in the reverse direction.

Even prior to British colonization of India and other regions of the East, Arabic scholars associated with the Islamic invasions carried important Indian concepts westward. As is now well known, the decimal system, which originated in India, was transmitted to Europe and became known as Arabic numerals. During the middle of the seventeenth century, the Mughal prince Dārā Shukōh had caused a Persian translation of the Upanishads, which found its way across the Middle East to Europe. Anquetil Durerron, a French scholar, published a Latin translation of this Persian translation in 1801–1802. This translation reached European thinkers like Schopenhauer, eliciting great interest in Indian thought in the nineteenth century. Several British officers of the empire, like Colonel Jacob, not only learned Sanskrit but also translated important texts into English. In the later part of the nineteenth century, a group of European and American scholars became interested in Indian philosophical thought, and more particularly in occult phenomena associated with Yoga. They formed a group called the Theosophical Society, which became instrumental in introducing Indian thought in America. As is well known, American thinkers such as Walt Whitman and David Thoreau became well acquainted with Indian thought.

William James was initially exposed to Indian thought through such connections. In 1883 James met Swami Vivekananda after he became well known in the United States due to his famous speech at the World Council of Religions in Chicago. In his *Varieties of Religious Experience,* James (1958) refers to the extraordinary states of consciousness experienced by Indian Yogis and saints such as Ramakrishna Paramahamsa, the guru of Swami Vivekananda. Carl Jung visited India in 1938 and is widely credited for introducing psychological concepts from India and other parts of Asia to the West (Jung, 1978).

Psychology in India in the Postcolonial Period

There was a rapid expansion of education in India after the end of the colonial rule. As part of this overall expansion, psychology showed phenomenal growth. Durganand Sinha (1986) cites the following statistics for the period from 1947 to 1982: the number of universities offering graduate degrees in psychology rose from 3 to 57; the enrollments in graduate degree programs rose from 1,122 in 1961 to 4,194 in 1981; and during the same two decades the number of doctorates awarded went up from twelve to ninety-six. Dalal (2002) estimates that in India in the early 1990s there were about 4,500 psychologists. There were few national and several provincial associations of psychologists, and forty-four psychology journals were being published. In addition to the universities, psychology was taught at several prestigious institutes such as the well-known Indian Institutes of Technology (the IITs), the National Institute of Educational Research and Training (NCERT) in Delhi, and the National Institute for Mental Health and Neuro-Science (NIMHANS) in Bangalore. Sinha (1986) cites statistics about research trends in the 1950s and the 1960s, which show clinical (19 percent), personality (18 percent), social (13 percent), industrial (12 percent), and experimental (10 percent) as the most common areas of published research papers.

Throughout the post-independence period, psychologists in India have been increasingly exposed to the outside world, and their work reflects the effects of internationalization. At least three sources of international input may be noted: first, a growing number of Indian students have been going to England, the United States, and Canada to pursue higher degrees, often with the assistance of foreign or Indian scholarships; second, visits by foreign scholars, some of them conducting cross-cultural research, have increased; third, Indian psychologists participate in international fora, particularly the International Association of Cross-Cultural Psychology.

The dominance of Western models that began in the colonial days continued well into the postcolonial decades. A common trend was to replicate studies published in British or American journals following their experimental procedures or paper and pencil tests. The imitation was often blind, although some attention was given to adapt imported tests to local conditions. But adaptation was often cosmetic and earned the epithet "adaptology." There is no need to describe the typical topics or contents of research output of this era to an international audience, since it is simply "more of the same" that they must have encountered in prestigious international journals, especially American and British.

During the 1970s a majority of Indian psychological studies began to be perceived as Western imports that had no connection with life in India. Dalal (2002) quotes Ashis Nandy's pithy words published in the latter's article in 1974: "Indian psychology has become not merely imitative and subservient, but also dull and replicative" (p. 5). In his authoritative review of the literature of the 1971–1976 period sponsored by the Indian Council of Social Science Research, the well-known psychologist Udai Pareek (1980) concluded that there were "signs of a growing crisis in psychology" insofar as psychology had "failed to make a thrust in the national life" (Vol. 1, p. ix). As editor of the comprehensive review of the field, Pareek made a series of recommendations for a healthy development of psychology in India: psychologists should keep in touch with social reality, work on urgent social issues, make use of India's rich inheritance of the knowledge of self and its epistemological traditions, and so on (Vol. 2, Ch. 13).

Pareek's call for this new direction for psychology was well heeded. In the 1980s and 1990s, Indian psychologists turned to the study of a host of pressing social problems, such as the psychology of poverty and inequality, social change, issues in family planning, leadership in village society and in industrial organizations, issues in organizational psychology—and the list goes on. There is not enough place in this essay to review the progress in these fields of study. From an international standpoint, it is necessary to consider how the problem of blind application of Western models was addressed and whether Pareek's call for developing psychology on the basis of the native intellectual tradition was heard.

The problem of the misfit of imported theories and methods is by no means unique to India; it was a common complaint in many "developing societies" where psychologists had followed Euro-American models. The need for development of psychology in tune with the local culture has been widely recognized and often labeled "indigenization." It has become a widely discussed topic especially in the field of cross-cultural psychology. Insofar as a majority of psychologists in India, as well as many other "developing" countries were trained in Western models, they could not suddenly shift to indigenously developed theories and methods. It was but natural for them to continue using concepts and tests borrowed from the West, albeit with gradually increasing sensitivity to local cultural context. The Canadian psychologist John Adair saw indigenization as a gradual process, and in collaboration with his Indian colleagues, he developed a scale to measure the degree of indigenization. Adair and his colleagues concluded on the basis of content analysis of a sample of over 300 journal articles that there was progress in indigenization of psychology in India, albeit at a slow pace (Adair, Puhan, and Vohra, 1993). Surely concern over the dominance of American psychology and attempts to develop psychology appropriate to indigenous cultures and societies is common not only to Third World countries but also in the Second World countries of Europe (Moghaddam, 1987). It is important to note in this context that, as Adair and his associates clarify, their focus is on the indigenization of an "imported discipline" and not on "endogenous development" of psychology based on indigenous sources.

A call for the development of psychology based on the indigenous intellectual tradition did not begin with Pareek's review mentioned before; in the mid-1960s Durganand Sinha (1965) had appealed for the "integration of modern psychology with Indian thought." Although scholars such as Jadunath Sinha (1958; 1961) and Ramachandra Rao (1962) had already begun to rejuvenate psychology embedded in the ancient tradition prior to Sinha's call, new efforts in explaining crucial traditional insights in contemporary context were needed. Such efforts were forthcoming in the 1980s and have continued to flourish with increased vigor. Notable among such efforts are the publications by Anand Paranjpe (1984; 1988; 1998a) and K. Ramakrishna Rao (1988; 2002). By this time the literature in this category is already rich and growing; it would need separate essays—even a volume—to review it. This new trend involves not only the interpretation of traditional concepts and theories in contemporary idiom but also their integration within a broader, global perspective that tries to put East and West together without separation or presumed superiority of one over the other. Some efforts are also under way to put empirical test concepts, such as that of traditional personality typology (Mohan and Sandhu, 1986), or theories, such as the theory of action without emotional attachment to results based on ancient sources like the *Bhagavad-Gītā* (Pande and Naidu, 1992). It is by systematic and thoughtful integration of concepts, theories, and methods originating across history and geography that psychology can move toward globalization of psychological knowledge.

Globalization of psychological knowledge would be meaningless if only the Western theories keep being exported to the Third World and get adapted and adopted there with no reciprocal movement of ideas. As noted earlier in this essay, ideas of psychological significance have been transported since ancient times through the colonial era from India to the West. Given the imbalance of power between the East and the West, it would be small wonder if Indian and other Eastern concepts had not found place in Western countries. Nevertheless, the link established by William James's interest in Indian views of the higher states of consciousness continued after a long gap. As is widely known, Timothy Leary and Richard Alpert (a.k.a. Baba Ram Dass) went to India in 1967 after being fired from Harvard in connection with their research on the effect of drugs on consciousness (Ram Dass, 1974). Although the youthful interest in Ravi Shankar's sitar and other things Indian faded with the growing up of the peaceniks of the Vietnam War era, some serious academic interest in Yoga, meditation, and the "altered states of consciousness" persisted (Goleman, 1977; Tart, 1969). Textbooks on theories of personality opened up to the East by including chapters on Eastern theories of personality (Fadiman and Frager, 1976; Hall and Lindzey, 1978). Although Hall and Lindzey's move in this direction seemed like a step in the door of the prestigious academic world of American psychology, the later version of their popular text seemed to shut that door (Hall et al., 1985). However, the popularity of Maharishi Mahesh Yogi's Transcendental Meditation has continued to inspire a long series of studies in Vedic Psychology,[3] although this field, like that of Transpersonal Psychology, has remained at the fringe of academic psychology.

Problems in, and Prospects for, the Globalization of Psychological Knowledge

Disciplines have a history of their own as do nations, and like nations new disciplines arise and old ones transform; the boundaries of disciplines change over time, as do those of nations. Internationalization of psychology must deal with these dynamic boundaries or be stopped in its tracks. The boundaries of traditional psychology in India were defined by a spiritual quest, which is alien to the mainstream of modern psychology, especially in America. Those influenced by such alienation are likely to view pre-modern psychology as described earlier in this essay as out of bounds for psychology as they view it. In my view, consciousness and cognition, affect, and conation—or the trilogy of mind as Hilgard (1980) called it—form the core subject matter of psychology. These have been historically common areas of interest in India as they have been in the West (Paranjpe 1998a). The history of American psychology has witnessed a period of domination by the behaviorist—especially Skinnerian—model, where consciousness was pushed out of psychology's domain and where cognition, affect, and conation were viewed sans subjectivity, reducing them to, respectively, perception, activation of the body, and behavior without volition. However, the tide of behaviorism is said to have ebbed, and consciousness and self have returned to mainstream psychology. Yet the alienation of Western psychology from spirituality continues and poses as an obstacle to the possible integration of prominent Indian insights into a global mainstream of psychology. In my view, such alienation does not imply that the East is spiritual and the West is material as the stereotype goes; spiritual and material needs are common around the globe—although to different degrees in different cultures. Here again, history is the guide for understanding the periodic variations in the dominant features of a discipline.

In his historical analysis of Western spirituality, Pierre Hadot (1995) has pointed out how spiritual exercises have been part of the Western tradition from ancient to contemporary times—from Socrates right down to Foucault. It is not only that the spiritual quest is alive and well in the West, a careful look would show considerable similarity between the aims and the methods of spirituality in East and West. To say the least, "know thyself" was as important an injunction in ancient Greece as it was in India; meditation, as some form of "dialogue with oneself" (Hadot, 1995, p. 91) has been common in Western spiritual practices as in the Indian tradition. As well, inner tranquility or peace of mind—*amerimnia* as Hadot refers to it—was one of the most sought-after goals of spiritual practices (p. 130). Hadot has shown in detail how the Stoics and the Epicurians developed philosophies of life along with a variety of spiritual practices to help achieve existential benefits such as peace of mind. According to Hadot,

Christians incorporated such pagan practices in their repertoire when they started to develop a "philosophy" of their own. During the late medieval times, as controversies raged in Europe over faith versus reason (Jones, 1969, pp. 197–207), philosophy was segregated as a purely rational inquiry, leaving its traditional spiritual components entirely to the church. Against this background, it makes sense that contemporary books on the history of philosophy tend to omit the spiritual exercise aspect of ancient philosophers. Further, philosophy and science were sharply separated from religion around the seventeenth century in Europe when emerging science spearheaded by Galileo came into serious conflict with the church. Such historical developments are typical of the intellectual history of Europe and remarkably alien to the intellectual history of India (Paranjpe, 1984).

As William James's writings clearly show, modern Western psychology had no aversion for either philosophy or religion when he founded it in the later nineteenth century. However, psychology in the twentieth century, enamored by the technological benefits spawned by various advances in physics and biology, developed a staunch alliance with natural sciences. As noted by C. P. Snow (1959), the world of science and technology drifted away from that of the arts and the humanities. Against this background, Western psychology moved away not only from religion and philosophy but also from the arts and the humanities, perhaps with the exception of psychoanalysis. Given all this, it is hardly a surprise that the close association of psychology in India with spirituality, philosophy, religion, and the arts would appear antithetical to the spirit of modern Western psychology. Having imported Western psychology lock, stock, and barrel, psychology in modern India shared the alienation from spirituality, philosophy, religion, and the arts. While this was enough for the sequestering of modern from traditional psychology in India, the colonial mentality widened the rift further.

Except for the work of Ashis Nandy (1998), the flourishing field of postcolonial studies has not affected psychology in any significant way. There are, however, some postcolonial insights relevant to the topic on hand. Following Edward Said's (1978) well-known work, *Orientalism*, Richard King (1999) has shown how, within the "orientalist" imagery of the colonial era, "mysticism" was created as a category associated with private, irrational, and quietist as opposed to public, rational, and activist features. A clear illustration of such characterization is seen in Bertrand Russell's writings, where he portrays mysticism as an anti-rational philosophy committed to inaction (Russell, 1921; 1935). Besides, the word "mystical" has acquired several negative connotations, such as incommunicable, secret, and esoteric—although many mystics defy such characterization (Paranjpe, 1984). As well, insofar as consciousness as such was thrown out of psychology's boundaries as defined by behaviorism, higher states of consciousness, which are commonly thought of as mystical, became even more remote for the enterprise of psychology. Behaviorism, as is well known, was closely allied with the philosophy of logical positivism (Smith, 1986), and psychologists influenced by behaviorism often share logical positivism's ideal of the "unity of science." This is clearly illustrated in the strong yearning for a unified psychology expressed by Arthur Staats (1983). The positivist notion that all science must speak with one voice tends to militate against the differing perspectives warranted by indigenous psychologies from around the world. To say the least, ideals such as the unity of science borrowed from logical positivism would tend to rule out the diversity of perspectives demanded by an international and cross-cultural dialogue in psychology. Without a tolerant pluralism, the globalization of psychological knowledge will be little more than a new form of imperialism.

NOTES

1. For an English translation of the principal Upanishads, see Radhakrishnan (1994).

2. The *Bṛhadāraṇyaka* Upanishad (4.3.3) takes the highest pleasure attainable by a strong, well-endowed and highly educated youth with all the worldly means such as wealth and power at his disposal as one unit of pleasure, and estimates bliss experienced in the Fourth State as 100 quintillion multiples of this unit. A similar account is found in the *Taittirīya* Upanishad (2.8). Such a description may be viewed either as an ancient rating scale or hyperbole. Nevertheless, it speaks of the immensely positive nature of such an experience.

3. A long list of publications, including many on Vedic psychology related to Transcendental Meditation, is readily available on their website: http://www.tm.org.

REFERENCES

Adair, John. G., Biranchi N. Puhan, and Neharika Vohra. 1993. "Indigenization of psychology: Empirical assessment of progress in Indian research." *International Journal of Psychology*, 28, 149–169.

Bharatamuni. 1956. *Nāṭyaśāstra of Bharatamuni with the commentary Abhinav-abhāratī by Abhinavaguptācārya* (2nd ed.). K. S. R. Sastri (Ed.). Baroda, India: Oriental Institute. (Date of original publication of Bharata's work unknown.)

Dalal, Ajit K. 2002. "Psychology in India: A historical introduction." In Girishwar Misra and Ajit K. Mohanty (Eds.), *Perspectives on indigenous psychology.* New Delhi: Concept.

Fadiman, James, and Robert Frager. 1976. *Personality and personal growth* (1st ed.; 3rd ed. 1994). New York: HarperCollins.

Goleman, Daniel. 1977. *The varieties of meditative experience.* New York: Dutton.

Gosvāmī, Rūpa. 1981. *Bhaktirasāmṛtasindhu.* Shyamdas (Ed. and Commentator). Vṛndāvana, India: Shyamlal Hakim. (The exact date of original publication unknown.)

Greenwald, A. G. 1980. "The totalitarian ego: Fabrication and revision of personal history." *American Psychologist,* 35, 603–618.

Hadot, Pierre. 1995. *Philosophy as a way of life: Spiritual exercises from Socrates to Foucault.* A. I. Davidson (Ed.); M. Chase (Trans.). Oxford, U.K.: Blackwell.

Halbfass, Wilhelm. 1988. *India and Europe: An essay in understanding.* New York: State University of New York Press. (Original work published 1981)

Hall, Calvin S., and Gardner Lindzey. 1978. *Theories of personality* (3rd ed.). New York: Wiley.

Hall, Calvin S., Gardner Lindzey, J. C. Loehlin, and M. Manosevitz. 1985. *Introduction to theories of personality.* New York: Wiley.

Harré, Romano (Ed.). 1986. *The social construction of emotions.* Oxford: Basil Blackwell.

Harris, R. Baine (Ed.). 1982. *Neoplatonism and Indian thought.* Norfolk, VA: International Society for Neoplatonic Studies.

Hartnack, Christiane. 2001. *Psychoanalysis in colonial India.* Delhi: Oxford University Press.

Hilgard, Ernest R. 1980. "The trilogy of mind: Cognition, affection and conation." *Journal of the History of the Behavioral Sciences,* 16, 107–117.

Hume, Robert Ernest (Trans. and Ed.). 1931. *The thirteen principal Upanishads* (2nd ed.). Oxford: Oxford University Press.

James, William. 1958. *The varieties of religious experience.* New York: New American Library. (Originally published 1902.)

James, William. 1983. *Principles of psychology.* Cambridge, MA: Harvard University Press. (Originally published 1890.)

Jones, W. T. 1969. *A history of Western philosophy: The medieval mind* (2nd rev. ed.), Vol. 2. New York: Harcourt, Brace and World.

Jung, C. G. 1978. *Psychology and the East.* R. F. C. Hull (Trans.). Princeton, NJ: Princeton University Press.

King, Richard. 1999. *Orientalism and religion: Postcolonial theory, India, and the "mystic East."* New York: Routledge.

Leahey, Thomas Hardy. 1987. *A history of psychology: Main currents in psychological thought.* Englewood Cliffs, NJ: Prentice Hall.

Macaulay, Thomas Babington. 1972. "Minute on Indian education." In T. B. Macaulay, *Selected writings* (pp. 237–251). John Clive and Thomas Pinney (Eds.). Chicago: University of Chicago Press. (Original "Minute" presented in 1835.)

Moghaddam, Fathali M. 1987. "Psychology in the Three Worlds as reflected by the crisis in social psychology and the move toward indigenous Third World psychology." *American Psychologist,* 42, 912–920.

Mohan, V., and Sandhu, S. 1986. "Development of scale to measure *sattvic, rajasic* and *tamasic guna.*" *Journal of Indian Academy of Applied Psychology,* 12, 46–52.

Nandy, Ashis. 1998. "The savage Freud: The first non-Western psychoanalyst and the politics of secret selves in colonial India." In A. Nandy, *Return from exile* (pp. 81–144). Delhi: Oxford University Press.

Pande, Namita, and Radha Krishna Naidu. 1992. "Anasakti and health: A study of non-attachment." *Psychology and Developing Societies,* 4, 89–104.

Paranjpe, Anand C. 1984. *Theoretical psychology: The meeting of East and West.* New York: Plenum.

Paranjpe, Anand C. 1988. A personality theory according to Vedānta. In Anand C. Paranjpe, David Y. F. Ho, and Robert W. Rieber (Eds.), *Asian contributions to psychology* (pp. 185–214). New York: Praeger.

Paranjpe, Anand C. 1998a. *Self and identity in modern psychology and Indian thought.* New York: Plenum.

Paranjpe, Anand C. 1998b. "Theory and history of psychology and the denial and affirmation of the self." In Robert W. Rieber and Kurt Salzinger (Eds.), *Psychology: Theoretical-historical perspectives* (pp. 135–187) (2nd ed.). Washington, DC: American Psychological Association.

Pareek, Udai (Ed.) 1980. *A survey of research in psychology, 1971–76* (2 Vols.). Bombay: Popular Prakashan.

Potter, Karl H. 1980. "Karma theory in some Indian philosophical systems." In Wendy Doniger O'Flaherty (Ed.), *Karma and rebirth in classical Indian traditions* (pp. 241–267). Berkeley: University of California Press.

Radhakrishnan, S. (Ed. and Trans.). 1994. *The principal Upanishads.* Delhi: HarperCollins India. (First published 1953.)

Ramachandra Rao, S. K. 1962. *Development of psychological thought in India.* Mysore: Kavyalaya.

Ramakrishna Rao, K. 1988. "Psychology of transcendence: A study in early Buddhism." In Anand C. Paranjpe, David Y. F. Ho, and Robert W. Rieber (Eds.), *Asian contributions to psychology* (pp. 123–148). New York: Praeger.

Ramakrishna Rao, K. 2002. *Consciousness studies: Cross-cultural perspectives.* Jefferson, NC: McFarland.

Ram Dass. 1974. *The only dance there is.* Garden City, NY: Doubleday.

Russell, Bertrand. 1921. *Mysticism and logic and other essays.* London: Longmans, Green.

Russell, Bertrand. 1935. *Sceptical essays.* London: Unwin.

Safaya, R. 1976. *Indian psychology.* Delhi: Munshiram Manoharlal.

Said, Edward W. 1978. *Orientalism.* London: Routledge.

Sartre, Jean-Paul. 1964. *Nausea.* L. Alexander (Trans.). New York: New Directions. (Originally published 1938.)

Sinha, Durganand. 1965. "The integration of modern psychology with Indian thought." *Journal of Humanistic Psychology,* 5, 6–17.

Sinha, Durganand. 1986. *Psychology in a Third World country.* New Delhi: Sage.

Sinha, Jadunath. 1958. *Indian Psychology,* Vol. I: *Cognition.* Calcutta: Jadunath Sinha Foundation. (First published, 1934.)

Sinha, Jadunath. 1961. *Indian Psychology,* Vol. II: *Emotion and Will.* Calcutta: Jadunath Sinha Foundation. (Date of original publication unknown.)

Smith, Laurence D. 1986. *Behaviorism and logical positivism: A reassessment of the alliance.* Stanford, CA: Stanford University Press.

Snow, Charles Percy. 1959. *The two cultures and the scientific revolution.* New York: Cambridge University Press.

Śrīmad Bhāgavatam. n.d./1972– (10 Vols.). A. C. Bhativedanta Swami Prabhupada (Ed. and Trans.). New York: Bhativedanta Book Trust.

Staats, Arthur W. 1983. *Psychology's crisis of disunity: Philosophy and method for a unified science.* New York: Praeger.

Tart, Charles T. (Ed.). 1969. *Altered states of consciousness.* New York: Wiley.

Woods, James Houghton. 1972. *The Yoga-system of Patañjali.* Delhi: Motilal Banarsidass. (Originally published 1914.)

Chapter 4

History of Psychology in Turkey as a Sign of Diverse Modernization and Global Psychologization

Aydan Gulerce

Although there has been a growing awareness of the constructive role of writing history in many fields, this chapter stems from an observation that progress in the interdependent areas of historical studies, in the direction of critical theory/practice (Horkheimer, 1982) which is not "critical enough" (Gulerce, 2001) and of new cultural history which is not so "new" (Dow, 1898; Kelley, 1996; Robinson, 1912; Ware, 1940), currently range from very limited to none. In other words, critical/cultural history needs to be further "glocal" (simultaneously both, global and local) and transformative. The task might seem rather huge as it demands a radical transformation of the common "Western modern scientific world view" that has been hegemonizing and isolating all human intelligibilities around the globe. Yet it is not impossible. Indeed, change in the area of psychological science is already happening as previous works—namely by Danziger (1990), Hacking (1995), Rose (1996), and others—demonstrate. Some of the contributors in this volume have had significant roles in that regard. Nevertheless, the field can benefit further from truly transdisciplinary, theoretically sound, culturally sensitive, and diverse, critical-practice oriented, political, philosophical, conceptual, and feminist insights from around the globe.

In a limited attempt toward that direction, in this chapter I revisit historical developments in the field of psychology in Turkey. The hope is to be able to point at an alternative modernization narrative of the society and their mutually co-constructive influences. Otherwise, there can be found various reviews of the history of psychology in Turkey (e.g., Acar and Sahin, 1990; Basaran and Sahin, 1990; Kagitcibasi, 1994; Le Compte, 1980; Tan, 1972; Togrol, 1983; Vassaf, 1987).

The interpellation and normalization of American psychology is so strong in Turkish society (Gergen et. al., 1996) that Turkish psychologists do not get to study systematically and think about the long historical period prior to the common celebratory historical marker of the establishment of a Western chair of experimental psychology at a Turkish university. Furthermore, Turkish psychology is even more ahistorical, acultural, and asocial than American psychology, so that even the very idea of critical and cultural history of psychology in Turkey seems oxymoronic, as a good example of overidentification. Thus, a thorough reinsertion of the people and their works that have been left out from the historical discourses, let alone the sociohistorical conditions that made them possible, calls for a serious effort. This is quite apart from any possible contribution to the redefinitions of (Western) psychology in general and to its historical accounts that it might make. It is a multidisciplinary, multinational, and multilingual project, requiring fluency in Turkish, Arabic, Ottoman, Persian, Russian, and some other European and Asian languages. Clearly, such work is beyond the scope of the present chapter. Nevertheless, it is more important in what follows not only to see a list of characters or events but also to understand them as signs of the societal and global historical conditions for, and transformations of, "Turkish psychology." That calls for a critical reading acquired by paying particular attention to both the signifiers and the signifieds in the language of semiotics that together make up those signs (Barthes, 1968; Lacan, 1956).

Psychology in Modern Turkey

One can easily say, in reference to Ebbinghaus's (1908) famous saying about modern psychology in the Western world, that psychology in Turkey has a much "longer past" and an even "shorter history." The reviews of the history of modern psychology in Turkey that I mentioned above unanimously date 1915 as the beginning of psychology in Turkey. H. Z. Ulken's (1966) comprehensive early works on the history of modern thought in Turkey, and of Islamic thought, gave some important leads, however, that psychology did exist prior to that. N. Bilgin's (1988) work on a bibliography of psychology in Turkey between 1928 and 1978 also deserves special recognition in this regard.

We obviously will leave a detailed discussion of the pre-Hellenistic, pre-Islamic, and Islamic long past outside. It is still possible to come up with a historical narrative that views the development of psychology in Turkey as a modern discipline (in the Foucauldian sense). It begins in the last quarter of the nineteenth century and hence is still much earlier than 1915. Prior to focusing on the history of psychology in isolation, however, some summative words about the overall historical and sociopolitical context are in order here.

The frequently used term "Westernization" originally referred to changes that occurred in the Russian Empire in the last two decades of the seventeenth century and in the Ottoman Empire in the second half of the eighteenth century. While India experienced colonization (not Westernization), Iran, China, and Japan did not face Westernization or colonization in the same sense. During those times, the West itself was in the early stages of "becoming the West" (Belge, 2002). This came a century later with the French Revolution and the Industrial Revolution. Further, the Industrial Revolution had an impact on the Ottoman Empire's decline. The dissemination of the world capitalist system, as well as the modernity project that developed following the Enlightenment in Europe, led to transformations in the institutional and economical structures of Ottoman society. Both the Ottoman and Russian Empires, being in closer proximity to Europe than to Iran, China, and Japan, could not stay out of the war in Europe and needed some reforms in order to survive as empires or remain "intact."

Indeed, I. Tekeli (2002) narrates the process of turning the multireligious, premodern society of the vast Ottoman Empire into the nation-state that is modern Turkish society in four distinct phases. At first, the societal problems that were stemming from (European) modernity were not recognized as external influences. Then, during the reigns of Sultan Selim II and Sultan Mahmut II, the connections between internal problems and modernity were understood and various reforms were made. The institutionalization of individual ownership and rights, the differentiation of public and private spaces, and the replacement of the military personnel with the bureaucratic public administrators were among the first significant changes. During this second phase, European societies were not merely examined; many students were sent abroad (mostly to France), and modern educational institutions were established. Under the influence of Western knowledge, law, and art, the internalization of modernism as the guiding political orientation became apparent. The third phase corresponds to the ruling periods of Abdulmecit, Abdulaziz, and Abdulhamit II. It points to the "internal" political opposition—the Ittihat ve Terakki Cemiyeti (the Society of Union and Progress)—to the Ottoman Empire that developed as an underground movement in Anatolia and in Europe. The final phase is the period of the fragmentation of the Ottoman Empire, World War I, and the establishment of the Republic of Turkey (1923). Together with the change of legitimate power from the sultan to the democratic public preferences, modernization became a radical national project of young Turkey. Thus, while the expectations of modernization were the prevention of the fragmentation of the Ottoman Empire before World War I, they centered on the economic development of the new nation-state until World War II. Many revolutions and reforms that took place under Ataturk's great leadership aimed at a radical reconstruction of the society as a moder nation-state.

We may now turn to understanding how psychology has been struggling to find itself a disciplinary niche in Turkey and review the historical process in five, rather distinct, periods.

Ottoman Beginnings and the European Influence

During the systematic Ottoman modernization efforts, many Turkish scholars were sent to Europe for advanced studies; as well, several Western (i.e., American, Austrian, British, French, German, and Italian)–run high schools, institutions of higher education, and cultural centers were established, mostly in Istanbul. Robert College (now Bogazici University), for example, was founded in 1863. The medium of education in these "foreign" schools was, and still is, the language of the "sponsor" (Western) society. In 1868, Dar-ul Funun-i Osmani (now Istanbul University) was established.[1] Here the first public lectures on psychology were given in the evenings during the month of Ramadan in the following year by Aziz Efendi. Not surprisingly perhaps, the early writings on psychological matters took place in the philosophical and political works of the Ottoman intelligentsia and resemble the emancipation of psychology from philosophy in the West. In spite of this, a course on psychology did not appear in university curricula for another forty years (Ergin, 1977).

The first book of psychology (in the Western sense), in which the term "psychology" was used, was written by Hoca Tahsin (known also as Ahmet Nebil) in 1872. It was called *Psikoloji, yahut Ilm-i Ahval-i Ruh* [Psychology, or the science of the states of the soul] and was written in the Ottoman language. It was followed by Yusuf Kemal's (1876) *Gayet-ul Beyan fi Haki-kat-ul Insan* [Definitive explanation of the true essence of human kind]. These appeared around the same time as Wundt's *Principles of Physiological Psychology* in 1874 and the establishment of his psychological laboratory at the University of Leipzig in 1879. Three other people from the same period who were active in disseminating the psychological perspective are Baha Tevfik, Ahmet Mithat, and Mustafa Sati (known also as Sati-El-Husri). Baha Tevfik worked toward establishing ethics, based on psychological science. He wrote a monograph in 1915 called, *Felsefe-i Ferd* [Philosophy of the individual], made some translations such as *Feminizm* [*Feminism* by D. Lacquerre] and was the "senior editor" of a journal called *Zeka* [Intelligence], which was established in 1912. He also wrote the first Turkish textbook on psychology (the date is not available, though my guess would be 1911). It was titled *Ilm-i Ahval-i Ruh'un Mukaddimesi* [Introduction to the science of the states of the soul] and included sections on scientific taxonomy; the place and significance of philosophy; the definition and subject matter of psychology; consciousness; difference of psychology from physiology; determinism; methodology in psychology; experience; deduction; branches of psychology; tendencies and ambitions, will power and free will; the soul of the human being; generalizability or universality of the soul; aesthetics, motion, and the philosophy of beauty; reflection; memory; desire and motivation; belief; imagination; and the sense of perception. Mustafa Sati has written on the topics such as students' abilities, intelligence, and educational psychology in the journal called *Mektep* [The school]. He perhaps was the first person in Turkey to employ aptitude tests. He is known for his translations from Binet, Ribot, and James, as well as for his classical handbooks on pedagogy and ethnography.

During this period, most published psychology books were translations rather than original works. The first translated psychology book was *Cocuk: Meleket-i Uzviye ve Ruhiyesi* [The child: Capacities of the body and the soul] and was translated from G. Compayre by Ahmet Mithat in 1902. Mithat also wrote *Nevm ve Halat-i Nevm* [Sleep and sleep states], which contained deliberations on the various meanings of the soul and consciousness. Abdullah Cevdet Karlidag was one of the founders of the Ittihat ve Terakki that was a strong advocate of Western civilization and modernity as mentioned above. He was a prolific writer and also the translator of over fifty books, including three by Gustav LeBon and one by

L. Büchner. His colleague Huseyin Cahit, who was fluent in French, English, and Italian, and other contemporaries like Mustafa Hayrullah Diker, Ali Haydar, Avni Basman, and Mustafa Sekip Tunc, translated significant numbers of the important psychology books of the time, including works by H. Bergson, A. Binet, E. Boutroux, E. Clarapède, J. Dewey, H. Ebbinghaus, S. Freud, H. Hoffding, W. James, and T. Ribot.

Rise of Nationalism and the Independence Movement

During the downfall of the Ottoman Empire, many German social scientists came to Istanbul as part of Germany's educational aid. Among them was the psychologist Georg Anschütz, who established an experimental psychology laboratory at Istanbul University in 1915. This event marks the foundation of psychology in Turkey in the accounts that I referred to earlier. He left Turkey after World War I and later pursued his career in Nazi Germany. However, during the two-and-a half years that he taught in Istanbul, he wrote only one article and did not have many students. Because of World War I, only nine students graduated from the philosophy department (of which psychology was a part) between 1915 and 1918. In 1915, the Binet-Simon intelligence test was translated (but not adapted or standardized) into Turkish (Tan, 1972). The same year also marks the establishment of the first sociology department by Ziya Gokalp, whose work had a significant effect on the development of social sciences in modern Turkey. He worked with important figures in the faculty of literature, including another German scholar, Günther Jacobi (history of philosophy), Ahmet Emin Yalman (statistics), Kopruluzade Fuat (history of Turkish literature), Kazim Sinasi (historical method), Ismail Hakki Baltacioglu (pedagogy), and Mehmet Emin (history of philosophy). He founded the Institute of Sociocultural Studies, where the approach to sociocultural phenomena was very similar to the interdisciplinary cultural studies of our own time. The collapse of the Ottoman Empire created many socioeconomic problems, and the social sciences needed to be relevant to these problems.

If one particular person is to be credited as the founder of (modern) psychology in Turkey in a celebratory historical narrative, it would be Mustafa Sekip Tunc, not Anschütz. Tunc started to teach at Istanbul University in 1919, where he established the chair of general psychology.[2] Tunc had studied psychology in the J. J. Rousseau Institute in Geneva. Together with Emin and Baltacioglu, he had already been publishing the journal *Dergah* [Dervish convent] between 1905 and 1918, prior to taking up his position at the university. *Dergah* writers formed a group around the ideas of Boutroux, James, and especially of Bergson, against Gokalp's positivism and evolutionism. Gokalp was a disciple of Durkheim. For him, there was "no individual, but community." Thus, Tunc opposed this particular view of the relationship between the individual and the society and the related view that sociology was the most important social science (Ulken, 1966). During the Turkish War of Independence, Tunc and the *Dergah* group used Bergson's notion of élan vital to explain Turkish resistance to the invasion by European states.

After the establishment of the Turkish Republic in 1923, the Teacher Training Institute in the capital, Ankara, began to offer courses in developmental psychology, educational psychology, and testing and measurement. An evaluation report on Dar-ul Funun-i Osmani was provided by a Swiss scholar, Albert Malche, in 1933. Following this report, university reform took place and Dar-ul Funun was turned into Istanbul University. During this transformation, some of the faculty lost their jobs. Their positions were taken by Turkish scholars who returned after studying abroad and by German refugees who came to Turkey following the rise of the Nazis.

Wilhelm Peters, for example, was a psychologist from Jena University. After leaving Germany, he went to England but then moved to Istanbul, where he established the first Experimental Psychology Institute with a laboratory and a library in 1937. He also helped with the establishment of the first psychological association and journal in Turkey (Togrol, 1983); the journal was established in 1940 (Bilgin, 1991). Walter Miles from Yale University and Mumtaz Turhan, who completed his Ph.D. in the Gestalt tradition in Wertheimer's school in Frankfurt, were other figures of the time who taught psychology of perception.

Interest in Sociocultural Change and Field Research

Racist and nationalist ideology reached its peak in the 1940s, both during and after World War II. Turkey managed to stay out of the war. However, the ideologies of both parties were in competition to find support among the Turkish intelligentsia. Indeed, some took sides on German fascism, some on Anglo-Saxon democracy. The two important Turkish psychologists' critical contributions against the nationalist trend mark a separate phase for the history of psychology in Turkey.

One bright student who received a state scholarship to study abroad was Muzaffer Sherif. He went to Harvard University after receiving his M.A. from Istanbul University in 1929. However, he took more political science and sociology courses than psychology while he was there. This was the period of the Great Depression, and so he became interested in unemployment. He returned to Turkey to teach at the Ankara Gazi Institute. However, on his way back, he visited the University of Berlin and became interested in the use of slogans by Hitler's regime. He consequently chose the following research question for his doctoral thesis, "How do slogans help with attitude change and the rise of social norms?" although his thesis was more conservatively titled "A Study of Some Social Factors in Perception." He returned to the United States, initially to Harvard and then to Columbia University, where he completed his Ph.D. as a Rockefeller Fellow in 1935. Sherif turned his thesis into the well-known book, *The Psychology of Social Norms* in 1936. He then studied in Paris before taking up an appointment in the newly opened faculty of languages, history, and geography at Ankara University. Sherif was in Turkey from 1937 to 1944. During this time, he studied the effect of technology on rural peasants' perception and judgment in five villages (Acar and Sahin, 1990), translated some books, directed theses on the standardization of Terman-Merril Army beta tests, and established a psychometrics laboratory.

Sherif worked together with other leading figures in social sciences in Ankara. These include the sociologists Behice Boran and Niyazi and Mediha Berkes, the ethnologist W. Eberhart, the folklorist Pertev Naili Boratav, the anthropologist Muzaffer Senyurek, and the philosopher Nusret Hizir. All of them were politically minded and influenced by Marxist ideas, although that was not acknowledged openly. This group also differentiated its structural/functionalist approach from and against the dominant "humanistic knowledge" orientation in Istanbul University. They criticized the scholastic transfer of European social/philosophical knowledge of the nineteenth century and advocated empirical production of scientific knowledge based on analyses and the formulation of novel relations (Tekeli, 2000). Sherif voiced his political interest in the social movement in journals entitled *Adimlar* [The steps] and *Yurt ve Dunya* [The nation and the world], and in his book, *Degisen Dunya* [The changing world]. He defended the view that the production of local knowledge should come prior to the transfer of knowledge from elsewhere, and he made suggestions for higher education in this regard. In his third book that came out in 1943, *Irk Psikolojisi* [Race psychology], Sherif boldly argued against any race being superior to others. His critiques of the Turkish state policies of the time led to him being prosecuted by a military court. Pressure by the Harvard Alumni Association and the Allies' advantageous position toward the end of the war helped to secure his release after a month and a half in solitary confinement. He was then awarded a Fellowship by the U.S. State Department to work with Hadley Cantril at Princeton University. Thereafter, his works and achievements in the United States, which were clearly not political any longer, and his influence on experimental social psychology, are better known to the international reader.

In the meantime, Mumtaz Turhan of Istanbul University received a second Ph.D. from Cambridge University after studying with Sir Frederic Bartlett from 1940 to 1946. When he returned to Turkey, he made a significant shift in his orientation and research interests under the influence of the social psychology education he had received in England. He conducted cultural anthropological field research in the villages of Erzurum, observing and interviewing the villagers who had migrated from the Caucasus 150 years ago. He explained the resistance to culture-mixing during "cultural contact" with psychological factors. He also defended the importance of studying sociocultural change in Turkey and wrote three major books on the subject: *Kultur Degismeleri* [Cultural changes] in 1951, *Maarifimizin Ana Davalari* [The main problematics of our education] in 1954, and *Garplilasmanin neresindeyiz?* [Where are we in Westernization?] in 1961. In contrast to Gokalp, he argued for a conceptual distinction between culture and civilization. He believed that it was wrong to view the West as if it represented one nation and one homogenous culture. Its technology could cross national borders, but it was much more difficult for its cultures to travel in the same way. He also provided sociopolitical insights for Turkey's underdevelopment and strategies against the dominant ideological discourse. He suggested that a bureaucratic mentality could explain Turkey's resistance to Westernization since Tanzimat.[3]

American Influence and the Institutionalization Process

In the 1950s, Turkey adopted a multiparty system. The government, and hence psychology, were mostly in alliance with American research and technology. Thus the inclination toward indigenization and the social interest of psychology were lost. The new generation of psychologists who were educated mostly in American universities gave priority to scientific rigor than to the social relevance of their research. The political climate of fear of Russian domination and communism and the perception of Americans as powerful rescuers and inclinations toward individual freedom at the time also helped with that. Following Turkey's participation in the Korean War and its accession to NATO, American psychologists came to teach at the Ankara Gazi Institute. Turkish students were selected on the basis of intelligence test scores for scholarships to study in the United States (Vassaf, 1987). Early European influence and psychology books were replaced with American textbooks. During this period, psychology was recognized as an academic subject (Acar and Sahin, 1990), and priority was given to its organization in higher education (Bilgin, 1983) and to the training of high school teachers of psychology, sociology, and philosophy (Basaran and Sahin, 1990). The Turkish Psychological Association was established in Istanbul in 1956.

In the 1960s, Hacettepe University and the Middle East Technical University were established in Ankara. Their staff was supported with some faculty from American universities and by Fulbright funds. In that decade, following the bilateral agreement with Germany in 1961, Turkey underwent significant international and domestic migration. Large numbers of village workers went first to West Germany and then to other European countries. There was also internal migration to the metropolitan regions of the country. While one of Sherif's psychology students, F. Basaran (1969), carried out research in rural villages on various attitudes and social change, it was another researcher in sociology who helped to establish a new era in experimental social science. Inspired by Sherif's methods, M. Kiray (1964) studied urban transformation through industrial development. The State Planning Organization and the Turkish Social Science Association were established, and both supported the empirical research on rural and urban transformation. Despite the topics of interest having more relevance to Turkish society, the theories, concepts, and methodology were still within the Western positivist paradigm.

With the inclusion of new universities and psychology departments, and the increasing number of U.S.-educated psychologists in them, American influence was widespread and has dominated psychology in Turkey ever since. Psychology courses have also been a part of the curricula of other departments and faculties, such as education, guidance and counseling, sociology, social work, business administration, mass communication, and medicine. In some universities the medium of education is English. It would not be totally wrong to state that an implicit split and antagonism between the psychology departments in these so-called Westernized universities and in others has been disguised until today behind the claim of the latter's lack of scientific rigor. Indeed, a separate professional body was organized in Ankara in 1976 under the title the Association of Psychologists, mainly out of a sense of frustration with the Istanbul University–based association. Both associations were "united" recently into the Turkish Psychological Association. The Turkish Psychological Association currently has approximately 1,750 members. A significant part of its membership consists of academics, with the remainder working in applied settings, such as hospitals and private clinics in the major cities. Given that Turkey's population is over 70 million, the ratio of practicing psychologists to population is still much lower than that of the industrialized countries.

In the 1980s, the struggle for further democratization and development was arrested as a result of a military coup and the constitutional changes that followed it. In the meantime, the first National Psychology Congress was held in 1981 and has been meeting biannually since then. The Turkish Higher Education Council, which was founded in 1982, centrally awards and recognizes academic degrees in only five specialties of psychology: developmental psychology, experimental psychology, applied (clinical, organizational, and school) psychology, social psychology, and psychometrics. In spite of this, academic freedom enables faculty and departments in universities to offer courses in most areas of interest and expertise in psychology. In addition, there are few publication outlets for psychologists in Turkey, and the expectations of foreign journals and publications further lead Turkish psychologists to reproduce and adapt Western research questions and models.

N. Bilgin (1991) reported that 46 percent of Turkish psychologists work in medical settings, 16 percent are in academia, 15 percent work in preschool child services, 8 percent are in counseling and guidance services, 8 percent work with special groups, 6 percent are in private practice, and only 1 percent work in organizations. Current observations indicate more diversity, with the inclusion of new sectors and more psychology graduates finding better jobs in the business settings, public relations, and human resources departments, even if the majority still work in the health care system. Despite the (uneven) attempts of the association with different governments in recent decades, psychologists' professional status in society has not improved significantly. University entrance is decided by a nationwide central exam, and candidates express their preferences for particular universities and departments prior to finding out their results. Psychology is not favored by the most able students and is the first choice of very few. Also, most psychology graduates either work in other service sectors or are educated housewives, as 85 percent are female, according to Bilgin (1991). Considerable female dominance of the field in the country is understood as an important reason for the low status and the salaries of the psychologists (Kagitcibasi, 1994). Perhaps it could be seen as one of the signs of a much deeper sociocultural/political/historical resistance to psychological autonomy (individuation) of the society and the individual. I comment on that in more detail below. There are various detailed observations made by American and Turkish psychologists on the development of psychology and the major issues of research and practice in Turkey until the 1990s elsewhere (e.g., Acar and Sahin, 1990; Basaran and Sahin, 1990; Bilgin, 1983; Le Compte, 1980; McKinney, 1960).

Globalization, Postmodernity, and the Popularization of Psychology

Since the 1990s, the impact of economic globalization and the dissemination of postmodern technologies and Western/liberal values on Turkish society has led to at least four tendencies that seem most relevant to the present topic. First, in parallel to the general liberal economic tendencies of decentralization and the weakening of the power of the central structure of the nation-state, privatization in the education and health care sectors became inevitable. This occurred in spite of the long tradition and ideology of a strong centralized state. At present, Turkey has eighty universities in fifty-two cities; fifty-three of them are state universities and twenty-seven are private or foundations. There are nineteen psychology departments, twenty-one psychological counseling and guidance departments, and one social work department in these universities. While the interest of the private universities in psychology is very limited and restricted to the needs and values of the market economy, state universities lack sufficient staff. This is largely due to the constant transfers and recruitments by the private universities, which provide significantly higher salaries, benefits, and better academic environments. The state universities also lack research funds, autonomy, and egalitarian policies for knowledge production. A large proportion of the students who are taught in the state universities go on to become high school teachers or even unemployed. Few graduate programs attract even a small number of students since the majority who are interested in further training and education go abroad. There is a further "brain drain" in that many of them do not return or, if they do return, they work in the private sector.

This may be a good place in the text to acknowledge the unheralded but enormous contributions of a pioneer clinical psychologist, Prof. Isik Savasir. Her impact is often omitted in historical texts or limited to the standardization of some major clinical tests (Savasir, 1981; Savasir and Sahin, 1987). She devoted her short professional and academic life to the improvement of the status, ethical standards, and emancipatory power of professional psychology; the localization and standardization of psychological assessment and evaluation; and the training of highly skilled clinical psychologists to function in a therapeutic milieu. Despite her legacy, however, independent private practitioners providing psychological services without necessary qualifications are still common in the absence of close professional supervision and regulations. In contrast, most hospital settings are still orthodox in their male- and psychiatry-dominated hierarchical models. Psychologists are treated as test-administering technicians or auxiliary personnel at best. Needless to say, psychology and psychological counseling cannot enter the health and education systems with preventive community approaches and interventions. They rely on the traditional individual treatments of "intrinsic pathology." Although there has been a growing interest in family therapy over the last decade, it is still very small. In social practice, the medical model and atomistic modernist philosophy are still well preserved.

Second, despite the increasing gap between the poor and the rich, the consumer behavior and individualistic values of capitalism have been pervasively contaminating the entire society. As the business, marketing, and advertisement sectors turn to applied psychology for its "manipulative power" to increase sales, basic research is being further embedded in the mainstream cognitive-behavioral discourse and moves in the direction of the neurosciences. Yet the individual does not appear only as the consumer but also as a "novel sociopolitical agent" with increased demands for further democracy, the emancipation of the individual, and better quality of life in this traditionally communal and less-differentiated society. However, psychology's "instrumental function" has been recognized by policy makers only in the interest of national development through the improvement of maternal literacy and child-rearing practices to enhance the growth of children, as well as raising "good citizens." An intervention project for early mother-child education has been given wide governmental and societal support and the transformative (i.e., Westernizing) role of psychology has been partially recognized in this regard. Indeed, one of the leading figures in that enrichment project, a prominent cross-cultural psychologist C. Kagitcibasi, was honored by the APA in 1993 for her distinguished contributions to the international advancement of psychology. In addition, following a major earthquake in 1999, the mobilization of voluntary post-traumatic psychological support to individuals by the Turkish Psychological Association has helped increase the prestige of the profession in the eyes of the public.

Third, the privatization and plurality of mass media channels with poor ethical and quality regulations have been saturating popular culture with all types of psychological discourse and vulgar "information." Many self-help books, pop psychology magazine articles, and the psy-complex in Western societies (Rose, 1985) have been rapidly translated. The prolonged detachment of academics and professionals from real social problems and from the people have inevitably led to the void being filled by media figures and celebrities who, like Gramsci's organic intellectuals, show an absence of critical metacommentary or interpretation. From the everyday to the international political discourses, psychologization has rapidly taken over Turkish society. Excessive and interchangeable uses of technical terms and concepts, as well as the ones that gain or lose their meaning in translation, create further conceptual confusion, which at times leads to crises.

Fourth, the postmodern influence among avant-garde academics and universities led to the establishment of new interdisciplinary programs and centers. These cultural, cognitive, neuroscience, environmental, women's, urban, European studies, and the like, incorporate some subjects of interest to psychology. Overall, this may appear as a positive response to the disciplinary fragmentation of the twentieth century and the intellectual short-sightedness that modernism has created. However, psychology itself is a fragmented discipline. Its many subdisciplines and theoretical camps have common interests with just about every discipline. It has a serious lack of disciplinary integration and identity in the world in general. This is especially true in Turkey due to its limited sources and some of the problems that have already been discussed. Therefore, these new groupings and intellectual communities are rapidly giving way to new knowledge boundaries. The sense of a discipline of psychology and/or its subject/object face a new challenge of serious redefinition, if not a total disappearance in social practice. The discipline's subject is further split into concepts as partial subjects/objects like brain-mind, cognition, body, subject, identity, self, et cetera. Not only that, these objects are being adopted and appropriated by interdisciplinary communities without even needing a psychologist or any general psychological insights or worldview.

Reflective Summary and Further Remarks

What must be already obvious is that the adventure of psychology as a discipline in Turkey has been under the direct influence of international political relations and the affiliations of the country as much as the enduring historical, religious, and cultural discourses. Apparently it has not "developed" as much as it has in modern Western societies. Nor has a truly indigenous psychology been realized, in spite of various culturally sensitive and sociopolitically relevant empirical and theoretical studies related to issues of migration, gender, family, psychological health, and social transformations. The latter is not something "negative" that needs to be corrected and treated as a deviance from the modern/Western norms. There are insights to be found in this divergence so that the international audience can come up with an alternative to the standard view that psychology is universal and transcultural. It would require some reflexivity with regard to the modernist philosophy, science, and practice that developed in the West.

Alternatively, it may be worthy of a note that the Westernization and modernization of various countries, such as Japan, India, and China, have followed different paths from that of the Ottoman and Turkish societies. This is frequently understood in terms of the historical and ideological tension between the Christian and Buddhist worlds being less intense than the one between Christianity and Islam (e.g., Ulken, 1966) Indeed, the otherized "Orient" in the discourse of *Orientalism* (Said, 1978) referred to the Near East and Middle East, not to the Far East.

As discussed earlier, the Ottoman and Turkish societies "voluntarily adopted" Westernization and were not colonized. Indeed, in order for an Orientalist discourse to exist in the West, it needed and found an Occidentalist discourse within the "host" society, such as Ataturkism or (Mustafa)

Kemalism, which was strongly supported by the elite in modern Turkey (Gulerce, 2004). However, there was neither an intellectual Enlightenment period nor an Industrialization period in the Ottoman Empire that would have led to the establishment of liberalism or a bourgeoisie and industrial working class. Thus there was no concept of the individual as a citizen with human and moral rights, but the complying *kul* (*janissary*, the conformed subject) in the undifferentiated *tebaa* (the social community of the conformed subjects) in the Ottoman Empire.

In Western modernity, the project of construction of a nation-state paralleled and needed the construction of its individual citizens. That can be understood as the major sociopolitical function of the discipline of psychology. Radical and top-down reforms of Ataturk and the following state plans, however, gave priority to the constitution of the secular social state of law, populism, and economic development. In other words, the regulation of the public space through the legal, political, economical, and pedagogical discourses seemed more important. Thus the private space (and the psychology of the individuals) has been either left to, neglected, ignored, respected, or regulated by traditional, religious, moral, medical, and psychological discourses. It would be helpful to review the historical adventure of psychology in Turkey from this perspective.

Clearly, modern psychology remains trapped within the hegemonic individualistic, foundationalist, essentialist, and positivistic epistemology that cannot enter macropolitical discussions. Unfortunately, the domination of social theory and political and economic analyses prevents the existence of discussions about the innovative, creative, and liberatory potential of modern psychology for both the individual and society. Being interpellated by scientific, cultural, official, traditional, and ideological discourses all at once, most psychologists in Turkey are not yet able to reflect on their practice in order to overcome the entrapping paradox. Rather, they continue to blindly imitate standard mainstream practices in order to survive, thus reproducing the common academic discourse.

Psychoanalysis, in contrast, be it unconsciously sensed as a way to "individuation, psychological autonomy, freedom, and human rights" or consciously understood as "individualism, capitalistic ethics, free market economy, and the weakening the centralized state" in this authoritarian society, has not found itself a niche in Turkey until very recently. A good portion of the population outside the major cities is still unpsychologized. However, Turkish wit, literature, proverbs, collective unconscious, everyday cognitions, popular cultural discourse, and metaphoric common sense have a great deal in common with the discourse of psychoanalysis (Gulerce, 2005).

Writing, reading, and interpreting history never have been "objective" endeavors. We may not even always be aware of the biases involved. Psychology, being a young discipline of the past century, is commonly historicized within Western modernity. Furthermore, its internationalization in particular, just as globalization in general, is understood as its dissemination from the Western center toward the periphery. This, too, is itself a major modernist bias. However, an adoption of macrohistorical lenses, together with a "postmodernist" anachronic sense of time and critical definition of psychological science and practice, would give us an entirely different perspective. The history of psychology in Turkey is a highly promising and yet undiscovered field in that regard.

NOTES

1. That is the same year in which Gordon Allport visited Robert College—now Bogazici University—before taking up his fellowship at Harvard in the following year. But Allport taught sociology and English while he was in Turkey and did not mingle much with Turkish academics.

2. Islamic science education was carried out in *medreses* since 1542 until then.

3. "Tanzimat" (an Arabic word that means reordering) refers to the period of 1839–1876, during which systematic reforms took place in order to change the economic, social, and political structure of the Ottoman State toward a resemblance to Western European states.

REFERENCES

Acar, G., and Sahin, D. (1990). Psychology in Turkey. *Psychology and Developing Societies*, 2, 241–256.

Barthes, R. (1968). *Elements of semiology.* New York: Hill and Wang.

Basaran, F. (1969). *Psychological research about attitude change in Diyarbakir villages.* Research Report VIII. Ankara: Ankara Universitesi.

Basaran, F., and Sahin, N. (1990). *Psychology in Turkey: Country status report.* Social and Human Sciences in Asia and the Pacific RUSHAP Series, 34. Bangkok: UNESCO.

Belge, M. (2002). Batililasma: Turkiye ve Rusya (Westernization: Turkey and Russia). In U. Kocabasoglu (Ed.), *Modernlesme ve baticilik* [Modernization and Westernism] (pp. 43–55). Istanbul: Iletisim.

Bilgin, N. (1983). Psychology research and publications in Turkey. *Proceedings of the First National Psychology Congress* (pp. 11–27). Izmir: Ege Universitesi Edebiyat Fakultesi Yayinlari.

Bilgin, N. (1988). *Baslangicindan gunumuze Turk psikoloji bibliyografyasi* [Bibliography of Turkish psychology from its beginnings to today]. Izmir: Ege Universitesi Matbaasi.

Bilgin, N. (1991). Country profile: Turkey. *Psychology International*, 2, 9.

Danziger, K. (1990). *Constructing the subject: Historical origins of psychological research.* Cambridge: Cambridge University Press.

Dow, E. W. (1898). Features of the new history: Apropos of Lamprecht's "Deutsche Geschichte." *American Historical Review*, 3, 7–15.

Ebbinghaus, H. (1908). *Psychology: An elementary text-book.* Boston: Heath.

Ergin, O. (1977). *Turkiye maarif takvimi* [The eduation calender of Turkey], Vol. 5. Istanbul: Eser Kultur.

Gergen, K., Gulerce, A., Lock, A., and Misra, G. (1996). Psychological science in cultural context. *American Psychologist*, 51, 496–503.

Gulerce, A. (2001). Towards critically critical psychology. *International Journal of Critical Psychology*, 1, 121–125.

Gulerce, A. (2004). Minding the mind-less: A transformationalist reflection on critical discourse analysis. Paper presented at the First International Conference on Discourse and Cultural Transformation, October 9–13, Zhejiang University, Hangzou, China.

Gulerce, A. (2005). On the absence of a presence/presence of an absence: Psychoanalysis in Turkish context. Paper presented at the Eleventh Biennial Conference of the International Society of Theoretical Psychology, June 19–25, University of South Africa, Cape Town, South Africa.

Hacking, I. (1995). *Rewriting the soul: Multiple personality and the sciences of memory.* Princeton: Princeton University Press.

Horkheimer, M. (1982). *Critical theory.* New York: Seabury Press.

Kagitcibasi, C. (1994). Psychology in Turkey. The origins and development of psychology: Some national and regional perspectives. *International Journal of Psychology*, 29, 729–738.

Kelley, D. R. (1996). The old cultural history. *History of the Human Sciences*, 9, 101–126.

Kiray, M. (1964). *Eregli, agir sanayiden once bir sahil kasabasi* [Eregli, a town on the shore prior to the heavy industry]. Ankara: DPT Yayinlari.

Lacan, J. (1956). *The language of the self: The function of language in psychoanalysis.* Baltimore: Johns Hopkins University Press.

Le Compte, W. A. (1980). Some recent trends in Turkish psychology. *American Psychologist*, 8, 745–749.

McKinney, F. (1960). Psychology in Turkey: Speculation concerning psychology's growth and area culture. *American Psychologist*, 15, 717–723.

Robinson, J. H. (1912). *The new history: Essays illustrating the modern historical outlook.* New York: Columbia University Press.

Rose, N. (1985). *The psychological complex: Psychology, politics and society in England, 1869–1939.* London: Routledge and Kegan Paul.

Rose, N. (1996). *Inventing our selves: Psychology, power, and personhood.* Cambridge: Cambridge University Press.

Said, E. (1978). *Orientalism.* Harmonsworth: Penguin.

Savasir, I. (1981). *Minnesota cok yonlu kisilik envanteri el kitabi: Turk standardizasyonu* [Minnesota Multiphasic Personality Inventory manual: Turkish standardization]. Ankara: Sevinc Matbaasi.

Savasir, I., and Sahin, N. (1987). *Wechsler cocuklar icin zeka olcegi el kitabi* [Wechsler Intelligence Scale for Children manual]. Ankara: OSYM.

Sherif, M. (1936). *Psychology of social norms.* New York: Harper.

Tan, H. (1972). Development of psychology and mental testing in Turkey. In L. J. Cronbach and P. J. D. Drenth (Eds.), *Mental tests and cultural adaptation* (pp. 3–12). The Hague: Mouton.

Tekeli, I. (2000). Degismenin sosyologu: Mubeccel Belik Kiray [Sociologist of change: Mubeccel Belik Kiray]. In F. Atacan et al. (Eds.), *Mubeccel Kiray icin yazilar* [Writings for Mubeccel Kiray] (pp. 9–40). Ankara: Baglam.

Tekeli, I. (2002). Turkiye'de siyasal dusuncenin gelisimi konusunda bir ust anlati [A metanarrative about the development of political thought in Turkey]. In Uygur Kocabasoglu (Ed.), *Modernlesme ve baticilik* [Modernization and Westernism] (pp. 19–42). Istanbul: Iletisim Yayinlari.

Togrol, B. (1983). Turkiye'de psikolojinin gelisim vetarihcesi: Istanbul Universitesi [History and development of psychology in Turkey: Istanbul University]. *Proceedings of the First National Psychology Congress* (pp. 82–91). Izmir: Ege Universitesi Edebiyat Fakultesi Yayinlari.

Ulken, H. Z. (1966). *Turkiye'de cagdas dusunce tarihi* [History of modern thought in Turkey]. Istanbul: Ulken Yayinlari.

Vassaf, G. Y. H. (1987). Turkey. In C. Gilgen (Ed.), *International handbook of psychology* (pp. 89–97). Westport, CT.: Greenwood Press.

Ware, C. (Ed.). (1940). *The cultural approach to history.* New York: American Historical Society.

Chapter 5

Origins of Scientific Psychology in China, 1899–1949

Geoffrey Blowers

While psychology in China can be thought of as a traditional subject linked to the long-standing teachings of Confucius, Mencius, Laozi, and their followers, the modern discipline that emerged out of Euro-America only began to make an impact in the first decade of the twentieth century. Chinese philosophers had not made any special study of mind-body problems, nor had they sought an empirical analysis of them against European Enlightenment science. Like other sciences from nineteenth-century Europe, psychology was "unrecognizable to the Chinese, who had to discover, adopt and adapt it along with other strange new things from the West." (Reardon-Anderson, 1991, p. 6) What first attracted them to it came through translated works bought into the country usually for reasons, most historians of Chinese psychology have argued, having to do with moral development and educational reform in the last few decades of the Qing dynasty.

This chapter examines three routes that subsequently enhanced the transmission and institutionalization of this new science. First, translations of Western texts presented problems of establishing an equivalence of the meaning of terms and concepts. Once the language underwent changes, translations were made easier and, in the wake of the May Fourth movement soon after the establishment of the Republic of China, the number of translated texts increased significantly. Second, because of educational reforms, graduate training was rounded out by teacher education, into which the teacher training institutes (or "normal" universities) fit. Psychology, which came to be seen as an applied discipline, was thought useful in unspecified ways to teaching and learning and so became part of the teacher-training curriculum. Because the number of places available even under the reforms (modeled on the Japanese system) was far short of the numbers applying, many went abroad to Japan to study. These students brought back translated texts, some of which were Japanese translations of Western texts. Meanwhile, Japan also sent teachers to teach in Chinese universities. Third, after the formation of the republic, psychology became established at a few prestigious universities as a discipline independent of education, which led to the setting up of the first laboratories and the creation of a number of journals. An analysis of these journals reveals the extent to which Chinese psychologists during the late Qing and Republican periods attempted to imitate Western studies yet made copious use of translations.

Translations: Getting the Terms Right

The earliest psychology text—Y. K. Wen (Yan Yongjong)'s translation of Joseph Haven's (e.g., 1862) *Mental Philosophy*—appeared in 1899. Haven (1816–1874), a pastor, had taught psychology at Amherst College. His book became a widely used text after its publication in 1857. His Chinese translator, Yan Yongjing (1838–1898) had been educated in an American church school in China before going in 1854 to study at Kenyon College, Ohio. After his return in 1862, Yan maintained his interest in religion and education, preaching the gospel and founding schools. These activities led him in 1878 to Shanghai, where he rebuilt Ying Hua College as St. Johns College, later St. Johns University, and served as its vice chancellor for eight years. He was responsible for academic affairs and the teaching of psychology.

Haven's book dealt with the nature of mental science and the analysis and classification of mental "power," couched in the language of the faculty psychology of its day. It had chapters on consciousness, attention, and conception (thinking); memory and imagination; synthesis (generalization); and analysis (reasoning). Its last section was devoted to existence, the nature of intuition, and the understanding of the beautiful and the right. It concluded with a discussion of human wisdom being greater than that of animals, as well as the brain and the nervous system and their effects on psychology. Haven also wrote about sleep, dreams, sleepwalking, and mental illness.

The text in translation is exemplary of two developments. The choice of material was based on its utility seen as the time as an aid to moral guidance. In this it shared with many other texts from the West its being introduced to enhance "self-strengthening" a term commonly used in this period expressed as the *ti-yong* principle, the Chinese characters *ti* meaning "essence" and *yong* "utility." The term strongly suggested that there was an underlying structure to Chinese philosophical and moral values, which gave continuity to its civilization, and that adaptation to all sorts of Western practices did not fundamentally threaten it. This made it possible for foreign advisors, teachers, and educators generally to come to China (Spence, 1990).

Haven's book also presented the problem of translating psychology into the Chinese language—of finding appropriate equivalent terms that would not distort the original meanings. The term "psychology" was new, and Yan chose three Chinese characters not previously conjoined—*xin-lingxue*, meaning, literally, "heart-spirit study." His choice of spirit as the basic subject of psychology might have come out of his earlier influential reading at Kenyon College: Aristotle's *de Anima* and Bain's new journal, *Mind*. He had also translated Herbert Spencer's *Education: Intellectual, Moral, and Physical*. Taking up Haven's theme that humans were superior to animals in their possession of emotions and will, so they also have a soul. "Because of this, Man can know, think, understand things, be happy and fearful, love and hate, make decisions and act. So the study of heart-spirit is the study of what it is and how it functions."[1]

This was a radically new development and over the next eight years, Yan's terminology had some currency. But the second Western psychology text to appear in China, Harold Høffding's *Outline of Psychology* (e.g., 1891), probably relying on the Japanese translation which had now become prominent (see below), translated psychology as *xinlixue*, *li* having replaced *ling*, though this did not remove problems of ambiguous meanings (Blowers, 1991). The change of one character now rendered psychology as "heart-knowledge (principles)-study," but both *xin* and *li* had long histories of meaning, including from the time of Mencius, ethical principles of conduct arising out of competing views of human nature. These range from the Confucian ethic of intrinsic goodness to a belief in the heart's propensity for evil, the latter most fully expressed in the writings of Xunzi (298–238 BCE) (Creel, 1954). The heart-mind performed a natural evaluative role, including the making of sensory distinctions, yet all evaluations would appear to be made in accordance with how one should act in relation to others. These understandings have generally framed the Chinese intellectual outlook and help explain why there has been no theory of mind to explain the "soul" and seemingly no need to distinguish between conscious and unconscious thought (Munro, 1969; Petzold, 1987).

This beginning marked two developments for Western psychology into China: the selective borrowing of a psychological literature for utilitarian purposes, rather than for a general philosophical orientation, and the reshaping of its meaning through translation difficulties. Teaching about the mind was not to understand its workings per se as much as to foster the notion of a healthy mind, which would instigate correct patterns of behavior. This was entirely in keeping with Confucian doctrines and served the general pedagogical purpose at the time. In selecting texts with concepts for which there were no Chinese equivalents, decisions were arbitrarily taken to coin new terms by borrowing Chinese characters with similar but by no means identical semantic features. This marked the beginning of an indigenizing process common to many forms of translation, which only became apparent after the trickle of translated academic books at the end of the nineteenth century turned into a flood in the early part of the twentieth.

Students and Teachers: Reliance on Japan

Although the first university psychology department in China did not open until 1920, psychology was taught to many students who had an opportunity in the first decade of the twentieth century to study in the new system of teacher training schools, or "normal" universities. This system was based on the Japanese model, and, consequently, psychology at this time was strongly influenced by the kind of psychology being taught in Japan (for example, Abe, 1987; Gao, Yin, and Yang, 1985; Saneto, 1981; Zhao, 1992). Traditionally, education had always been confined to a privileged minority who entered preparatory schools for the government's civil service examination. It came under scrutiny after the Opium War of 1860, when government officials for pragmatic reasons felt the country needed strengthening against incursions by foreign powers. This led to the formation of the *tongwenguan*—the government schools for learning foreign languages and customs—in Peking, Shanghai, and Canton, as well as various military and technical schools in other regions.

Although this did not initially encroach on the older style system, which was primarily concerned with the learning of classical literature and calligraphy, the situation changed radically after China's defeat in its engagements with France in 1894 and Japan in 1895. At that time, the Qing court proposed educational reforms along the lines of those introduced earlier into Japan following the Meiji restoration. This was to involve a form of compulsory education for a specified number of years, a deemphasis on educating elite for government service, the formation of the Imperial University in Peking, a National Bureau of Translation, and opportunities for large numbers of Chinese to study overseas. Although these reforms were thwarted shortly after they were proposed, by a coup effected by the Empress Dowager Cixi, in 1899, the crushing of the Boxer Uprising in 1900 by foreign powers occupying Peking made it even more pressing that they be enacted.

As if further encouragement were necessary, the success of Japan in its war against Russia in 1904 made it clear to a China short of international bargaining power that it was in need of emulating the modernization of its militarily stronger opponent. Working to create a system of continuity from kindergarten to university, the education reformer Zhang Zhidong in 1904 brought into place a set of school regulations [zouding xuetang zhangcheng] that ensured twenty-one years of education modeled on the Japanese system and included six or seven years of higher education into which the normal schools were incorporated. Teacher education became part of the system for producing well-rounded graduates and was thought necessary to help provide large numbers of suitably trained teachers who would take their place within this newly created system. Zhang was likely guided in this move by two pro-Japanese educational publications, *Dongyou conglu*, an educational report edited by Wu Rulun, a scholar and headmaster of Lianchui academy in Baoding, who went on to become the vice chancellor of the Imperial University of Peking, and *Jiaoyu shijie* [World of education] a bi-weekly journal that first appeared in 1901 and ran for eight years. Wang Guowei, a polymath and translator, with interests in philosophy, mathematics, literature, and psychology, was one of its editors.

Wang taught ethics and psychology in Tongzhou and Sushou Teachers Colleges and was fond of the philosophy of Kant and Schopenhauer. Among his translations was Harold Høffding's *Outlines of Psychology* in 1907, which introduced a broad range of psychological topics in vogue at the time of the book's original appearance in Danish in 1882 (Wang used the English translation by Loundes). Høffding presented a view of psychology as a new experimental science using subjective methods and psychophysical principles. It ran through ten editions in Chinese translation until 1935 and was enormously influential as a basic psychology text. Wang's other psychology translation appeared in 1910. *Educational Psychology* was an American-authored text that had first appeared in Japanese translation from which Wang took his source (the date of original publication is unknown). It combined psychological theory with practical examples in the classroom of how to apply the theory. The introduction stressed an important link between psychology and education (which may have been its appeal to the Japanese translators in the first instance): "A teacher must understand the rationale of a particular exercise or a particular curriculum to make it effective. As a result, education cannot be independent of psychology" (Zhao, 1992, p. 22). There were chapters on classification of mental phenomena, the material basis of mind, sensation, affect, memory, and will. Wang's terminology followed that of his Japanese translators, in spite of limitations of the Chinese language for translating new concepts (it had yet to undergo its modern reshaping whereby it represented most concepts in dyadic—two-character—form; see below). The Japanese were already in the habit of using several characters to represent a single concept.

Wang read widely and translated many texts, not just in psychology. But his interest in psychology and the use to which he put it illustrate why translations were a significant route to foreign psychological knowledge: to improve teaching (Hsiao, 1983). Changes to the educational system made possible the expansion of the teachers colleges, which, in turn, provided an opportunity to incorporate psychology into the teacher-training curriculum.

In two other important ways, Japan forged links between psychology and education in China at this time. The expansion of the universities to accommodate intensive teacher training created a temporary shortage of suitably qualified teacher trainers. At the same time, the expansion was not sufficient to meet the demand of those seeking places under the reforms. Japan cooperated in helping to meet both demands. It allowed large numbers of Chinese students to enter its own universities, and it supplied teachers to the universities and to the various levels of the Chinese school system, many of whom were serving in universities and schools in Japan. At its peak in 1905, some 500 to 600 Japanese teachers were employed in China's schools, universities, and military academies. Something like 7,000 to 8,000 Chinese students were studying in Japan, most of them in programs of intensive teacher training (Abe, 1987).

One Japanese scholar academic, in particular, had a seminal role in the transmission of psychological ideas to China at the time. The reopening in 1902 of the Imperial University of Peking included a newly added Normal School for intensive teacher training, in compliance with the educational reforms. Hattori Unokichi, an associate professor at the Liberal Arts College of Tokyo, was invited to be the Normal School's associate dean. He assumed this position for seven years, playing an important part in teacher training with nine Japanese teachers under him. Having studied sinology earlier in Beijing, he was the first Japanese to lecture on psychology in China, and a copy of his lectures, translated by his assistant, later chancellor, Fan Yuanlian, exist in a threadbound printed form to this day (Hattori, 1902). They contain a summary and chapters divided into the theory and function of cognition [zhi], emotion [qing], and will [yi]. Hattori saw a parallel between mind and brain and discussed the function of consciousness. He also drew on several examples from Chinese classical sayings to explain psychological phenomena—for example, a saying by Daxue: "If your mind is not there, you see nothing despite the fact you are looking; you hear nothing despite the fact that you are listening. You taste nothing despite the fact you are eating" (Zhao, 1992, p. 16). By combining knowledge of Western psychological science of the day with the traditional wisdom of ancient Chinese philosophers, Hattori's book was exemplary of the *ti-yong* principle applied to teaching. His lectures were used as a textbook in the Imperial University and were compulsory reading for all students of the college. Although psychology was not well understood by educational planners, its subject matter seemed relevant to educational problems.[2]

Also in this period, four other Japanese psychology books were translated into Chinese. All four stressed a link to education. Kubota Sadanori's *Xinli jiaoyuxue* [Pedagogical psychology], which first appeared in 1903, offered a description of basic Western theory applied to problems of teaching. It included chapters on mind-body relationship, memory, and attention, as well as certain specific functions or "abilities" (to summarize, make decisions, and generate hypotheses). Ohse Jintaro and Tachigara Noritoshi's *Xinlixue jiaokeshu* [Textbook of psychology] followed it. Defining psychology as the "science of the study of mental phenomena," their comprehensive text covered a broad range of fields of psychology. It emphasized research methods and a basic physiological knowledge of the nervous system, as well as describing a number of areas of applied psychology. It also mentioned the relationship between general psychology and the nurturing and educating of children and thus would have been a suitable textbook for the teacher colleges (Zhao, 1992).

Also appearing that year was the anonymously authored *Xinjie wen-ming deng* [Illuminating the mind], whose ten chapters are laid out as a series of psychology lectures. Its subject matter began with animal behavior and went on to deal in some detail with consciousness, cognition, emotion, and will, as well as theories of social psychology and personality. Inoue Enryo's *Xinli zhaiyao* [Outline of psychology] appeared in translation in 1902. Inoue was a prolific writer and popularized ideas of philosophy, religion, and psychology. He wrote extensively about Buddhism and about ghosts.[3] His definition was that the study of psychology should clarify the movement and function of the mind. His descriptions of psychological processes were full of his Buddhist preoccupations, and the text made no associations to education.

Transmission of psychological ideas also came by way of Chinese students studying in Japan. Chen Huang, though not a student of psychology, translated Japanese articles that interested him, and this governed his choice of material, which he eventually published under the pen name Leshu in 1905 as *Xinli Yijie* [Psychology made easy], an accessible and popular work of its time. The publisher in Tokyo was Qingguo Liuxueshen Huigan [Qing Students' Guildhall] a student-formed organization engaged in editing and translating works for distribution in China.

From this time on, Japan's role in bringing psychology to China began to wane. This was for several reasons. There was concern about the falling quality of those returning to China and doing more poorly in the civil service examinations. This led to a raising of the educational requirements of those who were eligible to go in the first place. The Japanese educational authorities encouraged a shift away from short-term intensive courses so that fewer Chinese students could afford to go. There were occasional problems with the quality of some of the Japanese teachers in China, some of whom had become unemployable after the 1902 textbook scandal in Japan, in which many people in the educational administration had been accused of accepting bribes from publishers. But perhaps the most significant factor was the rise of the United States' influence in Chinese education. Protestant missionaries had come and opened new universities. The United States deployed some of its money from the Boxer Indemnity to finance Tsinghua College and to instigate a scheme to enable Chinese students to study in America. As Abe concluded: "The political and social confusion following the revolution of 1911 brought an end to the era of Japan's contributions to Chinese education" (1987, p. 80). However, to this day, even though only about a dozen or so universities in China teach psychology as an independent discipline, the link to teacher education remains.

Psychology in the Republic: Departments, Laboratories, and Journals

Chinese higher education improved after the establishment of the Republic of China in 1912, and this greatly affected teaching and research in psychology. Both the *pai hua* movement to raise the vernacular Chinese language to a literary form and the May Fourth student movement against the Versailles settlement of previous German possessions in Shandong being handed over to Japan led to calls for a universal education, importing of more foreign ideas, and textbooks and materials to be relevant to everyday life (Lutz, 1971). The adoption of *pai hua* made it easier to substitute Chinese for English as the medium of instruction in government schools, particularly in the teaching on Western subjects. By 1922, under an order from the Ministry of Education, all primary and secondary school texts were to be written in the vernacular.

Although the earlier Japanese connection had ensured that education continued to expand in response to growing teaching demands, there were few facilities to carry out systematic investigations or set up laboratories. This was, seemingly, because the Chinese trained in Japan had largely been influenced there by the European emphasis on philosophy and literature (Reardon-Anderson, 1991). This was in sharp contrast to those schools that were to become supported by American-trained faculty, which were oriented toward professional education. Several schools opened psychology departments during this period.

National Southeastern University, founded in 1915 as Nanking Higher Normal College [Nanjing Gaodeng Shifan], opened the first psychology department in 1920 under the education faculty. The college was the first tertiary educational institution to be set up without a direct foreign subsidy. It became a university in 1921 and was renamed National Central University in 1928 by merging several colleges in Jiangsu province (Reardon-Anderson, 1991). In spite of a basement fire in 1923, which destroyed equipment and research data, psychology rapidly developed with its curricula split into two streams: offering education-based subjects and science-based subjects. A laboratory was built with a separate area for the rearing of animals and the study of comparative psychology. New books and journals were purchased, and the books lost in the previous fire were replaced (Zhao, 1992).

After the merger of schools resulting in the creation of National Central University, the two streams of the curriculum, initially grouped under the science faculty, were moved to the education faculty in 1932 as there were more students there who were willing to study the subject. Pan Shu (1897–1998), who obtained his Ph.D. from the University of Chicago and who would go on to develop the basis for the study of theoretical psychology particularly after the formation of the People's Republic of China, was head of the department.

Other notable psychologists working at Nanking in this period were Xiao Xiaorong (1897–1963), who succeeded Pan as head in 1932. He had obtained a master's degree at Columbia University, gone to Berlin to study Gestalt psychology, and then obtained a Ph.D. at the University of California, returning in 1931. Ai Wei (1890–1955) and Guo Yichen (1894–1977) were also on the faculty. Ai obtained his Ph.D. at Washington University in 1925 but also did postdoctoral work in statistics at the University of London in 1932. He devoted his entire life to academic work and promoted research into testing. Guo had studied for his Ph.D. in Germany, familiarizing himself with the work of the Gestalt psychologists and made philosophy a significant part of his own largely theoretical work. These two men represented a new generation who had studied abroad, absorbed the latest ideas of their own psychology teachers, and returned to university jobs intent on opening laboratories and carrying out similar lines of research. However, prevailing conditions led many to become practical in their research concerns. Much of the research in the early 1930s at NCU was carried out on psychological tests and intelligence testing of primary and secondary schoolchildren at both group and individual levels. Special tests were also designed for recruitment of suitable personnel into the army (Han, 1984; Ma, 1992).

The National Peking University, successor of the Imperial University, established its first psychology department in 1926 in a grouping with education and philosophy. As early as 1917, Chen Dachi (1886–1983), a graduate of the Tokyo Imperial University, had built a simple laboratory and a year later offered a course in experimental psychology. Funds increased by 1932, and basic laboratory equipment was purchased, allowing up to thirty students to run their experiments at the same time. However, the shortage of students enrolling led the university council to merge psychology with the department of education. Courses in general and experimental psychology were core subjects for students majoring in education and philosophy, and more than forty students took these two courses each year.

Tsinghua (Qinghua) University established an educational psychology department in 1926. The best endowed of all China's universities, thanks to a U.S. remittance on part of the indemnity owed by China for damages arising from the Boxer Rebellion made conditional upon its being spent on education, Tsinghua "throughout its history bore the character and privilege of these origins" (Reardon-Anderson, 1991, p. 114). Tang Yue (1891–1987), the Cornell and Harvard–educated psychologist who held an appointment in the Beijing Normal University philosophy department alongside his job as chief editor of the Shanghai Commercial Press's philosophy and education section, became actively involved in setting up the psychology department and gave it a clear direction for both its teaching and research work. The core curriculum included courses in psychological concepts, elementary experimental psychology, abnormal psychology, social psychology, developmental psychology, animal psychology, and history of psychology. There were also advanced experimental psychology seminars on new ideas and psychological problems for postgraduate students. A biannual journal, *Jiaoyue Xinli* [Education and psychology] began in 1928 under its chief editor Zhu Junyi, who was head of psychology at that time. In 1931, a team of professors and students collaborated on producing a Chinese dictionary of psychology based primarily on translated materials.

Psychology became established at several other leading schools in the 1920s, with similar curricula, usually allied to educational departments. Three of these were in Beijing. A psychology department in the generally well run Mission college, Yenching University, was established in 1927. Within ten years, it had acquired many books and some journals and had begun some research activity under the supervision of the psychologist and linguist Lu Zhiwei (1894–1970), who trained at the University of Chicago. The work focused on Chinese language structure, observations of young children's social behavior, and adaptations to imported tests. Fujen University, founded in 1925, had a psychology department under the faculty of education in 1929 and was active in research as it drew many Chinese scholars to its doors. Similar developments took place at Peking Normal University [Beijing Shifan Daxue], where psychology had begun in 1920 under Zhang Yaoxiang, with a strong emphasis on educational psychology allied to research in education.

Only with the setting up of laboratories was any kind of systematic research possible. In August 1921 at a summer seminar in education held at Nanking Teachers College, a group of students invited their teachers to join with them creating the Chinese Psychological Society. Zhang Yaoxiang (1893–1964), of Peking Higher Normal University who had trained at Columbia University, was elected to its chair and made chief editor of the society's journal, *Xinli* [Psychology]. The journal was intended as a forum for those professionally engaged in psychological research and became the means through which society members could engage in discussion. Among its aims outlined in the first issue was the notion that psychology "is the most useful science in the world. Not only can it be applied to education, but also to business, medicine, fine arts, law, the military and daily life. . . . [The journal was created] to let others share these applications" (Zhao, 1992, p. 48). Its readers were encouraged to focus on three areas of study: first, the older material in the historical literature of the country should be brought to life; second, newer material from other countries should be studied; third, new theories and experiments should be developed out of a synthesis of the first two.

Xinli ran through fourteen issues from 1922 until 1927, during which time it published over 150 original articles, 20 percent of which the editor wrote himself. In addition, there were over 330 summaries of articles published in a variety of other journals and magazines, which proliferated during the early days of the republic and had been the main source of the importing of foreign knowledge in a variety of fields. Chief among these were *Jiaoyu Zazhi* [Education journal], *Dongfang Zazhi* [Eastern journal], and *Xin Qing Nian* [New youth], which employed a more popular and less scholarly style. *Xinli* carried a "communications corner" where reports from psychology in other parts of the world were printed and a reader's column, which aimed at "answering all questions in psychology and giving readers a chance to freely express themselves" (Zhao, 1992, p. 49). Questions were rich and varied, revealing a readership that was intellectually curious: "Why does one feel a distance for strange roads and closeness to familiar ones?" "Can thirst really be quenched by looking at cherries, and hunger sated by drawing cakes?" "What psychology is it that drives parents to love their last born child?" On gender differences: "Should we narrow the gap or keep the distance?" On habits: "Why is it difficult to maintain good habits?" Answers came from readers themselves, who wrote in offering their speculations, there being little expertise or scientific knowledge available to guide understanding. *Xinli* aimed to encourage less specialized or experienced authors to submit their work and did not rely solely on well-placed academics for its material, attempting to strike a balance between the student of psychology and the interested nonprofessional.

With its rich, varied, yet ordered contents, which included a systematic division between theoretical and applied articles, and its lavish illustrations which appeared in every issue, *Xinli* proved popular for its short life. Its contents reflected the debates among Chinese psychologists in the 1920s centering on tests, instincts, and the nature of mind. In spite of a diligent editor, the work could not meet regular publication deadlines, and with insufficient funds, unstable political conditions, and poor business in bookstores, the journal's final issue appeared in January 1927. With its demise, the Chinese Psychological Society also ceased functioning.

The 1920s was a particularly difficult time in the life of the country. In 1926, the Northern Expeditionary Army, under Commander-in-Chief Chiang Kai-shek and Russian advisers, had begun to move northward from its southern base in Kwangtung (Guangdong), its primary objective being, as stated in Chiang's proclamation in Changsha that August, "to liberate China from the warlords and win its rightful place of equality among nations with friendship for all" (Wilbur, 1986). Further disruptions came in 1931 when Japanese insurgents fired on Shanghai, causing damage to the city. In spite of poor and uncertain conditions, for the period up to the outbreak of the Sino-Japanese war in 1937, there was a renaissance of research activity. This came about because of the formation of research institutes under a centralized system, along with the enthusiasm of small groups of teachers and students in psychology departments in various universities to start up their own psychology laboratories and journals. Given the difficulties, it is perhaps not surprising that there should have been such a large concentration of psychological studies in this period devoted to practical applications.

The founding in 1928 of Academia Sinica, under President T'sai Yuan-p'ei (Cai Yuenpei), marked the beginning of systematic science research in modern China. Its mission was to "implement science investigations, direct, coordinate and encourage academic research." It comprised thirteen institutes, one of which was the Institute of Psychology, headed by Tang Yue.[4] Although it was initially set up in Peking with research focused on animal learning, and neurological studies, the institute moved in 1933 to Shanghai under a new director, Wang Ginghsi, and expanded its focus to include psycho-physiological research on animals; it moved again in 1934 to Nanking. In 1935, research on industrial psychology began with the collaboration of Tsinghua University.

In 1934 at National Central University, the *Half-Yearly Journal of Psychology*, edited by Ai Wei, began publication. At the same time, the university daily newspaper began publishing a two-page weekly supplement, *Xin Li Fu Kan*, which concentrated on psychology translations of articles of psychology applied to business and industry. For example, "The Rise of Chinese Industrial Psychology" described fieldwork studies carried out under the joint supervision of the Central Research Institute Psychology Center and Qinghua University Psychology Department in the Beijing Nankou machinery factories and the Shanghai and Nantong weaving factories. In 1936, the Psychological Society of Shanghai Daixia University educational psychology department published the *Quarterly Journal of Psychology*, edited by Zhang Yilian, for the public. The motto of this journal was: "Use psychology to improve daily life." As with the first psychology journal, in addition to original articles and translations, there were many abstracts of articles published in more popular magazines. In the same year, Beijing University and Yanjing University psychology departments organized a "China Psychology Post Office," which published the *Chinese Journal of Psychology*, edited by Chen Chiwei. With the revival in January 1937 of the China Psychological Society, this journal became its official organ. Similarly, in Nanking, the China Test Society's journal *Tests* began in 1932. From 1932 to 1934, the Central Research Institute Psychology Research Centre published the *Journal of the Central Research Institute Psychological Research Centre*, devoted to research reports of animal learning and neural physiology. The earliest study in this field was Guo Renyuan's "The Embryonic Development of Birds," which observed the development of movements of chick embryo, taking a strongly anti-instinctual position. From 1934 to 1936 and then after 1939, there as the book *Special Articles on Psychology Education Experiments* published by the National Central University School of Education Laboratory.

War: 1937–1945

After the July Seventh event of 1937, Japanese forces occupied the eastern seaboard regions of China, where the hub of most university and scientific research centers were located. The Kuomintang forces retreated inward, taking with them schools, research scientists, scholars, teachers, and intellectuals. Many of the universities formed coalitions in their new habitat. Beijing, Qinghua, and Nankai Universities left Beijing and formed the Changsha Temporary University, then moved in 1938 to Kunming and formed the South West Joint University. National Central University and the Central Research Institute Psychological Research Centre were moved from Nanjing to Chungking (Chongqing), the wartime headquarters of the Nationalists.

During the war period, Chongqing and Kunming became the new centers of teaching and research. The psychologists who followed the move to Kunming taught and conducted various seminars. But no psychology journals or related publications coming out of this group have been found. Meanwhile in Chongqing, National Central University published the *Educational Psychology Study Journal*, edited by Ai Wei. As with the situation in the 1930s generally, the focus of the articles in this journal was on applied psychology, particularly in education.

At that time, the Chongqing People's Government Education Department invited Ai Wei to conduct studies of Han characters and the educational issues arising out of the use of classical versus modern Chinese language. For twenty years, Ai had insisted on studies of these two issues, which he felt were central to the country's concerns for continuing psychological research. In February 1940, he organized an educational psychology experimental class of sixth-year secondary school students (who were all children of the staff in Central University) to carry out observational studies of their learning skills in the subjects of Chinese language, English language, and mathematics, and also of free activities in the classroom. Although resources were limited under the trying conditions of the war, an article by Xiao Xiaorong in 1940 celebrated the twentieth anniversary of the department by referring to its current resource strength: "Now there are 1993 pieces of equipment for psychological experiments and tests, 153 models, 1,477 tools for experiments; the library [has] 1,023 Chinese books, 795 English books, 131 German books, 39 Chinese journals, 776 English journals, and 483 German journals."[5]

During this period, the Chongqing government became increasingly concerned about widespread corruption and so began to encourage studies in "psychological construction" and personnel management and to set up research and publications to this end. Essentially part of the propaganda machine, its aim was to encourage strengthening the belief in victory; combating corruption; strengthening the body, the mind, and the spirit; and building up a strong will and national self-esteem. One off-shoot of this, in 1942, was the creation of the Chinese Psychological Construction Society and the *Psychological Construction Journal*, the focus of which was "to put our spirit and national character into practice." Also in 1940, the Personnel Psychology Study Society was formed, which had the duty of "providing knowledge of personnel psychology and skills to the army, politicians, students, industry, and medicine . . . so as to raise efficiency . . . and lay a strong foundation for psychological construction." This society edited books, including Xiao Xiaorong's *Personnel Psychology Problems* (1944–45) and *The Scientific Foundation of Psychological Construction* (1945–46). In 1943, under the auspices of the "Police Intelligence Test Office," Xiao began a six-year study on the selection and training of police staff to increase police efficiency. There were also comparative studies on national psychology, which aimed at strengthening national spirit and nurturing national pride (Zhao, 1992).

During the war, the Institute of Psychology was also on the move, and this greatly disrupted its work. Even so, research on embryonic behavior and how its development was regulated by the central nervous system continued, while in industrial psychology, the activity was reduced to archiving past research data. In 1944, most of the institute's books and instruments were destroyed due to Japanese attack, and the institute was forced to move to Chungking again. Only in 1946 did the institute resume normal operation, and at that time, research still focused on neurology. The institute published a psychological journal in ten volumes. Many of its articles were published in other psychological journals in China and the United States (Zhao, 1992).

With the defeat of Japan, the universities, which had been operating in the hinterland, returned to their eastern locations and in 1946, in spite of damage to many of the original buildings, classes resumed. Nonetheless, "events outside the university overwhelmed efforts within. Civil war and hyperinflation drained funds from education, making it impossible to carry on teaching and research. Students demonstrated, government troops cracked down, and soon the Communists were in Peiping" (Reardon-Anderson, 1991, p. 367). In spite of great hardships in the previous twenty-year period, it had been one of large-scale psychological research activity harnessed to university education and national science support. This had arisen out of the widespread belief in education as "a means of solving the many social, moral and political problems of the nation," as one outside observer had noted after an official visit in the 1920s (Monroe,

1922). The emphasis had been on applied psychology, and the central feature of this work was testing. There had been seen a need to test children of all ages for educational purposes, as well as adults for recruitment into appropriate forms of military and other service. This had led to serious inquiry into the nature of testing, and a journal and a society devoted to these ends were established. At the same time, a large number of translated articles of psychology from other countries filled a substantial portion of the journals of the period and the popular pieces written in cultural magazines. For the most part, leading psychologists retained a correspondence with their former teachers abroad, and departments shared their journals and encouraged when possible open exchanges with institutions abroad.

This alliance of psychology with politics was to continue after the formation of the People's Republic of China but with a much narrower focus and a rigidly applied political orthodoxy, one which was not to be cast off for another thirty years.

NOTES

1. Translator's introduction to Haven's *Mental Philosophy*. Cited in Zhao (1992).

2. Hattori's lectures also proved popular in Japan and were read by Japanese students, as well as Chinese students studying there.

3. Cai Yuanpei translated several of the latter volumes into Chinese.

4. The others were the Institutes of Mathematics, Astronomy, Physics, Chemistry, Geology, Zoology, Botany, Meteorology, History and Philology, Social Sciences, Medicine, and Engineering.

5. Cited in Zhao (1992), chapter 13, p. 89 [translation by M. Y. Cheung].

REFERENCES

Abe, Hiroshi (1987). Borrowing from Japan: China's first modern educational system. In R. Hayhoe and Marianne Bastid (Eds.), *China's education and the industrialized world* (pp. 57–80). Armonk, NY: M. E. Sharpe.

Blowers, G. H. (1991). Assessing the impact of Western psychology in Hong Kong. *International Journal of Psychology,* 26(2), 254–261.

Creel, H. G. (1954). *Chinese thought from Confucius to Mao Tse Tung.* London: Eyre and Spottiswoode.

Gao, J. F., Yin, G. C., and Yang, X. H. (Eds.) (1985). *Zhongguo Xinlixueshi* [The history of psychology in China]. Beijing: People's Press.

Han, J. Z. (1984). Contemporary Chinese psychologist Xiao Xiaorong. *Dazhong Xinlixue Zazhi* [Journal of popular psychology], 3, 44–45.

Hattori, U. K. (1902). *Xinlixue Jiangyi* [Psychology lectures]. Shanghai: Shangwu Yinshuguan [Commercial Press].

Haven, J. (1862). *Mental philosophy including the intellect, sensibilities and will.* Boston: Gould and Lincoln.

Høffding, H. (1891). *Outlines of psychology.* London: Macmillan.

Hsiao A. (1983). *Wang Guowei Pingzhu* [Commentary of Wang Guowei], Zhejiang Wenyi Chubanshe [Zhejiang Culture and Arts], 7.

Lutz, J. G. (1971). *China and the Christian colleges, 1850–1950.* Ithaca, NY: Cornell University Press.

Ma, W. J. (1992). Explorations in military psychology by Xiao Xiaorong. *Dazhong Xinlixue Zazhi* [Journal of popular psychology], no. 4.

Monroe, P. (1922). *A report on education in China.* New York: Institute of International Education.

Munro, D. J. (1969). *The concept of man in early China.* Stanford, CA: Stanford University Press.

Petzold, M. (1987). The social history of Chinese psychology. In Mitchell G. Ash and William R. Woodward (Eds.), *Psychology in twentieth-century thought and society* (pp. 213–231). Cambridge: Cambridge University Press.

Reardon-Anderson, J. (1991). *The study of change: chemistry in China, 1849–1949.* Cambridge: Cambridge University Press.

Saneto, K. S. (1981). *Chugokujin Nihon Ryugakushi* [The history of Chinese students' study in Japan]. Tokyo: Kuroshio Shuppan.

Spence, J. (1990). *The search for modern China.* New York: Norton.

Wilbur, C. Martin (1986), The Nationalist Revolution: from Canton to Nanking, 1923–28. In D. Twitchett and J. K. Fairbank (Eds.), *The Cambridge History of China*, Vol. 12, part 1, p. 547ff.

Zhao, L. R. (1992). *Xhonggua xiandai xinlixue de qiyuan he fazhan* [The origin and development of modern psychology in China]. *Xinlixue Dongtai* [Journal of Developments in Psychology], special issue 4, 1–114.

Chapter 6

Behavior Analysis in an International Context

Ruben Ardila

Cognitivism is considered the dominant paradigm in psychology at the beginning of the twenty-first century. It supposedly replaced the former paradigm, behaviorism, which dominated in psychology until the 1960s. It has been stated that behaviorism is "dead," it is out of fashion, and it has been replaced by a more complex and holistic model, which is cognitivism.

Nothing is more misguided than this. In the first place, it is not accurate that behaviorism had been the dominant approach in psychology until the 1960s. In fact, during this period many other models were influential, such as structuralism, psychoanalysis, Gestalt and humanist psychology, not just behaviorism. Important developments took place in basic behavioral research linked to the names of Watson, Hull, Spence, Skinner, and Tolman and in applied research and technological applications. So behaviorism was not the only model, and certainly it cannot be said that it was predominant at a worldwide level: it only was predominant in some centers of great development in scientific research in psychology.

Alternatively, it is also not true that behaviorism has "passed away." At the moment, behaviorism is active in basic and applied research, in novel technological developments, and in conceptual and philosophical analysis of great depth. Behaviorism has not died; as Mark Twain said: "Reports of my death have been greatly exaggerated."

Behaviorism is the philosophy of the science of behavior or experimental analysis of behavior (Skinner, 1974). Today, the term "behavior analysis," which is more general, is more frequently used, and it is the term that will be used in this chapter. Behavior analysis has given origin to a science of great development, with its own conceptual and methodological structure, its principles and explanations, and its theorization and laws. It has well-established centers, training programs for psychologists, laboratories, congresses, journals, professional associations, and the like. It continues to be a part of psychology, but it also has a relationship with other fields of knowledge such as education, social work, sociology, and anthropology. Behavior analysis is not only psychology, and today's psychology is not only behavior analysis.

International Context

As in many other sciences and professions, it was in the United States and other English-speaking countries that important advances have been made in behavior analysis over eight decades. Anglo-Saxon culture provided the appropriate context for developing a system of explaining psychological phenomena that were based on the facts, using valid and trustworthy methods, and it produced contrastable and comparable results. The results could be proven, and they were also susceptible to being falsified (as Popper wanted). Skinner had great ambitions of changing the human being and its world (for example, *Walden Two*, 1948, and *Beyond Freedom and Dignity*, 1971, both by Skinner). All this had a positive resonance in the culture of the United States in the twentieth century.

We find the origins of the behavioral approach in other nations like Russia (Pavlov and Bechterev), France (Pieron), South Africa (Wolpe and Lazarus), and England (Eysenck). The great British scientists like Darwin, Spencer, and Huxley can also be considered part of a related line of thought.

Behavior analysis is being cultivated today in many parts of the world. As an example, the international organization, the Association for Behavior Analysis (ABA) had members from forty-two countries in 2003: Argentina, Australia, Bahrain, Bangladesh, Belgium, Brazil, Canada, Cayman Islands, Colombia, Costa Rica, Finland, France, Georgia, Germany, Greece, Guam, Hong Kong, Iceland, India, Ireland, Israel, Italy, Japan, Jordan, Mexico, the Netherlands, New Zealand, Norway, the Philippines, Poland, Portugal, Russia, Saudi Arabia, Singapore, South Korea, Spain, Sweden, Switzerland, Taiwan, Turkey, the United Kingdom, and Venezuela (Malott, 2004).

The 2003 ABA Convention had participants from twenty-six countries. ABA has also organized International Conferences: 2001 in Venice (Italy), 2004 in Campinas (Brazil), and 2005 in Beijing (China).

In many countries, there is an abundance of jobs in applied behavior analysis in settings such as schools, hospitals, businesses, and institutions for developmental disabilities. In sport training centers, pharmacological laboratories, and health promotion programs, for example, behavior analysis occupies a central place.

Professional Training

In spite of all that has been said so far, professional training programs in behavior analysis are not plentiful. In the 2003 ABA directory, there were seventeen graduate training programs in non-U.S. countries: five in Latin America, two in the Middle East, four in Europe, four in Australasia, one in Southern Asia, and one in Canada (ABA, 2003).

The pioneering programs were organized in the United States. Six stand out as having greatly influenced the development of the area in research, conceptualizations, applications, and the positioning of behavior analysis in society. They are located in the following universities: University of Kansas, University of Washington, Southern Illinois University at Carbondale, Western Michigan University, West Virginia University, and the University of Florida.

Many of these programs are at the master's level; others are at a doctoral level. Ph.D. programs in behavior analysis are not common. In every case, the aim is to train graduate students in the philosophy of behavior analysis, in basic scientific research both with nonhuman and human participants, and in the applications to socially relevant problems.

In graduate programs of psychology, social work, education, law, sociology, anthropology, and other fields, training in behavior analysis is offered, but there is no intention to train experts in this area. For the specific case of psychology, it is possible to say that all the advanced training programs offer specialization—even though it is fragmented—in behavior analysis. This is offered along with other approaches and ways of studying psychological phenomena that do not follow the behavioral approach.

The greater part of the advanced studies programs are of a broad spectrum, and many of them are relatively eclectic. The advanced studies programs in psychology based strictly on behavior analysis are probably more the exception than the rule.

The scientific knowledge and theoretical conceptualizations are presented to the scientific community in specialized journals. In the following section I discuss the place of these publications in the world context of behavior analysis.

Journals

Specialized journals offer a forum for the publication of laboratory discoveries, theories, applications, and ideas; in general, they provide an opportunity to evaluate the "state of the art" of a discipline. The *Journal of the Experimental Analysis of Behavior (JEAB)* was founded in 1958 because experimental work with single-case designs and inductive methodology was not welcome in "mainstream" psychology. The leading journals in the area, such as the *Journal of Experimental Psychology* and *Psychological Review*, did not like this work, which was derived from a Skinnerian experimental analysis of behavior perspective, since it did not conform to the orthodox view of methodology.

Ten years later, in 1968, the *Journal of Applied Behavior Analysis (JABA)* started publishing; it is a journal for applied work following behavioral methodology. It includes applications in education, work, and human development and in the clinical, industrial and organizational, business, social, community, juridical, and sports fields, among others.

Journals in an international context started in Europe with the publication of *Behaviour Research and Therapy*, under the leadership of H. J. Eysenck (1963). In Latin America, the *Revista Mexicana de Análisis de la Conducta / Mexican Journal of Behavior Analysis* (1975) was published, with articles in Spanish and English. The invited editor of the first issue was Sidney W. Bijou. In his editorial he wrote:

There is little doubt that the *Mexican Journal of Behavior Analysis* will give added momentum to an already fast moving trend toward improved education and training in psychology, and particularly in behavior analysis, in Mexico and other Latin American countries. Research reports, both basic and applied, and treatises on theoretical issues not only provide a means of communication among students, instructors, investigators, and behavioral practitioners but will also make possible more rapid communication between behaviorally orientated Latin American psychologists and those in other countries, particularly in Canada, Europe, Japan, and the United States. . . . This new journal will make possible the direct dissemination of the advances in behavior analysis and applied behavior analysis, wherever they are taking place. (Bijou, 1975, p. 6)

Later on, numerous journals appeared, in different countries of the world. Within an international perspective, the following journals deserve to be mentioned: *Behavior Analyst, Analysis of Verbal Behavior, Behavior and Philosophy, Behavior and Social Issues, Behavior Modification, Behavior Therapy, Child and Family Behavior Therapy, Japanese Journal of Behavior Analysis* (Japan), *Scandinavian Journal of Behavior Therapy* (Sweden), *Journal of Organizational Behavior Management, Verhaltenstherapie* (Germany), *Science et Comportement* (France), *Psicología Conductual* (Spain), *Análisis y Modificación de Conducta* (Spain), *International Journal of Clinical and Health Psychology* (Spain), *Acta Comportamentalia* (Mexico), *European Journal of Behavior Analysis.*

In a survey of this topic, 121 journals related to behavior analysis were identified (Malott, 2004, p. 30). Division 25 of APA publishes *PsycScan: Behavior Analysis and Therapy,* formerly on paper and now in an electronic version. It contains abstracts of publications on behavior analysis and many of them from an international perspective.

All of this work, published throughout the world, is an indication of the internationalization of behavior analysis. In this connection, I examine the research, and the applications of behavior analysis, in several parts of the world: Europe, Latin America, the socialist world, Japan, Africa, Australia and New Zealand, and India.

Europe

Europe is a continent with many cultures, many linguistic contexts, and a varied history. For those who see the phenomenon from the outside, Europe's unity is a "miracle" that deserves to be studied. Unity in diversity is maintained. This is without a doubt one of the modern world's ideals: to look for that which unites human beings and not that which divides them.

The European Association for Behavior Therapy (EABT) stands out on the continent. Its objective is to create an international forum in Europe for the discussion of matters that are relevant to empirically based behavioral focuses in the areas of health, education, and related fields, both at the individual and the community level. The EABT organizes an annual conference and maintains relationships with behavior therapy associations in Europe and other parts of the world.

The European Congresses of Behavior Therapy are held with participants from Europe, the United States, and other parts of the world. A large number of people usually participate in these congresses, and there is scope for the presentation of work on behavior therapy's main topics, as well as occasional papers on basic research in experimental analysis.

The leading European countries have been the United Kingdom, Germany, Sweden, Norway, Denmark, Belgium, and, more recently, Spain. France has probably been the least receptive nation to experimental analysis, as has been graphically described by Freixa i Baqué (1985). Nevertheless, it is surely right to say that experimental analysis has been quite important in all European countries, especially in the last few years.

Congresses are organized at the regional, national, and continental levels. Research is carried out. Courses are taught in psychology departments, medical schools, social work schools, and educational departments.

France is probably one of the countries that are least receptive to the experimental analysis of behavior (Richelle et al., in press). This is clear in relation to Europe and probably in the world as a whole. Although a great deal of research in experimental psychology has existed for several decades, and important investigations have been carried out, the work of Skinner was not correctly understood. Stereotypes, prejudices, and lack of information concerning the analysis of behavior were the rule, rather than the exception, among French psychologists and among the French intelligentsia in general. The country that produced Claude Bernard, Henri Piéron, and Paul Fraisse, to cite just a few, did not understand the way of applying the method of experimental science to human affairs.

The French Association of Behavior Therapy was founded in 1972 by Pierre Pichot with just fifty members (Cottraux, 1990). Almost twenty years later, it had 600 members and a significant impact in the psychiatric —not so much the psychological—community. The work of M. Agathon was decisive in this growth of behavior therapy in France. Some psychiatrists were trained in the United States and in Great Britain, and they begin to offer behavior therapy in private practice and psychiatric hospitals. The University of Lille was the first academic center to organize university courses in behavior therapy. Other universities followed in its wake.

The reaction of the psychoanalysts was very negative. As Cottraux (1990) indicates:

Behavior therapists were considered by psychoanalysts as simple minded educational therapists dealing with residual behavioral handicaps left by successful psychoanalytic cures of neurotic patient's deep mental structures. They were supposed, at best, to cure meaningless marginal symptoms and, at worse, to obtain symptom substitutions that would lead the patients back to the couches where they belonged. (p. 189)

French psychology was structuralist in its frame of reference and psychoanalytic in practice. The Anglo-Saxon methodology of research was known but not utilized. Biologically oriented psychiatrists were ahead of psychologists in their interest in behavior therapy, particularly when the word "cognitive" was added to the title of the association: French Association of Behavioral and Cognitive Therapy. Social learning theory was very influential in the change from "behavioral" to "cognitive behavioral." As matter of fact, three-fourths of the members of the French Association are psychiatrists, and this is a very different situation from any other country (psychologists usually are the majority of members of behavior therapy associations). Psychology even now is in France a part of the "human sciences," not the natural sciences.

The main experimental work, however, uses more traditional approaches and not the paradigm of the experimental analysis of behavior. Research at the universities centers on perception, human learning, individual differences, psychometrics, social psychology, and the like. Although some animal work is done by psychologists and other scientists, it is not Skinnerian in the majority of the cases (Guilbert and Dorna, 1982).

In relation to other European nations, the situation in Germany has changed considerably in the last few years, especially due to the emphasis placed on applied aspects of psychology which were not formerly as important. The Scandinavian countries have developed the subject to a high level and have maintained their traditional experimental emphasis without neglecting practice.

The case of Spain is particularly interesting. During the last three decades, Spanish psychology has advanced considerably and Spain has became a leader country, at the world level, both in basic research and in professional applications. Behavior analysis occupies a central role in Spanish psychology.

Private practice in behavior therapy is more recent in Europe than it is in the United States and Latin America. Even so, different European nations have psychologists whose primary professional activity is behavior therapy and behavior analysis applied to education and, to a lesser degree, to the social/community and industrial/organizational fields.

There is a great deal of diversity in Europe, and this brief account provides only a sketch of an area of complex research and application in which the research facilities, publications, congresses, applications, resources, libraries, university teaching in experimental and applied analysis, social receptivity, and legislation governing practice vary a great deal from one country to another.

Latin America

One of the areas of the world in which behavior analysis has had greater social impact and has generated more research is Latin America and the Caribbean—that is, all the Americas except Canada and the United States. In this large part of the American continent, important events have taken place that have influenced the development of experimental analysis and its applications:

1. Fred S. Keller's visits to São Paulo University (1961) and the University of Brasilia (1964). Keller began his basic and applied work in experimental analysis of behavior in Brazil. During his second visit, he initiated the Brasilia Plan, coordinated by Carolina M. Bori, focusing on the Personalized System of Instruction (PSI) or Keller System.
2. Sidney W. Bijou's work in Mexico. Bijou stimulated experimental analysis at the laboratory research and applied levels, especially in the field of developmental retardation. Bijou also trained psychologists at Veracruzana University (Xalapa, Mexico), including Emilio Ribes and Florente López.
3. Work done by many young Latin American professionals who studied in the United States in centers oriented toward experimental analysis and returned to their countries to work in universities and applied science institutions. These psychologists came from Chile, Brazil, Venezuela, Peru, Puerto Rico, Colombia, Panama, Dominican Republic, and other nations. They became leaders in experimental analysis in their countries and broadly contributed to the development of this field.
4. The founding of the Latin American Association of Behavior Analysis and

Modification (ALAMOC by its initials in Spanish) on February 19, 1975, in Bogota, Colombia. ALAMOC has helped bring behavioral analysts together from all over America. It publishes a bilingual journal, *Aprendizaje y Comportamiento / Learning and Behavior*. It has organized the following Latin American congresses on behavior analysis and modification:

   a. Panama City, Panama; December 14–17, 1977
   b. Bogota, Colombia; June 23–27, 1979
   c. Santiago, Chile; November 30–December 4, 1981
   d. Lima, Peru; April 25–28, 1984
   e. Caracas, Venezuela; October 6–9, 1986
   f. Montevideo, Uruguay; June 18–22, 1989
   g. Guayaquil, Ecuador; November 5–8, 1991
   h. La Paz, Bolivia; June 5–10, 1994
   i. Viña del Mar, Chile; October 15–18, 1996
   j. Caracas, Venezuela; March 17–20, 1999
   k. Lima, Peru; October 29–November 1, 2001
   l. Guayaquil, Ecuador; October 22–25, 2003
   m. Montevideo Uruguay; May 4–7, 2005

5. The organization of the International Symposia on Behavior Modification initiated by Emilio Ribes and Sidney W. Bijou. The first one took place in Xalapa, Mexico, in 1971. The participants were top-level international researchers. Unfortunately, these symposia have not been organized recently. The books that include the work presented are still important sources of information on behavior analysis and its applications to socially relevant subjects.

6. The founding of the *Revista Mexicana de Análisis de la Conducta / Mexican Journal of Behavior Analysis* in 1975.

7. The organization of national societies of behavior analysts. In most of these countries there are associations that conduct research, organize national congresses, and develop both experimental and applied analysis. Worthy of mention are the Mexican Society of Behavior Analysis, the Association of Behavior Analysis of São Paulo, the Dominican Behavior Association, the Puerto Rican Association for Behavior Analysis and Therapy, the Peruvian Society for Behavior Analysis and Modification, the Colombian Association of Behavior Analysis and Therapy, and the Uruguayan Society for Behavior Analysis and Therapy.

8. Training centers, generally in psychology, medicine, and education departments. Behavior analysis is a required subject for all undergraduate degrees in psychology. For psychiatric training, it is usually offered at the resident level

(graduate) but not as often. In education departments it has been welcomed due to its applicability in the fields of developmental retardation.

The training in experimental analysis of behavior that psychologists receive is frequently criticized. It is suggested that they learn techniques and procedures with a short-term applied emphasis and that experimental and laboratory aspects and the conceptual and methodological bases are ignored. This criticism is not always justified. In general, situations vary a great deal between Latin American countries and it is not easy to generalize. The most rigorous training is, without a doubt, given in Mexico and Brazil.

9. The applications in the field of education, clinical psychology, cultural design, rehabilitation, health psychology, social behavior, po-litical behavior, industrial and organizational psychology, forensic psychology, sport psychology, and many others. Experimental analysis came to Latin America more as a field of application than as a laboratory science, in spite of the efforts of leaders in the area to give a solid experimental basis to the discipline.

10. The organization of experimental communities, the most important of these being Los Horcones. It was founded in Mexico, near the city of Hermosillo, in the state of Sonora in October 1973. It has become one of the most important experimental communities in the world, possibly the most important.

It must be clear that behavior analysis is well developed in Latin America and its growth continues. Additional information can be found in Ardila (1974, 1999, 2000).

The Socialist World

The so-called Second World (socialist) previously covered Russia, China, Vietnam, North Korea, Cuba, and others. Despite their geographical diversity, there were certain common tendencies associated with ideological factors. However, the political changes that began in the 1990s produced deep transformations in the life of these countries. This has affected universities and professional practice and has surely had an impact on the experimental analysis of behavior and its social acceptance.

The socialist world traditionally mistrusted Western science and psychology. They believed that it was based on capitalist, bourgeoisie values and that its aim was to defend the status quo and exploit the working masses. The evaluation of Skinner in Russia (before Gorbachev) is presented in Yaroshevsky's work (1979). Yaroshevsky is certainly one of the socialist world's most influential historians of psychology. He wrote:

> Skinner's experimental model was not a simple projection of Pavlov's ideas, although it was formed under his influence. (p. 176)

> What is Skinner's authority based on? Of course, the high experimental level in his work is of great value, but this is not enough. The force of scientific influence has always had its roots in the application of a program that affects the manner of orienting research. (p. 177)

> Having taken the principles related to the problem of motivation (reinforcement) from Pavlov, it is surprising that Skinner has not been very receptive to Pavlov's other ideas. Positivist, he saw nothing more than the description of the correlation between stimuli and the quantity of saliva secreted by the experimental animal. (p. 181)

> Behaviorism has inevitably entered in conflict with the needs of scientific progress. (p. 182)

> Upon examining the vicissitudes in the behaviorist tendency, we discover the influence of general methodological principles through its variants and phases: the positivist interpretation of scientific knowledge and the mechanist philosophies of man, according to which the determining factors in human behavior in "life's maze." Both methodological orientations have, however, as demonstrated in the results which behaviorism has obtained, proven to be inconsistent. (p. 183)

These statements might be comprehensible if they were coming from a beginning psychology student in a developing country, but they were made by one of Russia's most prominent historians. This shows that the level of information at that moment was quite limited and that the evaluation was clearly biased by the dominant ideological outlook.

The situation in Cuba, without being as extreme as in Soviet Russia, is similar. In De la Torre and Morenza's paper (undated) on behaviorism in Latin America, it is stated:

> Skinner's radical behaviorism, with its promises of promoting and facilitating social change, became the most important psychological tendency in Latin America during the 1970s. (p. 1)

Many psychologists trained in the behaviorist tradition consider themselves, on the one hand, to be apolitical and, on the other, to possess the best techniques for promoting social change. (p. 2)

Skinner's radical behaviorism has been characterized by its dogmatism. In effect, classical behaviorism as well as its many variants has been, as no other psychological theory, radical and dogmatic. (p. 5)

In general, they believe that they are the most radical and that in a not very far future, the way in which men do justice, educate their children, organize the social and economic system, and carry out international relations will be based on the principles discovered by B. F. Skinner. (p. 6)

In spite of all the criticism, the experimental analysis of behavior is and was known and applied in socialist or ex-socialist nations. Basic research and practical work exists, especially in Russia. In Cole and Maltzma's manual (1969), the classic work on Pavlovian conditioning can be found (see, in particular, chapters 22 and 29). In some cases, experimental results that point out the importance of contingency relationships within the area of operant conditioning are shown. In a more modern context, much of the work done by Russian psychologists and physiologists points to the usefulness of operant principles in the explanation of behavior.

The journal *Soviet Psychology* dedicated one of its issues in 1990 (Vol. 28, No. 1), to the relationship between the perestroika and psychology. In this special issue, the importance of reorganizing the scientific work that can deal with scientific problems and modern practices was recognized. E. V. Subbotskii (1990), for example, stresses that "psychology needs basic research (but psychological research, not physiological, engineering or medical research bearing a psychological label put on it)" (p. 7).

In relation to the laboratory equipment used in Russia, L. P. Urvantsev (1990) points out that

the provision of equipment to psychologists has not improved. Without resolving this problem, it will be impossible to achieve any notable increase in the quality of empirical research. Much time is wasted in developing and preparing do-it-yourself experimental designs, which is by no means within the capabilities of everyone. This forced do-it-yourself situation belongs to the past of science. (p. 21)

The rest of the work of this round table on perestroika and psychology is equally critical and recognizes the importance of an aperture and a restructuring of Russian psychology. The need for access to foreign literature is discussed by several participants.

There is a great deal of literature on psychology from China, including recent work (Stevens and Wedding, 2004). In general, psychology in China has gone through at least five stages:

1. The beginnings (1921–1949)
2. Marxist reorientation (1949–1956)
3. Growth and development (1957–1966)
4. The so-called Cultural Revolution (1966–1976)
5. The renaissance and expansion of psychology (1976 to the present).

At present, most research—including that related to the psychology of learning—is done in the Institute of Psychology of the Chinese Academy of Science and in the major universities. The institute belongs to the Academy of Science, not to the Academy of Social Science, indicating its emphasis on experimental methodology from the perspective of natural science. There are also important research programs in universities in China.

The methods and procedures of operant conditioning are studied within the areas of developmental psychology and educational psychology, both being areas of significant development in China. To a lesser degree, studies on physiological and perceptual psychology are carried out. One of the most unusual challenges that China has faced is the acceptance of one-child families. Q. Jing, Ch. Wan, and R. Over (1987) present a detailed description of the psychological parameters that come into play, including the influence of reinforcers like the certified compensation and benefits that are given to ensure only one child per family.

Despite the criticism aimed at Cuba that was mentioned earlier, experimental analysis of behavior and applied analysis are known and practiced there. Cuba belongs to the Latin American Association of Behavior Analysis and Modification (ALAMOC). The "reflexological therapy" in Cuba is not exclusively Pavlovian conditioning but operant as well. Important media channels like the *Revista del Hospital Psiquiátrico de la Habana* have published operant-level work. Operant conditioning research has also been cited in many other articles.

The term *conductoterapia* (conduct therapy) is used in Cuba in a way that is similar to "behavior therapy." It is employed to contrast this area of work with traditional psychotherapy. There is basic and applied research in experimental analysis of behavior in Cuba with a relative level of refinement. Upon presenting his work on behavior analysis applied to developmental retardation, G. Valdés-Lombillo (1985) wrote:

> In our country, the first steps are being taken which tend to objectively value all the aspects contained in the application of behavior modification techniques with developmentally retarded subjects. This assessment must contemplate everything from the philosophical and theoretical aspects to the methodological aspects, as well as their resources and necessary and available conditions. . . . Behavior modification techniques start from neobehaviorism, specifically B. F. Skinner's work, who developed his entire theory from the distinction between respondent behaviorism and operant behavior and the formulation of instrumental conditioning. (pp. 119–120)
>
> We believe that the techniques of behavior modification and, specifically, applied behavior analysis (ABA) have great prospects of being introduced and developed in our country. (p. 125)

The development of psychology in socialist countries other than Russia, the People's Republic of China, and Cuba has been slow. For a description of psychology in Vietnam, Burma, and other Asian countries—socialist and nonsocialist—see G. H. Blowers and A. M. Turtle (1987).

Japan

The Asian country with the most developed psychology, including behavior analysis, is Japan. Its origins go back to the first Japanese students of Wundt (in Germany) and of Hall (in the United States). Matataro Matsumoto established the first psychological laboratory at the Imperial University of Tokyo in 1903 and a second laboratory at the Imperial University of Kyoto in 1906.

With respect to behavior analysis, M. Imada introduced Watson's behaviorism and opened an experimental psychology laboratory at Kwansei Gakuin University in 1923. J. Tanaka-Matsumi and K. Otsui (2004) wrote: "Japanese psychologists adapted the works of various learning theorists, including Ivan Pavlov, Clark Hull, Edward C. Tolman, and B. F. Skinner, and conducted laboratory experiments on classical and operant conditioning" (p. 195).

The Japanese Society of Animal Psychology was founded in 1933, and it is still active. The research conducted by Japanese psychologists on primate behavior has obtained international recognition. The Primate Research Institute (Kyoto University) has done research in the area for more than fifty years. As an example of this line of behavioral research, see T. Matsuzawa (2001). Other associations of psychologists with a large number of behavior analysts are the Japanese Association of Special Education (founded in 1963), the Japanese Society of Biofeedback Research (1973), the Japanese Association for Behavior Therapy (1976), the Japanese Association for Behavior Analysis (1979), and the Japanese Association for Behavioral Science Research (1994).

In Japan there are active groups of behavior analysts, working both in research and in several applied areas: learning disabilities, educational problems, clinical behavior therapy, organizational systems, early intervention with families of children with learning difficulties, psychopharmacology, and many more. Masayo Sato (from Keio University) was President of the Association for Behavior Analysis (ABA) in 1997. He was the first Asian president of ABA and helped to promote communication between Japanese behavior analysts and Western researchers and practitioners.

Two areas that can be considered as high priority fields in the experimental analysis of behavior in Japan are the behavioral effects of drugs and the behavioral processes in primates. Examples of work in experimental analysis done by Japanese psychologists are those of T. Fushimi on discriminatory stimuli in apes (1990) and K. Manabe on the concept of time in pigeons (1990).

Africa

Psychology is a relatively new discipline in sub-Saharan Africa, with the possible exception of South Africa. As G. B. Stead (2004) has indicated: "Psychologists continue to search for, and provide meaningful solutions to South Africa's social problems with a focus on social justice" (p. 59). Probably the same could be said about psychology in other African countries. We find applied programs in the areas of child development, family, education, teaching procedures, community development, social psychological processes, and HIV/AIDS, among others.

Referring to the main achievements of psychology in "Black" Africa, M. O. A. Durojaiye (1987) wrote:

[Teaching] has benefited from learning theories, and the motivational dis-coveries have been used to stimulate the student's desire to learn. The effects of practice, punishment, incentives and inhibiting and facilitating processes have contributed to our understanding of how children learn. (p. 31)

Some African psychologists research traditional areas like perception, learn-ing, thought, creativity, child-rearing norms, and behavior analysis (normal as well as abnormal). (p. 35)

In one of the most comprehensive books on clinical psychology in Africa (Peltzer and Ebigbo, 1989), a chapter on behavior therapy (Awaritefe, 1989) suggests that "behavior therapy as a valuable clinical and scientific effort, is projecting itself into all of Nigeria's universities where psychology is taught as an organized discipline" (p. 588). Probably the same is the case in other African nations, particularly Kenya, South Africa, Angola, and Zim-babwe (see also Dawes, 1998).

The *Journal of Psychology in Africa*, first published in 1988, contains re-search and practical work carried out in that continent. Behavior analysis and behavior therapy papers are published in this English-language jour-nal from time to time. Although behavior analysis and its applications are not common in sub-Saharan Africa, they are not entirely absent, either. The area is the process of development.

Australia and New Zealand

Well-established behavior analysis communities exist in Australia and New Zealand. A number of scientists from these countries publish in ma-jor behavior analysis journals such as *Journal of the Experimental Analysis of Behavior, Journal of Applied Behavior Analysis,* and *Behavior Analyst.* Also, in ABA there are a relatively large number of behavior analysts from Australia and New Zealand.

Distinguished Australian psychologist V. L. Lee, from Monash Univer-sity, wrote a book called *Beyond Behaviorism* (1988), which is a well-formu-lated defense of Skinner's radical behaviorism, as opposed to Watson's classical (E-R) behaviorism. This book, based on a rigorous philosophy of science, became a classic in the experimental analysis of behavior. A. F. Garton (2004) writes that "all who are Australia-trained will have been grounded in cognitive-behavioral therapy. Cognitive-behavioral therapy remains the treatment of choice for most psychologists in practice" (p. 447).

In New Zealand, the main behavior analysis centers are at the University of Auckland, the University of Otago, Canterbury University, and the University of Waikato. The New Zealand Psychological Society also has a very active behavior analysis division.

India

Both the wisdom of the ancient sages and present-day scientific research have been influential in the current profession of psychology in India. In relation to behavior analysis, D. Sinha (1986) writes:

> We must point out that the influence of behavior therapy on India's psychologists. Based on Pavlov's classical work, Skinner's operant conditioning model and the strong experimental substratum of learning theory, behavior modification techniques have earned a great reputation for clinical and therapeutic purposes in the curing of mental diseases, especially certain types of neurosis. Hindu clinical psychologists began to use aversive techniques . . . reciprocal inhibition . . . progressive relaxation . . . to name only a few techniques, in the treatment of drug addiction and alcoholism. They have gained popularity in recent years and in an area in which the impact of Western scientific psychology seems not only to be strong but also to increase day by day. (p. 53)

Conclusion

The aim of this overview of behavior analysis and its applications around the world is to contribute to the internationalization of psychology (Stevens and Wedding, 2004), including its history. I aim to show that this field is not a "typically U.S." phenomenon but is well established internationally. Behavior analysis as an area of scholarship and professional applications exists on five continents and in most of the countries of the world.

In Figure 1, I present the development of behavior analysis from Darwin, Sechenov, Mach, and others to the present. As can be seen, international developments have steadily increased since the 1970s (Ardila, 1999, 2000). While describing behavior analysis at Spanish universities nearly two decades ago, C. Pál-Hegedus (1987) stated that it was alive and well and "we expect it to continue" (p. 111).

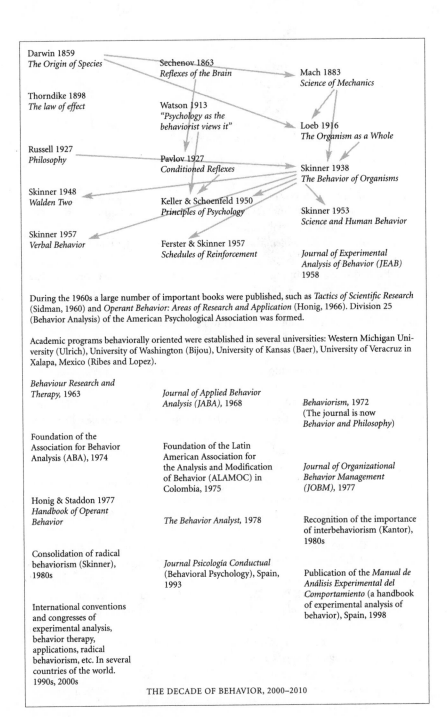

Darwin 1859
The Origin of Species

Thorndike 1898
The law of effect

Russell 1927
Philosophy

Skinner 1948
Walden Two

Skinner 1957
Verbal Behavior

Sechenov 1863
Reflexes of the Brain

Watson 1913
"Psychology as the behaviorist views it"

Pavlov 1927
Conditioned Reflexes

Keller & Schoenfeld 1950
Principles of Psychology

Ferster & Skinner 1957
Schedules of Reinforcement

Mach 1883
Science of Mechanics

Loeb 1916
The Organism as a Whole

Skinner 1938
The Behavior of Organisms

Skinner 1953
Science and Human Behavior

Journal of Experimental Analysis of Behavior (JEAB)
1958

During the 1960s a large number of important books were published, such as *Tactics of Scientific Research* (Sidman, 1960) and *Operant Behavior: Areas of Research and Application* (Honig, 1966). Division 25 (Behavior Analysis) of the American Psychological Association was formed.

Academic programs behaviorally oriented were established in several universities: Western Michigan University (Ulrich), University of Washington (Bijou), University of Kansas (Baer), University of Veracruz in Xalapa, Mexico (Ribes and Lopez).

Behaviour Research and Therapy, 1963

Foundation of the Association for Behavior Analysis (ABA), 1974

Honig & Staddon 1977
Handbook of Operant Behavior

Consolidation of radical behaviorism (Skinner), 1980s

International conventions and congresses of experimental analysis, behavior therapy, applications, radical behaviorism, etc. In several countries of the world. 1990s, 2000s

Journal of Applied Behavior Analysis (JABA), 1968

Foundation of the Latin American Association for the Analysis and Modification of Behavior (ALAMOC) in Colombia, 1975

The Behavior Analyst, 1978

Journal Psicología Conductual (Behavioral Psychology), Spain, 1993

Behaviorism, 1972
(The journal is now *Behavior and Philosophy*)

Journal of Organizational Behavior Management (JOBM), 1977

Recognition of the importance of interbehaviorism (Kantor), 1980s

Publication of the *Manual de Análisis Experimental del Comportamiento* (a handbook of experimental analysis of behavior), Spain, 1998

THE DECADE OF BEHAVIOR, 2000–2010

Figure 1. Development of Behavior Analysis

Behavior analysis is growing in both the developed and the developing countries. I am sure it is here to stay.

REFERENCES

ABA (2003). *Graduate training directory.* Kalamazoo, MI: Association for Behavior Analysis.

Ardila, R. (1974). *El análisis experimental del comportamiento: La contribución lati-noamericana* [The experimental analysis of behavior: The Latin American contribution]. Mexico: Editorial Trillas.

Ardila, R. (1999). *The experimental analysis of behavior.* Bogota: Foundation for the Advancement of Psychology.

Ardila, R. (2000). Conditioning and experimental analysis of behavior. In K. Pawlik and M. R. Rosenzweig (Eds.), *The international handbook of psychology* (pp. 100–116). London: Sage.

Awaritefe, A. (1989). Behavior therapy. In K. Peltzer and P. O. Obigbo (Eds.), *Clinical psychology in Africa* (pp. 586–602). Uwani-Enugu, Nigeria: Chuka Printing.

Bijou, S. W. (1975). Invited editorial. *Revista Mexicana de Análisis de la Conducta / Mexican Journal of Behavior Analysis,* 1, 5–6.

Blowers, G. H., and Turtle, A. M. (Eds.) (1987). *Psychology moving east: The status of Western psychology in Asia and Oceania.* Boulder, Colo.: Westview Press, Sydney University Press.

Cole, M., and Maltzman, I. (Eds.) (1969). *A handbook of contemporary Soviet psychology.* New York: Basic Books.

Cottraux, J. (1990). "Cogito ergo sum": Cognitive-behavior therapy in France. *Behavior Therapist,* 13, 189–190.

Dawes, A. (1998). Africanization of psychology: Identities and continents. *Psychology in Society,* 23, 4–16.

De la Torre, C., and Morenza, L. M. (undated). *El conductismo en América Latina: Mito y realidad* [Behaviorism in Latin America: myth and reality]. Unpublished ms., University of Havana.

Durojaiye, M. O. A. (1987). Black Africa. In A. R. Gilgen and C. K. Gilgen (Eds.), *International handbook of psychology* (pp. 24–36). New York: Greenwood Press.

Freixa i Baqué, E. (1985). El conductismo y el marxismo en Francia [Behaviorism and Marxism in France]. *Revista Mexicana de Análisis de la Conducta / Mexican Journal for Behavior Analysis,* 11, 175–237.

Fushimi, T. (1990) A functional analysis of another individual's behavior as discriminative stimulus for a monkey. *Journal of the Experimental Analysis of Behavior,* 53, 285–291.

Garton, A. F. (2004). Psychology in Australia. In M. J. Stevens and D. Wedding

(Eds.), *Handbook of international psychology* (pp. 437–451). New York: Brunner-Routledge.

Guilbert, P., and Dorna, A. (1982). *Significations du comportamentalisme* [Meanings of behaviorism]. Toulouse: Editions Privat.

Jing, Q., Wan, Ch., and Over, R. (1987). Single-child family in China: Psychological perspectives. *International Journal of Psychology, 22,* 127–138.

Lee, V. L. (1988). *Beyond behaviorism.* Hillsdale, N.J.: Erlbaum.

Malott, M. E. (2004). Toward the globalization of behavior analysis. *Behavior Analyst, 27,* 25–32.

Manabe, K. (1990). Determinants of pigeon's waiting time: Effects of inter-reinforcement interval and food delay. *Journal of the Experimental Analysis of Behavior, 53,* 123–132.

Matsuzawa, T. (2001). *Primate origins of human cognition and behavior.* New York: Springer.

Pál-Hegedus, C. (1987). El análisis experimental del comportamiento en las universidades españolas: "Los reportes sobre mi muerte son altamente exagerados" [The experimental analysis of behavior in Spanish universities: "The reports of my death are highly exaggerated"]. *Revista Latinoamericana de Psicología, 19,* 111–112.

Peltzer, K., and Ebigbo, P.O. (Eds.) (1989). *Clinical psychology in Africa.* Uwani-Enugu, Nigeria: Chuka Printing.

Richelle, M. N., Freixa i Baqué, E., Lambert, J.-L., and Pomini, V. (In press). Behavior analysis in the European French speaking area. *International Journal of Psychology.*

Sinha, D. (1986). *Psychology in a Third World country: The Indian experience.* New Delhi: Sage.

Skinner, B. F. (1948). *Walden two.* New York: Macmillan.

Skinner, B. F. (1971). *Beyond freedom and dignity.* New York: Knopf.

Skinner, B. F. (1974). *About behaviorism.* New York: Knopf.

Stead, G. B. (2004). Psychology in South Africa. In M. J. Stevens and D. Wedding (Eds.), *Handbook of international psychology* (pp. 59–73). New York: Brunner-Routledge.

Stevens, M. J., and Wedding, D. (Eds.) (2004). *Handbook of international psychology.* New York: Brunner-Routledge.

Subbotskii, E. V. (1990). Let's not be afraid of new paradigms. *Soviet Psychology, 28,* 6–9. (Russian original, 1988).

Tanaka-Matsumi, J., and Otsui, K. (2004). Psychology in Japan. In M. J. Stevens and D. Wedding (Eds.), *Handbook of international psychology* (pp. 193–210). New York: Brunner-Routledge.

Urvantsev, L. P. (1990). Some barriers on the path toward the development of psychological theory and applied psychology. *Soviet Psychology, 28,* 21–23. (Russian original, 1988).

Valdés-Lombillo, G. (1985). El análisis conductual aplicado: Una experiencia con sujetos con retardo en el desarrollo [Applied behavior analysis: An experience with developmentally retarded subjects]. *Memorias del II Congreso Nacional de Psicología de la Salud (Cuba)*, Vol. 1 (pp. 118–126). Havana: Hospital Psiquiátrico de la Habana–Editorial Científico-Técnica.

Watson, J. B. (1913). Psychology as the behaviorist views it. *Psychological Review*, 20, 158–177.

Yaroshevsky, M. G. (1979). *La psicología del siglo XXI* [Psychology in the 20th century]. Translated form the Russian. México, Grijalbo.

Chapter 7

Internationalizing the History of U.S. Developmental Psychology

John D. Hogan and Thomas P. Vaccaro

Contemporary research has emphasized the degree to which human development is embedded in its culture and historical period. The notion, once very popular, that we carry within ourselves the essential elements for all of our future behavior—a throwback to a biological model for development—is now seen as outmoded and naïve. Instead, we have begun to appreciate that our particular time and place in history may determine not just the way we develop but, to a large degree, the way we conceptualize development. Can such forces also determine the way we write the history of developmental psychology?

Psychology in the United States has a reputation for being insular. While we have always acknowledged our debt to other countries, particularly those in Europe, we have also tended to ignore them. We rarely read non-U.S. publications, particularly if they are not in English, and we tend to ignore non-U.S. research. Occasionally, we have acknowledged advances outside our borders, but usually when we are forced to do so. The work of Piaget has been used as an example of this, and it remains a good one. By the early 1930s, Piaget was invited to write a chapter for the prestigious U.S.-published *Handbook of Child Psychology* (Piaget, 1931). He contributed a chapter on "children's philosophies," but American psychology was too involved in behaviorism to pay him much attention. When we finally caught up to him, several decades later, he was already known throughout most of the world. Eventually, his work revolutionized American developmental psychology.

The case of Piaget should serve as a lesson for contemporary U.S. psychology. The world of psychology is changing. While the United States is the dominant power in the discipline—and it is expected to remain so—it is no longer the monolithic force that it once was. Other countries are expanding their involvement in psychology and have become increasingly relevant to the discipline. Some observers have begun to refer to two centers for contemporary psychology—the United States and Europe. Even countries that had little interest in psychology only a few decades ago have begun to show a strong interest now. This is true, for instance, for much of the Arab world.

In this chapter we explore some of the European origins of developmental psychology. We also discuss the early history of developmental psychology in the United States, with particular emphasis on its international links. We include a brief review of the work of some important non-U.S. contributors who are often missing in the U.S. version of developmental history. Finally, we explore some of the publication trends in U.S. developmental psychology, with particular emphasis on foreign contributions.

History of Developmental Psychology: Overview

Developmental psychology is typically given little space in textbooks in the history of psychology. When Freud and Binet are mentioned, for instance, they are usually identified for other contributions—Freud for his clinical work and Binet for his work with intelligence tests. Edwin G. Boring, the famous Harvard historian of psychology, may be responsible for part of that bias. An emphatic proponent of "pure" experimental psychology, Boring's historical outlook was marked by his opposition to the rise of applied approaches (O'Donnell, 1979).

Boring's influential textbook, *A History of Experimental Psychology* (Boring, 1929), promoted a reverence for the so-called experimental method that has remained in modern histories. As a result, textbooks on psychology frequently use the founding of the psychology laboratory at Leipzig in 1879 by Wundt as the centerpiece for the modern origins of psychology. While that description applies best to the beginnings of experimental psychology, it does not describe several other specialties, including developmental psychology. The developmental approach comes from a different tradition, but one that is no less important.

Attempts to describe development have a long history. Confucius (551–479 BC), the renowned Chinese philosopher and teacher, discussed such important developmental topics as nature versus nurture, stages of development, individual differences, life-span development, and age-appropriate behaviors (Miao and Wang, 2003). In ancient Greece, Plato (ca. 427–347 BC) wrote of the characteristics of children of different ages and was particularly concerned with appropriate child-rearing and educational practices for children (Borstelmann, 1983). Avicenna (Ibn Sina) (980–1037), the Arab physician and scholar, discussed the nature of speech difficulties, the importance of individual differences on learning and behavior, and the influence of heredity and environment on behavior (Ahmed and Gielen, 1998).

It is clear that attempts to describe developmental phenomena can be found in virtually every culture throughout recorded history. But these attempts are usually not considered to be examples of genuine developmental psychology. They lack scientific underpinning and methodology. When, then, does developmental psychology begin? The beginnings are elusive.

Some European Origins

In its purest and earliest form, developmental psychology was not experimental: that is, it did not involve experimental manipulation. Instead, it focused on the natural unfolding of the organism over time. And while it had close ties to the concept of maturation, it did not deny the role of experience. One of its central methods was the most fundamental scientific method of all—systematic observation. Jean Jacques Rousseau (1712–1778), the Swiss-born French philosopher and social reformer, is usually identified as the first Westerner to describe developmental stages in a manner similar to their modern form.

Several notable Germans followed in his footsteps. Joachim Heinrich Campe (1746–1818) was one of the first to call for objective observations of the physical and mental development of the child from birth (Jaeger, 1985). Johann Nicolaus Tetens (1736–1807) wrote about language development, nature-nurture issues, individual differences, and, particularly, life-span development. Although his writings were speculative, he also urged the adoption of more objective scientific methods to answer the questions posed by development (Baltes, 1983).

Friedrich August Carus (1770–1808), also a theorist of life-span development, promoted concepts of plasticity very similar to modern ones, although his work was largely unrecognized because of his premature death (Baltes, 1983). Dietrich Tiedemann (1748–1803) became known for his use of the "baby biography." This method, while far from unbiased, represented one of the first systematic attempts to describe the development of the child. Tiedemann's work spawned dozens of baby biographies that were written in the period before the 1880s (Dennis, 1949). Among them was Charles Darwin's nine-page paper on his son, William (Darwin, 1877). Despite the efforts of these pioneers, however, no systematic change resulted from these early works (Baltes, 1983).

Nonetheless, one of those contributors, Charles Darwin, had a significant impact on the field, far beyond that of his baby biography. His classic book, *The Origin of Species* (1859), was an important influence on several early developmental psychologists, including Wilhelm Preyer (1841–1897). In 1882, Preyer, a physiologist, published a book titled *Die Seele des Kindes* (*The Mind of the Child*). Based largely on observations that he made of his infant son over his first three years of life, Preyer's book was a landmark and one of the founding publications of the discipline. Preyer had been dissatisfied with earlier baby biographies and made it a point in his study to include only objective observations. While his publication aroused some criticism, both for its originality and accuracy, it remains a pivotal event in modern developmental psychology.

In 1982, a group of international scholars met at the University of Jena, in Germany, to present papers celebrating the 100th anniversary of the publication of Preyer's book. The volume that grew out of that conference (Eckardt, Bringmann, and Sprung, 1984) is a testament to Preyer's pioneering contributions. But the volume also discussed the contributions of another early important developmental researcher, Adolf Kussmaul (1822–1902). Kussmaul, a German physician, was the author of a sophisticated work of experimental child psychology in 1859, two decades before Preyer, Hall, or any of the other so-called pioneers published research in this area (Bringmann, Bringmann, and Balance, 1985).

Kussmaul's publication described his attempt to develop baseline information on newborns in various sensory areas such as taste, touch, hearing, and vision. Although his work has received some notice in various U.S. handbooks and histories of child development, his name is little known, and the evidence suggests that he is an underrated pioneer of the field. Curiously, although there was a ten-year difference in their ages, Kussmaul and Wilhelm Wundt knew each other quite well. While Wundt is generally believed to have despised developmental psychology, he actually conducted research in the area in the late 1870s (Bringmann, Bringmann, and Balance, 1985).

Early Developmental Psychology in the United States

International psychology had a strong presence in the early days of U.S. psychology. American pioneers such as William James and G. Stanley Hall drew many of their ideas from Europe, and they continued to demonstrate their international interests throughout their lives. And while many developmental concepts were taken from Europe, it is also true that American developmental ideas were exported to Europe in the early days; for example in the work of Hall and James Mark Baldwin.

William James (1842–1910), America's first great psychologist, was drawn to the subject largely through his reading of German researchers, such as Hermann Helmholtz (1821–1894) and Wundt (1832–1920). Other important pioneers of American psychology received their degrees in Europe, including James McKeen Cattell (1860–1944) and Lightner Witmer (1867–1956), both of whom studied at the University of Leipzig under Wundt. But the openness to European ideas and ways of thinking did not last for very long.

As U.S. psychology expanded and became more influential internationally, it displayed less interest in the psychology of Europe. Moreover, it began to develop in different ways. Its psychology was more practical and less philosophical than that of its European counterparts (Sexton and Misiak, 1984). By the late 1930s, with the flight of large numbers of European intellectuals to the United States, the transformation was all but complete. U.S. journals began printing fewer articles from non-U.S. sources, and fewer international editors appeared on the mastheads of journals. Eventually, the loss of these international connections was reflected in the history of psychology. Many important non-U.S. contributors were lost to students in the United States (e.g., Charlotte Bühler, Edouard Clarapède, William Stern), and others were overlooked for far longer than they should have been (e.g., Jean Piaget, Lev Vygotsky).

G. Stanley Hall

Although G. Stanley Hall (1844–1924) is appropriately given credit for leading the developmental movement in the United States, his contributions are sometimes seen as weak and short-lived (e.g., Berndt and Zigler, 1983). Such a view dramatically underrates his impact.

Hall first traveled to Europe while enrolled as a theology student in New York City. Later, after receiving his Ph.D. degree from William James at Harvard University in 1878—the first Ph.D. degree conferred in psychology in the United States—Hall returned to Europe to study under several German professors, principally in Berlin and Leipzig. The impact of his European experience would stay with him for the rest of his life.

When Hall returned to the United States in 1881, he began making promises about the new science of psychology based on information he had been exposed to in Germany. Specifically, he promised that psychology would be the medium through which parents and educators could raise children scientifically. His ideas were well received; a child-study movement was already under way in America, and Hall's ideas were a welcome addition to it. Before long, he would become the leader of this movement in America (Hogan, 2004).

Hall published an article titled "The Contents of Children's Minds," often identified as the first modern empirical article in U.S. child psychology (Hall, 1883). The research was specifically modeled after German publications that Hall had read earlier; even the title he used was virtually the same as the original German work. The response to Hall's work was positive and immediate. Before long, Hall's name became known throughout the United States. Eventually, the impact of his work was seen in the child-study movement in Europe and other parts of the world. (See, for instance, the discussion of the European "pedology" movement in I. Z. Holowinsky, 1993.)

His books on *Adolescence* (1904) and *Senescence* (1922) developed his theory and thoughts on the life span. In each case, he drew on the literature of the world, not just research in psychology. In 1909, at the 20th anniversary conference of the founding of Clark University, of which he was president, he invited Sigmund Freud to speak and presented him with an honorary degree, the only honorary degree that Freud ever received. It was a prescient act by Hall, anticipating as he did the importance of one of the most influential developmental theorists of all time.

James Mark Baldwin

James Mark Baldwin (1861–1934) is considered the other major pioneer developmental psychologist in America, after Hall. Although his ideas were in many ways more sophisticated and thoughtful than Hall's, his impact is not as readily apparent. He founded experimental laboratories at the University of Toronto and at Princeton University (and re-founded the one at Johns Hopkins left vacant when Hall left for Clark University). Early in his career, Baldwin conducted empirical research on infants. But as his career progressed, his approach to psychology became increasingly less experimental and more theoretical and philosophical, an inclination that was likely there from the beginning. His writings are considered rich but difficult, which may have contributed to his relative contemporary obscurity.

Baldwin was an important and influential U.S. psychologist in areas other than developmental psychology: he helped found three psychology journals and served as an early president of the American Psychological Association. Unfortunately, in 1909 a personal scandal interrupted his career. He left the country and worked first in Mexico. Eventually, he settled in France where he remained for the rest of his life. After his departure from the United States, he was ignored, with little or no further contribution to U.S. psychology, but his work was not entirely forgotten.

Several of Baldwin's ideas, including his work on genetic epistemology, adaptation, and "circular reactions," later found expression in the writing of Jean Piaget. Although Piaget and Baldwin were both in Paris at the same time, they never met. However, Piaget took courses with Pierre Janet, who had been influenced by Baldwin and who cited him often. Lev Vygotsky is also considered one of Baldwin's intellectual heirs, although Vygotsky had other influences as well. Still later, Lawrence Kohlberg would find Baldwin an important source for his research on moral development.

Despite the pioneer role that Hall and Baldwin had in American developmental psychology, their influence is frequently downplayed. The child-study movement in which they participated is often considered a failure. For some observers, there was no organized or systematic work in child development until the 1920s (e.g., Anderson, 1956). Particularly in the case of Hall, such a view ignores his influence on several very important students such as Lewis M. Terman (1877–1956) and Arnold L. Gesell (1880–1961). The work of Terman on the Stanford-Binet Intelligence Scale and Gesell in developing norms for infants and children can be seen as the fulfillment of the promise that Hall had made to the child-study movement at the beginning of his career.

Ninth International Congress of Psychology

One of the earliest pieces of evidence for the international nature of psychology was the organization of international congresses of psychology. The first was held in Paris in 1889 under the title, "International Congress of Physiological Psychology." Although held only ten years after the founding of Wundt's laboratory, there was little presented on Wundtian forms of psychology, as there was little evidence of developmental psychology. Instead, the four sections focused on muscular sensitivity, heredity (with Francis Galton as discussant), hallucinations and parapsychology, and hypnosis, the last comprising fully one-third of the papers (Hilgard, 1987). Of the 200 attendees, only two were known to be American: William James and Joseph Jastrow. The second international meeting, held in London in 1892 and attended by 300 registrants, was called the "International Congress of Experimental Psychology." This congress specifically included papers on developmental psychology given by Wilhelm Preyer and the American James Mark Baldwin.

Although the congresses have continued until this day, with most of the venues in Europe, only two have been held in the United States–the ninth (1929), held at Yale University, in New Haven, Connecticut, and the seventeenth (1963), held in Washington, D.C. The meeting of the Ninth International Congress was particularly noteworthy for U.S. psychologists. Not only did the American Psychological Association (APA) cancel its meeting in favor of the international one—the only time it has ever cancelled its meeting—but also three-fourths of the APA membership, 722 people, attended the meeting. In addition, there were 104 international registrants; many came from Europe, but they also came from India, China, Egypt, Australia, and Brazil (Hilgard, 1987).

Among the developmental psychologists present at that meeting were Edouard Clarapède (Geneva), the secretary of the congress; Kurt Lewin (Berlin); Jean Piaget (Paris); Henri Piéron (Paris); and William Stern (Hamburg). Two sessions were devoted to "child development." The first session was chaired by Karl Bühler and included a paper by Kurt Lewin and another by Lev Vygotsky and A. R. Luria (Moscow). A second session, chaired by John E. Anderson, included papers by A. G. Decroly (Brussels), Käthe Wolf (Vienna), Charlotte Bühler (Vienna), and M. L. Reymert (Wittenberg). There was also a session on juvenile delinquency that addressed some developmental issues. Despite the second-class status often given to developmental issues among the experimentalists, the congress demonstrated that some aspects of the specialty were being addressed by the international community in psychology.

Selected European Contributors to Developmental Psychology

Despite the importance of G. Stanley Hall and James Mark Baldwin to the beginning of American developmental psychology, the initial impetus for the specialty came from Europe. Moreover, for many years, European contributors were among the most important contributors. Many of them have gone unnoticed by contemporary students of development or, in the case of Alfred Binet, have not been given credit for their contributions to developmental research. Yet, their contributions were substantial, and their work deserves to be further recognized. A brief discussion of a few of these contributors follows. The list is far from exhaustive.

Edouard Clarapède: Developmental Psychology in Switzerland before Piaget

Psychology had a substantial history in Switzerland before the appearance of Jean Piaget. Théodore Flournoy (1854–1920) is considered the founder of Swiss psychology. Originally from Geneva, his family fled to France because of religious persecution. He received a doctorate in medicine and also studied briefly with Wundt. Eventually he returned to Switzerland where, in 1891, he occupied the first chair of experimental and physiological psychology at the University of Geneva. In 1892, he founded a psychology laboratory there, and one of his fellow workers was his cousin, Edouard Clarapède, later to become the founder of Swiss child psychology.

Born in Geneva, Clarapède also spent time at Leipzig. He received his doctorate in medicine from the University of Geneva in 1897. He spent a year in Paris, where he became acquainted with Alfred Binet, and maintained a profound respect for him for the rest of his life. Clarapède returned to Geneva and founded a journal, *Archives de Psychologie* with Flournoy. In 1905, he published his most important book, *Psychologie de l'enfant et pédagogie expérimentale* [Psychology of the child and experimental pedagogy]. The book would later have an impact on the experimental work of Jean Piaget. In 1912, Clarapède founded the Institut J. J. Rousseau, which ultimately became affiliated with the University of Geneva. He succeeded Flournoy as chair of experimental psychology at the University of Geneva. Later, he was succeeded by Jean Piaget.

Alfred Binet: French Developmental Psychology

Alfred Binet (1857–1911), the French psychologist, is known to most students of psychology for his association with intelligence testing. Few recognize that his contributions were far wider, ranging from psychophysics to hypnosis and including substantial work in developmental psychology, particularly cognitive development. His two daughters were subjects in some of his early work on intelligence, suggesting to him that qualitative differences in the way children approached problems were more important in predicting intelligence than sensory measures, as Galton had indicated.

Some of Binet's work in this area anticipated that of Piaget (Fancher, 1998). Binet viewed cognitive development as a constructive process, was particularly interested in the cognitive errors that children made, and developed tests similar to those used by Piaget in his famous conservation experiments. Although Piaget had never worked directly with Binet, who died before Piaget came to Paris, he worked with Binet's associate, Theodore Simon, and was later hired by Edouard Clarapède, a friend of Binet. It seems likely that Piaget developed at least some of his notions through a familiarity with Binet's work (Siegler, 1992).

In 1899, Binet joined an organization that acted as an advocate for children. He soon became its president and remained so for the next nine years, until his death in 1911. Among other activities, the organization encouraged educators to engage in research with children (Siegler, 1992). Binet's role in developing intelligence scales was related to his advocacy work with children. Binet also founded an experimental laboratory school, probably the first such school in Europe (Wolf, 1973, as quoted in Siegler, 1992).

In 1895, Binet and his associate, Victor Henri, published the first two articles in the new journal that Binet had founded, *L'Année Psychologique*, studies of memory in children (Fancher, 1998). He continued to edit the journal for seventeen years, and the journal is still in existence. Some of his research was considered so advanced for his time, that one historian would comment that it took experimental child psychology seventy years to catch up with some of Binet's insights (Cairns, 1983).

William Stern: German Pioneer of Developmental Psychology

William Stern (1871–1938) was a pioneer German psychologist who originated a comprehensive system of personalistic psychology. His work spanned an unusually broad range of subfields and was highly regarded in Europe during his time. In the United States, Stern has been known primarily for developing the concept of the intelligence quotient (IQ).

Stern was born in Berlin where he studied philosophy and psychology and completed his dissertation under Hermann Ebbinghaus in 1893. The most creative period in Stern's career followed his marriage to Clara in 1899. By 1907, Stern had published extensively in the relatively new fields of applied, child, differential, and forensic psychology. Stern's first visit to the United States came at G. Stanley Hall's invitation to Clark University in 1909, when Stern received the first of two American honorary doctoral degrees.

In 1915, Stern succeeded Ernst Meumann as the editor of the *Zeitschrift für pädagogische Psychologie* and, the following year, as the director of the psychological laboratory at the Hamburg Institute for Colonial Studies (Kreppner, 1992). Stern remained in Hamburg until he was expelled by the Nazis in 1933. Following a year in Holland, Stern emigrated to the United States where William McDougall secured a professorate for him at Duke University. During the years preceding his death in 1938, Stern attempted, through a series of lectures, to bring his work in personalistic psychology out of the shadow of his IQ invention (Allport, 1938).

In part, Stern's ideas on development were derived from observing his own children, which he did in collaboration with his wife (Eyferth, 1976; Kreppner, 1992). While contemporaries were more concerned with general laws of human development, Stern investigated development as a function of individual differences. Rejecting attempts to determine the distinct influence of heredity and environment, Stern emphasized the role of individual plasticity as environmental factors and inherited dispositions converge, a view that is quite current.

Although Stern became influential through students and collaborators who furthered his ideas, including Heinz Werner, Martha Muchow, Gordon Allport, and Kurt Lewin, most of his work was neglected following his death. He has not been recognized for his role in founding the field of developmental psychology (Cairns, 1999; Kreppner, 1992). A reason for his limited posthumous influence in the United States may have been that his ideas were more consistent with contemporary developmental psychology than with trends in U.S. psychology during his own lifetime.

Lev Vygotsky and Russian Developmental Psychology:
Importance of Context

Lev Semenovich Vygotsky (1896–1934) and colleagues, most notably Alexander Romanovich Luria (1902–1977) and Alexei Nikolaivitch Leontiev (1904–1979), founded a cultural-historical school of psychology that emphasized the role of social processes in cognitive development. In his brief career, Vygotsky made significant methodological and theoretical contributions that continue to be relevant in contemporary education and developmental psychology. However, only during the past two decades, has Vygotsky risen from relative obscurity to become one of the more influential figures in U.S. developmental psychology.

Vygotsky was born to a Jewish family in Orscha (now in Belarus). He demonstrated early academic prowess and obtained admission to Moscow University, which at that time limited enrollment for Jewish students with a quota and lottery system (Kozulin, 1990). Vygotsky's early work in psychology concerned consciousness and methodology. Subsequently, Vygostky was offered a position as a research fellow at the Moscow Institute of Psychology where he began his work with Luria and Leontiev.

The method Vygotsky and colleagues at the Moscow Institute of Psychology employed to study psychological functions was to analyze the cultural context and social activities through which such functions develop. According to Vygotsky, intrapsychic functions are internalized social processes, and the latter must be analyzed to understand the former (Wertsch and Tulviste, 1992). His interest was in the psychological tools (e.g., language) that mediate the transformation of lower into higher functions (Kozulin, 1986). A central, and perhaps the most widely known, concept in Vygotsky's work is the "zone of proximal development," which refers to the extent to which, with instruction from others, an individual can achieve beyond one's actual developmental level (Vygotsky, 1986).

In the 1930s, purges initiated by Stalin disrupted Vygotsky's research program at the Moscow Institute of Psychology (Kozulin, 1990). Vygotsky was forced to abandon his work on consciousness, as well as his cross-cultural research program with Luria, and to fashion his ideas to be more consistent with Marxist ideology. Leontiev relocated to the city of Kharkov in the Ukraine along with other disciples of Vygotsky. The Kharkov group established a research program in developmental psychology that furthered, and in some areas, revised Vygotsky's work. Vygotsky remained in Moscow where he died of tuberculosis in 1934 at the age of thirty-seven.

More than half a century passed before U.S. developmental psychology came to appreciate the contributions of Vygotsky's school of psychology. By the 1930s, U.S. psychology was dominated by behaviorism and was particularly unreceptive to Vygotsky's emphasis on culture and cognition. Furthermore, other than *Thought and Language*, no translations of Vygotsky's books were available in English before the late 1970s. Like William Stern, another reason for the relatively late discovery of Vygotsky in the United States may be that Vygotsky's ideas were ahead of their time and may be more relevant to contemporary research in developmental psychology.

Charlotte Bühler and Lifespan Developmental Psychology

Over the course of her highly productive career, Charlotte Malachowski Bühler (1893–1974) made several important contributions to developmental psychology. She developed innovative naturalistic research methods and was among the first psychologists to study psychological development across the lifespan. In the United States, Bühler has gained recognition as a leading figure in the humanistic psychology movement, but the depth of her contributions to developmental psychology has often gone unnoticed.

Charlotte Malachowski was born in Berlin on December 20, 1893. She was precocious and exhibited such early academic interests that her parents encouraged her to pursue higher education (Gavin, 1990). After completing her undergraduate studies at the University of Berlin, she relocated to Munich where she studied under Oswald Külpe and obtained her Ph.D. in 1918. Upon the sudden death of Külpe during her graduate studies, she was supervised by Karl Bühler whose published work she had long admired and whom she married in 1916.

In 1922, at the appointment of the Austrian government, Karl Bühler founded the Vienna Psychological Institute, which he directed with his wife until it was taken over by the Nazis in 1938 (Ash, 1987). Under their leadership, the Vienna Institute became one of the most productive and prominent research institutions in Europe. From 1924 to 1925 Charlotte Bühler collaborated with several U.S. psychologists, including Edward Thorndike and Arnold Gesell, on a Rockefeller fellowship at Columbia University. A year after she returned to Vienna, the Rockefeller Foundation provided her with a ten-year grant to fund her developmental research with children and adolescents. The Bühlers left Austria when that country was annexed by Nazi Germany in 1938 and eventually settled in California, where Charlotte gained employment as a clinical psychologist at the Los

Angeles County Hospital and as a professor at the University of Southern California (Gavin, 1990).

A central objective in Bühler's research was to derive a theory that encompassed personality and cognitive development, in all its stages, as a whole (Schenk-Danzinger, 1963). She conceptualized personality development in terms of phases of self-determination, whereby the purpose is the experience of fulfillment upon reaching life goals. At different times in her career, beginning with her research on childhood and adolescence, Bühler devoted herself to extensively studying the characteristics of different stages of development. Finding experimental methods too limited for such research purposes, Bühler developed novel methodological approaches, including techniques for systematic observations of infants and for analyzing diaries and biographies.

International Influences on U.S. Journals of Developmental Psychology

The insular quality of U.S. psychology has often been reflected in its journals. U. P. Gielen and M. Pagan (1993) have documented the tendency of U.S. journals to ignore contributions from other countries and to have editorial boards that consist entirely of U.S. psychologists. Developmental psychology has been as guilty of these practices as the other specialties. But a review of developmental journals suggests some interesting variations and trends.

The *Journal of Genetic Psychology,* founded by G. Stanley Hall in 1891, is generally regarded as the first U.S. journal of developmental psychology. It promoted an international perspective from the outset. Hall maintained that "no professor in a university is respectable if he does not know the latest discoveries in his subjects in all lands" (Hall, 1891, p, v.). Following Hall's death in 1924, the journal was reorganized, with a new editor and sixteen additional consulting editors, including four non-U.S. editors: Cyril Burt, University of London; Edouard Clarapède, University of Geneva; Henri Piéron, University of Paris; and Sante De Sanctis, University of Rome. The tradition of using a substantial number of non-U.S. editors continued until 1984, when the journal was sold to an educational foundation. But the number of non-U.S. editors appears to have had little influence on the number of international contributions to the journal.

From 1925 to 2004, the journal published 4,296 articles, with 652, or 15 percent, of them from non-U.S. sources. However, the averages mask the trends. In the period immediately after its reorganization (1925–1929), 13.4 percent of the journal articles were from international sources. This value dropped immediately in the decades that followed, rarely going higher than 5 percent. In the entire 1950s, for instance, the journal published only fourteen articles (3 percent) from non-U.S. sources (Vaccaro and Hogan, 2005). Since that time, non-U.S. contributions to the journal have risen— and quite sharply—in recent years. The following summary of the last forty-five years of non-U.S. publications in the journal demonstrates the rising trend: 1960–1969, 10.2 percent; 1970–1979, 12.9 percent; 1980–1989, 22.2 percent; and 1990–1999, 44.5 percent. The high rate of international publication continued in the half decade 2000–2004 at 43.0 percent (Vaccaro and Hogan, 2005).

For another early U.S. journal, *Child Development,* fewer than 1 percent of the articles published between 1930, the starting date of the journal, through the 1950s, were foreign based. However, by 1960–1964, almost 6 percent of the journal articles were from outside the United States. By 2000, that figure had increased to 19 percent. A survey of recent articles in a third journal, *Developmental Psychology,* exhibits a similar pattern with an increasingly greater proportion of articles contributed by authors with non-U.S. institutional affiliations. For instance, during the 1990s, 19.9 percent of the articles published in *Developmental Psychology* were by authors with foreign affiliations; this figure had increased to 28.7 percent during 2000–2004 (Vaccaro and Hogan, 2005).

Still other U.S. developmental journals have also begun to reflect a higher rate of international involvement. In fact, two relatively recent U.S.-based journals, *Infant Behavior and Development* (begun in 1978) and *Journal of Applied Developmental Psychology* (begun in 1980), describe themselves as "international journals." While many of the non-U.S. articles in the journals originate in Canada and countries with strong English-speaking traditions (e.g., Australia, South Africa, and the United Kingdom), many other countries are represented as well, including Israel, China, Japan, the Netherlands, Spain, France, Germany, and others. It is clear that U.S. journals can be a source for non-U.S. contributions if they choose to be. Moreover, it appears that the international communication that has been so much discussed in recent years is finally beginning to be reflected in the journals.

Summary and Conclusions

Developmental psychology originated in Europe as a nonexperimental field of study. Many of its U.S. pioneers were trained in Europe and remained influenced by international contributions to the field. With the growth of behaviorism in the 1920s and 1930s, U.S. psychology expanded rapidly and gradually dominated the discipline. By the late 1930s, interest in non-U.S. research in developmental psychology had declined substantially. Consequently, important contributors from abroad, some of whom have been discussed in this chapter, were discovered late or neglected entirely.

One reason for this U.S. insularity was that several areas of study, which are considered important in modern developmental psychology (such as cognition, language, and the role of culture and social context), were beyond the realm of orthodox behaviorism. Another reason was that U.S. psychologists became less versed in foreign languages and, hence, less able to appreciate research that was not published in English. However, the neglect of non-U.S. developmental psychology may also be attributed to the erroneous belief that contributions from abroad were negligible.

Current trends suggest that U.S. dominance in developmental psychology is fading. At the same time, U.S. isolationism has declined. European psychology is regaining the leadership it lost in the 1930s, and the potential for the growth of psychology in some parts of the world, particularly in developing nations, is enormous. The two largest countries in the world, China and India, with a third of the world's population between them, have a surprising small number of psychologists per unit of population. It is therefore likely that the study of developmental psychology will continue to expand internationally and quite possibly in directions different from those seen in the United States.

An important future challenge for U.S. developmental psychology will be to stay current with contributions to the field from abroad. Studying the history of developmental psychology from an international perspective is a way of gaining new insights into the growth of the discipline. It is also a way of introducing ourselves to colleagues from around the world, an act that is both academic and social and that will become increasingly essential in the years to come.

REFERENCES

Ahmed, R., and Gielen, U. P. (1998). *Psychology in the Arab countries*. Menoufia, Egypt: Menoufia University Press.

Allport, G. W. (1938). William Stern: 1871–1938. *American Journal of Psychology*, 51, 770–773.

Anderson, J. E. (1956). Child development: An historical perspective. *Child Development*, 27, 181–196.

Ash, M. G. (1987). Psychology and politics in interwar Vienna: The Vienna Psychological Institute, 1922–1942. In M. G. Ash and W. R. Woodward (Eds.), *Psychology in twentieth-century thought and society* (pp. 143–164). Cambridge: Cambridge University Press.

Baltes, P. B. (1983). Life-span developmental psychology: Observations on history and theory revisited. In R. M. Lerner (Ed.), *Developmental psychology: Historical and philosophical perspectives* (pp. 79–111). Hillsdale, NJ: Lawrence Erlbaum.

Berndt, T. J., and Zigler, E. F. (1983). Developmental psychology. In G. A. Kimble and K. Schlesinger (Eds.), *Topics in the history of psychology* (pp. 115–150). Hillsdale, NJ: Lawrence Erlbaum.

Boring, E. G. (1929). *A history of experimental psychology*. New York: Appleton-Century.

Borstelmann, L. J. (1983). Children before psychology: Ideas about children from antiquity to the late 1800s. In W. Kessen (Ed.), *Handbook of child psychology*, Vol. 1: *History, theory, and methods* (4th ed., pp. 1–40). New York: Wiley.

Bringmann, W. G., Bringmann, N. J., and Balance, W. D. G. (1985). Experimental approaches to developmental psychology before William Preyer. In G. Eckardt, W. G. Bringmann, and L. Sprung (Eds.), *Contributions to a history of developmental psychology* (pp. 157–173). Berlin: Mouton.

Cairns, R. B. (1983). The emergence of developmental psychology. In W. Kessen (Ed.), *Handbook of child psychology*, Vol. 1: *History, theory, and methods* (4th ed., pp. 41–102). New York: Wiley.

Cairns, R. B. (1999). The making of developmental psychology. In W. Damon and R. M. Lerner (Eds.), *Handbook of child psychology: Theoretical models of human development* (Vol. 1, pp. 25–105). New York: Wiley.

Darwin, C. (1859). *The origin of species by means of natural selection*. London: J. Murray.

Darwin, C. (1877). A biographical sketch of an infant. *Mind*, 2, 285–294.

Dennis, W. (1949). Historical beginnings of child psychology. *Psychological Bulletin*, 46, 224–235.

Eckardt, G., Bringmann, W. G., and Sprung, L. (Eds.) (1984). *Contributions to a history of developmental psychology*. Berlin: Mouton.

Eyferth, K. (1976). The contribution of William and Clara Stern to the onset of developmental psychology. In K. Riegel and J. A. Meacham (Eds.), *The developing individual in a changing world: Historical and cultural issues* (Vol. 1, pp. 9–15). The Hague: Mouton.

Fancher, R. E. (1998). Alfred Binet, general psychologist. In G. A. Kimble and M. Wertheimer (Eds.), *Portraits of pioneers in psychology* (Vol. III, pp. 67–83). Washington, DC: American Psychological Association.

Flournoy, T. (1905). *Psychologie de l'enfant et pédagogie expérimentale* [Psychology of the child and experimental pedagogy]. Geneva: Hundig.

Gavin, E. A. (1990). Charlotte M. Bühler (1893–1974). In A. N. O'Connell and N. F. Russo (Eds.), *Women in psychology: A bio-bibliographic sourcebook* (pp. 49–56). New York: Greenwood.

Gielen, U. P., and Pagan, M. (1993). International psychology and American mainstream psychology. *International Psychologist,* 34(1), 16–19, and 34(2), 5.

Hall, G. S. (1883). The content of children's minds. *Princeton Review,* 11, 249–272.

Hall, G. S. (1891). Editorial. *Pedagogical Seminary,* 1(1), iii–viii.

Hall, G. S. (1904). *Adolescence.* New York: Appleton.

Hall, G. S. (1922). *Senescence.* New York: Appleton.

Hilgard, E. R. (1987). *Psychology in America: A historical survey.* New York: Harcourt Brace.

Hogan, J. D. (2004). G. Stanley Hall: Educator, organizer, and pioneer developmental psychologist. In G. A. Kimble and M. Wertheimer (Eds.), *Portraits of pioneers in psychology* (Vol. V, pp. 19–36). Washington, DC: American Psychological Association.

Holowinsky, I. Z. (1993). Pedology in Europe and developmental psychology in Ukraine. *School Psychology International,* 14, 327–338.

Jaeger, S. (1985). The origins of the diary method in developmental psychology. In G. Eckardt, W. G. Bringmann, and L. Sprung (Eds.), *Contributions to a history of developmental psychology* (pp. 63–74). Berlin: Mouton.

Kozulin, A. (1986). The concept of activity in Soviet psychology: Vygotsky, his disciples and critics. *American Psychologist,* 41, 264–274.

Kozulin, A. (1990). *Vygotsky's psychology: A biography of ideas.* Cambridge: Harvard University Press.

Kreppner, K. (1992). William L. Stern, 1871–1938: A neglected founder of developmental psychology. *Developmental Psychology,* 28, 539–547.

Miao, X., and Wang, W. (2003). A century of Chinese developmental psychology. *International Journal of Psychology,* 38, 258–273.

O'Donnell, J. M. (1979). The crisis of experimentalism in the 1920s: E. G. Boring and his uses of history. *American Psychologist,* 34, 289–295.

Piaget, J. (1931). Children's philosophies. In C. Murchison, (Ed.), *Handbook of child psychology* (pp. 377–391). Worcester, MA: Clark University Press.

Preyer, W. (1882). *Die Seele des Kindes.* Leipzig: Grieben. English translation: *The Mind of the Child* (1889). New York: Appleton.

Schenk-Danzinger, L. (1963). Fundamental ideas and theories in Charlotte Buehler's lifework. *Journal of Humanistic Psychology,* 3, 3–9.

Sexton, V. S., and Misiak, H. (1984). American psychologists and psychology abroad. *American Psychologist,* 39, 1026–1031.

Siegler, R. S. (1992). The other Alfred Binet. *Developmental Psychology,* 28, 178–190.

Vaccaro, T. P., and Hogan, J. D. (2005). Publication trends in leading U.S. journals of developmental psychology. Poster presented at the Annual Meeting of the American Psychological Association, Washington, DC.

Vygotsky, L. S. (1986). *Thought and language.* Ed. and Trans. A. Kozulin. Cambridge, MA: MIT Press. (Original work published in 1934)

Wertsch, J. V., and Tulviste, P. (1992). L. S. Vygotsky and contemporary developmental psychology. *Developmental Psychology,* 28, 548–557.

Chapter 8

Psychology and Liberal Democracy

A Spurious Connection?

Adrian C. Brock

Does psychology have a special affinity with any kind of political system? At first glance, it would appear not. Since its appearance in Europe in the second half of the nineteenth century, psychology has existed under just about every kind of political system that has existed in various parts of the world. It has existed in the democracies of Western Europe, North America, and Australasia, and it has existed in Nazi Germany, as well as in the former Soviet Union and its allies. Clearly, psychology can exist under a variety of governments, but the question remains as to whether it is particularly compatible with any of them.

Nikolas Rose would suggest that it is. In many of his works, he has argued that psychology and what he calls "liberal democracy" are particularly compatible. Following Foucault, he suggests that the liberal democracies of the West have an aversion to the direct exercise of political power. Freedom and liberty are stressed. Because of this, their citizens have to be ruled in less direct ways. In fact, they often rule themselves through "technologies of the self" (Martin, Gutman, and Hutton, 1998). Thus in modern liberal democracies, what Rose calls the "psy disciplines"—psychology, psychiatry, and psychoanalysis—have an important role in "governing the soul" (Rose, 1999).

This presumed link between psychology and liberal democracy runs like a thread through Rose's work. For example, in chapter 4 of *Inventing Ourselves*, he writes:

> To conclude, let me sketch out the three principal forms of connection between psychological expertise and liberal democratic forms of government:

rationality, privacy and autonomy. First, in liberal democratic societies the exercise of power over citizens becomes legitimate to the extent that it claims a rational basis. . . . Second, liberal democratic problematics of government depend on the creation of "private" spaces outside the formal scope of the authority of public powers. . . . Third, liberal democratic problematics of government are autonomizing: they seek to govern through constructing a kind of regulated autonomy for social actors. The modern liberal self is "obliged to be free," to construe all aspects of its life as the outcome of choices made among a number of options. (Rose, 1996, pp. 99–100)

Although Rose is fundamentally interested in the liberal democratic societies of the West, he also has something to say about the former socialist countries of the east:

It appears that, as the apparatus of the party and the plan is dismantled, other forms of authority are born, other ways of shaping and guiding the choices of these newly freed individuals. . . . Perhaps we will find that the transition to market economies and political pluralism will require, as its necessary corollary, not just the importation of material technologies of liberal democracy but also their human technologies—the engineers of the human soul that are the other side of what we have come to term freedom. (ibid; p. 100)

These statements were made in a particular context. The chapter is based on a paper that Rose gave at a conference in the German Democratic Republic (East Germany) in 1990. I was present at that conference and could not resist the temptation to point out that Rose's audience consisted mainly of East German psychologists, that the discipline was flourishing in the GDR, and that there had been no need for liberal democracy for that situation to occur.[1] I could say that with some confidence because I had been an exchange student of psychology at the University of Leipzig and had previously attended other conferences in the GDR (Brock, 1991). It seemed to me that Rose had wandered into a situation that he did not understand.

I am sure that I am not the only person who raised objections of this kind, since Rose makes an attempt to address these objections in the introduction to *Inventing Ourselves*. The fact that these issues are considered in the introduction to a collection of previously written papers suggests that they were an afterthought. Rose (1996) is happy to acknowledge that psychology existed in Nazi Germany, but he is eager to play down its importance: "Psychotherapy, rather surprisingly, could be accorded a role under the Nazis . . . but it did not become a widely deployed technology for their regulation of conduct or subjectivity" (p. 14). Similarly:

> Geuter concludes that, while many psychologists did try to place their place their discipline in the service of organs of Nazi domination, psychology contributed little to stabilising that domination. . . . It was not systematically involved in the deployment of official propaganda, and psychologists are not known to have been used by the Nazis or the SS in persecution, torture or murder. (p. 14)

Then Rose turns his attention to the Soviet Union and its allies in Eastern Europe. He acknowledges that some psychology existed in the early years of the Soviet Union but points out that psychological testing and attitude questionnaires were banned:

> Although there was undoubtedly a rebirth of psychology after World War II, the governmental role of psy expertise in postwar communist nations remains to be analyzed. From the few detailed studies of local party apparatus that are available, there is little evidence that the psy experts were of much importance in the "pastoral relations" of the Communist Party bureaucracies through which everyday life was regulated in the former communist states of Eastern Europe in the period preceding their collapse. (p. 15)

Thus the special relationship between psychology and liberal democracy is preserved. No one pretends or could pretend that the relationship is mutually exclusive, but there is clearly an attempt to postulate an affinity between the two. Other evidence in favor of such an affinity can be produced. Johann Louw (chapter 1 in this volume) examines the spread of "psychologization" in South Africa and, following Rose, links it to the establishment of liberal democracy in that country in recent years.

It is true that most of the world's psychologists live in Northwestern Europe and North America under liberal democratic regimes. If we were to include the psychologists in Asia, Africa, Latin America, and Oceania who live under similar regimes, it would account for the vast majority of psychologists in the world.

In spite of this, I remain unconvinced. The basic problem, as I see it, is the one that is explained to first-year psychology students in their statistics class: correlation does not imply causation. This point has already been made by Louw and Kurt Danziger (undated manuscript) in relation to Rose's work:

> The problem here is the classical one of correlation. If all one's examples are taken from a category of cases in which two features coincide one can never be sure that there really is a direct link between them and that their association is not caused by some underlying, unexamined, factor. No matter how intelligible the link between psychological practices and certain forms of social regulation can be made to appear there is always the possibility that this link is merely the fortuitous outcome of their common dependence on circumstances that have escaped scrutiny (p. 5).[2]

Just because the majority of the world's psychologists live under liberal democratic regimes, it does not automatically follow that there is a significant relationship between psychology and liberal democracy.

I could similarly point out that the majority of the world's psychologists live in temperate climates. This would include North America, Europe, and Japan. There are fewer psychologists in the southern hemisphere, but this can be explained by the fact that the continents of the southern hemisphere have much smaller temperate zones. However, it is surely no coincidence that southern hemisphere countries with temperate climates, like Argentina, South Africa, and Australia, have more psychologists than the countries with tropical climates to the north. As with the liberal democracy theory, I can happily acknowledge that some psychology exists in these countries, but this does not alter the basic fact that most of world's psychologists live in temperate zones.

I do not want to seriously suggest that temperate climates encourage the spread of psychology, in spite of the strong association between the two. I simply wish to show how the argument works. It might be argued that a link between psychology and liberal democracy has more plausibility than a link between psychology and temperate climates, and this is undoubtedly true. Perhaps a more convincing way of casting doubt on the claim is to look at situations where psychology and liberal democracy do not co-exist. There are many countries with liberal democratic systems of government where psychology does not exist to any significant degree. Some examples are India, Turkey, the Philippines, South Korea, and Japan. The number of psychologists per million of population in these countries in the late 1980s was tiny compared with the number of psychologists per million of population in the Soviet bloc countries, such as Czechoslovakia, Poland, and the aforementioned GDR (Sexton and Hogan, 1992).

While it would be possible to look at an example of a country with a liberal democratic government where psychology hardly exists, this would not be particularly interesting to an audience of historians of psychology. I am therefore going to focus on an example of a country without a liberal democratic government where psychology not only has prospered and grown but also has permeated the whole of society. If it can be shown that such a country exists, it would cast serious doubt on the claim that there is a significant relationship between psychology and liberal democracy. Such a country does exist, and it is called "Cuba." I take it that no one would seriously suggest that Cuba has a liberal democratic government, not even the government itself.

I would like to stress that it is not my intention to make propaganda for or against the Cuban government. I make this point because a previous attempt to address these issues at a conference led to some audience members assuming that I was telling them how wonderful life in Cuba was and they were getting very irate (Brock, 2003). That is not my intention at all. My aim is simply to use the empirical evidence that the history of psychology in Cuba provides. I would also like to point out that I have not conducted any original research on the subject, though I made two trips to Cuba and spoke with several psychologists in Havana and Santiago while I was there. I also acquired a large collection of books, journals, and unpublished manuscripts that are difficult to obtain outside the country.[3] However, most of the information discussed here has been available in the English-language literature for many years (e.g., Bernal, 1985; Marín, 1987; Bernal and Rodriguez, 1992).

One of the most striking things about psychology in Cuba is its size. According to the well-known book by V. S. Sexton and J. D. Hogan (1992) on international psychology, Cuba had 186 psychologists per million of population. This is not far behind the United Kingdom which had 244, but it was ahead of Austria with 178, Ireland with 157, Greece with 60, and Japan with 36. I make these comparisons because Cuba is a poor, third-world country that has had to contend with an economic and information blockade for many years. All of the other countries are richer, first-world countries with liberal democratic governments.

The other significant point about psychology in Cuba is that it scarcely existed before the revolution of 1959. Following a visit to Cuba in the

1940s, the Harvard psychologist, W. H. D. Vernon wrote: "Psychology in Cuba, like psychology in other Latin American countries, has a history very different from psychology in the United States. It has no status as a separate discipline, and there is no journal given over to the publication of psychological data. Psychology is seen as a part of philosophy, sociology and education" (1944, p. 73). Some psychology was taught in the universities, and there were a few foreign-trained psychotherapists who catered to the rich. But the foundations of Cuban psychology as an independent discipline and as a profession were established in the years immediately after the revolution of 1959. Thus the first school of psychology in Cuba was established at the University of Las Villas in 1961, and the school of psychology at the University of Havana was established in 1962. The first group of students from the latter graduated only in 1966. However, by 1980 the Ministry of Public Health alone employed 310 psychologists and 350 psychometricians (Marín, 1987).

It is no secret why psychology was established in the immediate aftermath of the revolution or why it experienced such rapid growth:

> The shift from capitalism to socialism transformed all aspects of everyday life. Technology and science were now viewed as tools created to improve life and as having tremendous social value. Thus, psychology, as both a science and a profession, experienced a surge of development. This view is contrary to the attitude held before 1959, when psychology was seen as an esoteric field limited to the elite. (Bernal and Rodriguez, 1992, p. 86)

It will be recalled that Rose (1996) predicted that the demise of socialism would lead to the growth of psychology in the former socialist countries. Here we can see that it was socialism that led to the establishment of psychology and its subsequent development and growth.

The third point I wish to make is that, as the above quotation indicates, psychology is not something that exists apart from the rest of society in Cuba. Whatever other failings it might have, the Cuban revolution has delivered health care and education to the people in a way that no other government had done before. The fact that psychologists were involved in the provision of these services helped to ensure the establishment of the profession and its expansion and growth (Sommers, 1969). One of the areas in which Cuban psychology is particularly strong is community psychology, so much so that the *American Journal of Community Psychology* devoted a special issue of the journal to Cuba in 1985 (e.g., Bernal, 1985;

Garcia Averasturi, 1985; Marín, 1985). Cuba was seen, in many respects, as leading the way.

Since the revolution, psychologists have become involved in many aspects of Cuban society: "Psychologists may be found in non-traditional settings such as day-care centers, factories, schools, and political, cultural, and recreational organizations, as well as more traditional sites such as psychiatric institutions, hospitals, community health centers, universities, and research institutes" (Bernal and Rodriguez, 1992, p. 91). It is also clear that psychologists in Cuba are heavily involved in the regulation of everyday life: "Psychologists provide consultation, conduct research, and develop preventative programs in factories, cultural and recreational organizations, sport organizations and centers for the study of labor relations. . . . Psychologists in these centers aim to promote productivity, discipline and motivation" (Ibid., p. 90). There is also evidence of psychologists "engineering the human soul," in the way that Rose (1996, p. 100) uses the term, as well as the use of "technologies of the self."

In an article titled "The social function of the psychologist in Cuba," A. Mitjáns Martínez and M. Febles Elejade write that a major role of the psychologist is "the formation and development of the personality as part of the process of installing socialism in Cuba" (1983, p. 12). It may be recalled that Ernesto "Che" Guevara wrote a famous essay, "Socialism and man in Cuba," in which he argued that socialism would need a different kind of person (Guevara, 2001). When I discussed this essay with psychologists in Cuba, I was told that, although it was rarely cited, it formed the ideological background for much of their work.

Two of the main areas of research in Cuba since the revolution have been personality and moral development (see also Bernal, 1985). A major figure in this research was Fernando González Rey, who now lives in Brazil. One of his more interesting books is titled, *Moral motivation in adolescents and young people.* It ends, of course, with a chapter titled "The formation of moral ideals" (González Rey, 1982, p. 112). A work by the same author on the education and development of the personality contains chapters such as "Moral education of the personality," "Vocational and professional education," and "Education for health" (González Rey and Mitjáns Martínez, 1999). Psychologists in Cuba have been transforming people, and encouraging people to transform themselves, in socially desirable ways. There is nothing unique about liberal democracy in this regard.

I hope that by now the view that psychology has a special affinity with liberal democracy is untenable, or at least in serious doubt. How could it have been taken so seriously? Part of the problem is that historians of psychology have traditionally concerned themselves only with Northwestern Europe and North America. Rose's own work is heavily focused on Britain and the United States. It is perhaps unsurprising that people can be led astray with such a narrow data base. This is one reasons that an "internationalization" of the history of psychology is so desperately needed. In particular, there is a need for comparative studies of different societies (e.g., Dumont and Louw, 2001). It is only through comparative studies that we can find out what different societies have in common and what makes them unique.

Another problem seems to be the popular Western stereotypes of socialism that have their origins in the propaganda of the Cold War (e.g., Hayek, 2001). The people of Cuba are not like medieval serfs who simply do what they are told. They almost certainly have less freedom than people in liberal democratic societies, but this does not mean that they have no freedom at all. It also does not mean that the Cuban government is not concerned about what the Cuban people think. Like all governments, it has means of forcing people to comply with its wishes, but, like liberal democratic governments, it prefers to use them only as a last resort.

It is similarly absurd to suggest that rationality and the existence of a "private" sphere are not features of Cuban social life. We are not talking here about Europe under the "ancien regime," as Foucault was wont to do (e.g., Foucault, 1991). Cuba is a modern and a modernizing society. To that extent, it has much in common with modern liberal democratic regimes. A further possibility is that these problems are the result of a misapplication of Foucault's ideas. There is a world of difference between the ancien regime in Europe and modern nonliberal democratic regimes.

Having put one spurious connection aside, I am reluctant to suggest another. However, it seems to me that psychology is frequently associated with that constellation of beliefs that we call "modernity." Here I am referring to a belief in the value of economic development, industrialization, rationality, science, and technology. Where these beliefs exist, "modern" psychology is likely to appear, regardless of whether or not the government is liberal democratic.

This view must be tempered with the knowledge that local circumstances can make the situation different in each case. For example, psychology did not have a major role in Nazi Germany, even though Germany was a highly industrialized country and its science and technology were among the most advanced in the world. It had nothing to do with liberal democracy. Although experimental psychology appeared in Germany at an early stage in the history of psychology, German psychology continued to be a branch of philosophy until World War II. Danziger (chapter 11 in this volume) writes: "The spread of applied psychology encountered many obstacles in Germany. . . . As late as 1929 the German Psychological Society published a protest against the tendency to reduce the number of academic positions in psychology in favor of philosophy. But it defended psychology in terms of its philosophical, not its practical, value." Psychology as a discipline and as a profession made enormous strides under the Nazis, but the point from which it started was not particularly well advanced. German psychologists had not penetrated society in the way that their American counterparts had done, and this was equally true of the Weimar Republic as it was of the Nazi regime.

Local conditions vary from place to place. Even psychology can vary from place to place, and it seems plausible to suggest that the conditions of its establishment, as well as its growth, can also vary from place to place. In this situation, it is unwise to make sweeping generalizations of the kind that "psychology goes with x." I also hope that the above example will show the importance of looking at psychology in a variety of social contexts. Without that, we will fall prey to spurious connections of the kind that I have outlined.

NOTES

1. See also Busse (2004) and my review of this work (Brock, in press).

2. Unfortunately, these words were edited out of the published version of the manuscript (Louw and Danziger, 2000; Danziger, personal communication). I am very grateful to Kurt Danziger for the fruitful discussions that I have had with him on this subject. I am, of course, solely responsible for the opinions expressed.

3. The author who has written most extensively on the history of psychology in Cuba is Carolina de la Torre Molina (e.g., Torre, 1995; Torre Molina, 1991; Torre Molina and Calviño Valdés-Fauly, 2000). I am especially grateful to her for taking the time to talk with me and for helping me to obtain copies of her publications. See also the articles by Fernando González Rey (1995, 2000) and by Eduardo Cairo Valcárcel (1998).

REFERENCES

Bernal, G. (1985). A history of psychology in Cuba. *Journal of Community Psychology*, 13, 222–235.

Bernal, G., and Rodriguez, W. (1992). Cuba. In V. S. Sexton and J. D. Hogan (Eds.), *International psychology: Views from around the world* (pp. 85–94). Lincoln: University of Nebraska Press.

Brock, A. (1991). Imageless thought or stimulus error? The social construction of private experience. In W. R. Woodward and R. S. Cohen (Eds.), *World views and scientific discipline formation: Science studies in the German Democratic Republic* (pp. 97–106). Dordrecht: Kluwer.

Brock, A. C. (2003). Beyond liberal democracy: Psychology in revolutionary Cuba. Paper presented at Internationalizing the History of Psychology, symposium conducted at the annual convention of the American Psychological Association in Toronto, Canada, August.

Brock, A. C. (in press). Review of *Psychologie in der DDR* [Psychology in the GDR] by Stefan Busse. *Journal of the History of the Behavioral Sciences.*

Busse, S. (2004). *Psychologie in der DDR* [Psychology in the GDR]. Weinheim, Germany: Beltz.

Cairo Valcárcel, E. (1998). Análisis bibliométrico de la *Revista Cubana de Psicología.* Una modesta contribución para la tarea mayor: Escribir la historia de la Facultad de Psicología de la Universidad de la Habana [Bibliometric analysis of the Cuban *Journal of Psychology.* A modest contribution to the main task: To write a history of the School of Psychology at the University of Havana]. *Revista Cubana de Psicología,* 15, 168–176.

Dumont, K., and Louw, J. (2001). The International Union of Psychological Science and the politics of membership: Psychological associations in South Africa and the German Democratic Republic. *History of Psychology,* 4, 388–404.

Foucault, M. (1991). *Discipline and punish: The birth of the prison.* Harmondsworth: Penguin. (Original work published 1978.)

García Averasturi, L. (1985). Community health psychology in Cuba. *Journal of Community Psychology,* 13, 117–124.

González Rey, F. (1982). *Motivación moral en adolescentes y jóvenes* [Moral motivation in adolescents and young people]. Havana: Editorial Científico-Técnica.

González Rey, F. (1995). La psicología en Cuba: Apuntes para su historia [Psychology in Cuba: Notes for its history]. *Temas,* 1, 69–76.

González Rey, F. (2000). La psicología en Cuba: Un relato para su historia [Psychology in Cuba: A story for its history]. *Interamerican Journal of Psychology,* 34, 185–198.

González Rey, F., and Mitjáns Martínez, A. (1999). *La personalidad, su educación y desarollo* [The personality, its education and development] (3rd ed.). Havana: Editorial Pueblo y Educación.

Guevara, E. (2001). El socialismo y el hombre en Cuba [Socialism and man in Cuba]. In *Ernesto Che Guevara: Obras escogidas, 1957–1967* (pp. 361–384). Havana: Editorial de Ciencias Sociales. (Original work published 1965.)

Hayek, F. A. (2001). *The road to serfdom.* London: Routledge. (Original work published 1944.)

Louw, J., and Danziger, K. (Undated manuscript). Psychological practices and ideology: The South African case.

Louw, J., and Danziger, K. (2000). Psychological practices and ideology: The South African case. *Psychologie en Maatschappij,* 90, 50–61.

Marín, B. V. (1985). Community psychology in Cuba: A literature review. *Journal of Community Psychology,* 13, 138–154.

Marín, G. (1987). Cuba. In A. R. Gilgen and C. K. Gilgen (Eds.), *International handbook of psychology* (pp. 137–144). New York: Greenwood.

Martin, L. H., Gutman, H., and Hutton, P. H. (Eds.) (1998). *Technologies of the self: A seminar with Michel Foucault.* Amherst: University of Massachusetts Press.

Mitjáns Martínez, A., and Febles Elejade, M. (1983). La función social del psicólogo en Cuba [The social function of the psychologist in Cuba]. *Revista del Hospital Psiquiátrico de la Habana,* 24, 5–20.

Rose, N. (1996). *Inventing ourselves: Psychology, power and personhood.* New York: Cambridge University Press.

Rose, N. (1999). *Governing the soul: The shaping of the private self* (2nd ed.). London: Routledge.

Sexton, V. S., and Hogan, J. D. (Eds.) (1992). *International psychology: Views from around the world.* Lincoln: University of Nebraska Press.

Sommers, B. J. (1969). Psychology education and mental health services in Cuba in 1968. *American Psychologist,* 24, 941–946.

Torre, C. de la (1995). *Psicología Latinoamericana: Entre la dependencia y la identidad* [Latin American psychology: Between dependency and identity]. Havana: Editorial "Félix Varela."

Torre Molina, C. de la (1991). *Temas actuales de historia de la psicología* [Current topics in the history of psychology]. Havana: Ediciones ENPES.

Torre Molina, C. de la, and Calviño Valdés-Fauly, M. (2000). Reflexión sobre los logros, problemas y retos de la psicología en Cuba [Reflections on the achievements, problems, and challenges of psychology in Cuba]. *Interamerican Journal of Psychology,* 34, 169–183.

Vernon, W. H. D. (1944). Psychology in Cuba. *Psychological Bulletin,* 41, 73–89.

Chapter 9

Double Reification

The Process of Universalizing Psychology in the Three Worlds

Fathali M. Moghaddam and Naomi Lee

From a global perspective, psychology in the twenty-first century is characterized by two main features. First, on the world stage, psychology is dominated by the United States, which even before the collapse of the Soviet empire was described as the First World and the sole "superpower" of psychology (Moghaddam, 1987). Second, mainstream psychology, exported mainly from the United States, is now present in almost all Third World societies. Those interested in internationalizing the history of psychology must address the issue of how the United States became the dominant power in psychology and how mainstream psychology became global.

A first possibility, referred to by us as the "free-market model," is that this situation arose out of competition in a free market of ideas. In such a free market, different ideas are put forward and critically evaluated, and the best are adopted. The free-market model assumes that psychological research evolves independently from social, political, and economic forces. A second possibility, the "power-relations model," is that power relations between nations and groups have an important influence on the characteristics of contemporary psychology around the world. This second possibility suggests that the ideas that are supported by those who have greater power and influence on the world stage will become internationally dominant in psychology. The assumption here is that psychological research is fundamentally shaped by social, political, and economic forces.

Our contention is that the power-relations model is more accurate. We argue that, first, the reason U.S. psychology is being exported to different countries around the world has more to do with the status of the United States as the sole military superpower in the world than it has with the scientific merits of U.S. psychology. Second, the global spread of mainstream psychology, which assumes cause-effect relations to underlie thought and action, is an attempt to emulate what are thought to be the research practices of the natural sciences. Thus, as a discipline with lower status and power, psychology is attempting to emulate the natural science model that is associated with higher status and power.

We will discuss the power relations model within a three worlds framework (Moghaddam, 1987), developed to describe power disparities in the domain of psychology. The first world of psychology consists of the United States, which dominates on the world stage and exports psychological knowledge around the globe. The second world consists of the other industrialized nations, such as the United Kingdom, France, and Russia. These countries are important historic sources for modern psychology and still retain influence, particularly through former colonial ties, but their influence has faded considerably in the post–World War II era, compared with that of the United States.

Defining Double Reification

We apply the power-relations model in association with the concept of double reification, involving the exportation and propagation of cultural phenomena from one nation to another, and the later harvesting of the outcomes of this exportation through so-called international research, as validation for universalization. An example is the propagation of modern conceptions of human rights through international educational programs and, later, surveying social representations of human rights in the same societies to demonstrate the "universality" of rights (Spini and Doise, 2004). We use the term "double" reification to distinguish this between-nations process from reification that involves different groups within one nation (space limitations prevent us from discussing within-nation reification here).

Our perspective on the history of psychology is in line with what Gascoigne (1998) has aptly termed "science in the service of empire." A critical literature has emerged on the relationship between colonial expansion and science (e.g., Storey, 1996), arguing that science policy has been closely tied with political and military policy. Extending this theme, we argue that psychological science, and the history told of this science, has served both external and internal colonialism by supporting intergroup power disparities in both international and national contexts. At the international level, much of the psychology dominant in most African, Asian, and Latin American societies reflects the needs and values of Western powers (Moghaddam, 1990). At the national level, this psychology is imported through a Westernized Third World elite, and the imported psychology in large part remains within the modern sector and serves the elite rather than the majority of the population who live in the traditional sector of the economy and society (Moghaddam and Taylor, 1985; 1986).

Universalizing Psychology

The contemporary trend of exporting psychological knowledge from the first and second worlds to the third world of psychology has its roots in the historical goal of universalizing psychology. Research methods and findings evolving out of laboratories primarily in Germany in the later part of the nineteenth century, and in the United States from the early twentieth century, were exported to the rest of the world. Initially, ex-colonial ties helped European countries dominate the growth of modern psychology in their former colonies, as in the case of Great Britain and its influence on psychology in India, France, and French Canada. However, by the second half of the twentieth century, these former colonial ties were overshadowed by the supreme dominance of the United States on the world stage, so that, for example, psychology in India (e.g., Pandey, 2000) and French Canada (e.g., Vallerand, 1994) is now to a greater degree influenced by U.S. psychology.

The attempt to universalize psychology was based on the natural science model and the assumption that human thought and action are causally determined by factors that are the same for all humankind, rather than influenced by cultural conditions that can vary considerably across societies (such as in the domain of intelligence; Moghaddam, 2005, ch. 7). By the 1930s, and perhaps earlier, the causal assumption was formalized by the adoption of the terms "independent variable" (assumed cause) and "dependent variable" (assumed effect), imported probably from the field of statistics (Danziger and Dzinas, 1997; Winston, 2004).

Why the Causal Model?

The overwhelming dominance of causal psychology needs some explanation, particularly because from the very earliest days of modern psychology, the "dissenters" included important scholars, such as William James. As E. D. Cahan and S. H. White indicate, the dissenters were in a "politically weak position":

> The brass-instruments laboratory established scientific psychology in the university. It was concrete. One could show it to college presidents, colleagues, and students. . . . Dissenters . . . talked about the possibility and necessity of nonexperimental psychology, but they were in a politically weak position. . . . Experimental psychologists subscribed to well-known and revered principles of natural science. . . . They aspired to be technicians addressing themselves to facts, not values. (Cahan and White, 1992, p. 229)

A deeper exploration is needed to find out why this was and continues to be the case. The answer lies in subtle cultural trends, and the issues raised are also relevant to the exportation of causal psychology to Third World societies, which we discuss later in this chapter.

Particularly since the industrial revolution, the natural sciences gained immense prestige, first in Western and then also in Third World societies. Knowledge gained through natural science research helped to rapidly expand industrial production, leading to economic and military supremacy for Great Britain in the nineteenth century and the United States in the twentieth century. The application of natural science research enabled enormous new industries to flourish, improving the standard of living and health for many people. The evidence seemed clear: natural science research gave results. The prestige of scientists increased, both inside and outside academia.

Links between the social sciences, humanities, the arts, and in general "nonscience" disciplines and economic growth have been far more difficult to demonstrate. There may well be very strong links, but they are less direct and less visible. Within psychology, the economic and practical "real world" benefits of some specialties, such as clinical psychology, organizational psychology, and experimental research associated with ergonomics, have been more visible than the benefits of philosophical and theoretical psychology, which are closer to the humanities than to the natural sciences.

In the status hierarchy of universities, science and those professions associated with the application of science enjoy the highest prestige. Thus, in most major societies, government funding for natural science research is higher than for research in the social sciences, humanities, and the arts. In the United States and many other major societies, the salaries of university faculty follows the same trend, with highest to lowest salaries being paid to faculty in science, social science, humanities, and the arts (faculty in the professional schools of business, law, and medicine receive the highest salaries of all, presumably because of greater demand for them in the employment market).

Because the natural sciences enjoy high economic clout, relative to areas such as philosophy and literature, many psychologists have tried to associate their discipline with the natural sciences. Consequently, mainstream psychologists have adopted the paraphernalia of natural science methods, "laboratories," "white lab coats," "instruments," "subjects," "computer modeling," and the like, even in cases where the topic of study does not warrant such an approach.

Another important factor leading to the exportation of causal psychology is the assumption that cause-effect relations, and the laboratory methods associated with causal psychology, is culture-free and can be transferred from culture to culture as an independent, mobile package. Since the purpose of mainstream experimental procedures, at least since the 1930s, is to isolate causal factors and test their effects in isolation, and since this has meant the attempt to control and exclude all cultural factors except the independent variables, then it is not surprising that causal psychology and its associated methodology came to be seen as suitable from exportation to anywhere in the world. After all, as long as the independent and dependent variables are effectively isolated, what difference does it make if a study is conducted with native people in Australia, natives of New York, or natives of the southern Sahara?

Schools of Psychology and the Universal/Causal Assumption

The first half of the twentieth century was a time of tremendous change and growth in modern psychology (Koch and Leary, 1985), but a consistent trend was the dominance of causal over normative models and the persistent attempt at universalizing psychology (Moghaddam, 2002). The dawn of the new century saw the demise of Titchener's structuralism, and the second decade witnessed the launching of behaviorism (Moghaddam, 2005, ch. 6). The behaviorists, dominant in the United States, hoped that studies of stimulus-response (cause-effect) relations would eventually lead to the discovery of universal laws of learning. About the same time that Watson (1913) issued the "behaviorist manifesto," Freud delivered his influential lectures at Clark University (in 1909) and launched a new era for the psychoanalytic movement in North America. Despite some changes over time, Freud's psychology retained a core causal assumption that remained stable. Freud saw human behavior as causally determined, albeit often by unconscious factors that are not recognized or understood by the perpetrators themselves.

Thus, the two schools of psychology that were dominant, at least in the United States, for much of the first half of the twentieth century, behaviorism and psychoanalysis, assumed human behavior to be causally determined. Humanistic psychology, and to a lesser degree Gestalt psychology, followed a different path, emphasizing individual uniqueness and intentionality. However, these schools had less influence on developments in psychology in the United States than in Europe.

By the 1950s, the dominance of behaviorism in American academic psychology was being successfully challenged by the cognitive revolution. The path was prepared for the return of the mind to psychology by demonstrations in the 1930s and 1940s showing that even animals can be insightful and creative when given an opportunity to show a range of behaviors (e.g., Köhler, 1947), rather than only being given an option to press or not press a bar. In the same era, F. C. Bartlett (1932) in England demonstrated an important role for cognitive schemas in memory, and E. C. Tolman (1948) in the United States showed that rats navigate mazes using mental maps. The cognitive revolution had built up steam in the United States by the late 1950s, and cognitive psychology had become the dominant school of psychology by the end of the 1960s. From the platform of U.S. dominance, cognitive psychology was launched to world dominance by the 1980s.

But the dominance of cognitive psychology did not change the centrality of cause-effect relations and attempts at universalizing in mainstream psychological models; cognitive psychologists assumed causes to be universal cognitive mechanisms. For example, constructs such as short-term memory and cognitive dissonance are conceived as automatic causal factors rather than constructions that will probably change as cultural shifts take place (short-term memory has been reconceptualized through the concept of working memory, and the assumptions underlying cognitive dissonance are questionable even within U.S. culture; Moghaddam, 1998, ch.4).

The causal tradition continues with much of the research in neuroscience, where causes of thought and action are assumed to reside in biological processes. Findings from studies using fMRI (functional magnetic resonance imaging) and other brain-imaging techniques are often interpreted as demonstrating the "location" in the brain that causes particular thoughts and actions. Rather than the brain serving as part of the enabling conditions for thought and action, the brain is seen as the determinant. An example is a particular location or characteristic of the brain (e.g., abnormally small prefrontal cortex or low release of serotonin) as a causal determinant of aggression (Raine, Lenez, Bihrle, LaCasse, and Colletti, 2000).

Evolutionary psychology, increasingly influential since the 1980s, also adopts a causal approach. J. C. Gaulin and D. H. McBurney (2001) begin their text *Psychology: An Evolutionary Approach* with a question that guides all of their discussions: "What causes us to think, to react to others and behave in the ways we do?" (p. 1).

The strength of the causal approach in mainstream psychology is clearly reflected in introductory texts. For example, J. W. Kalat's (2005) popular introductory text includes a discussion of the debate concerning determinism in psychology, making it clear what he thinks is the only "scientific" position to take: "Let's note an important point here: The assumption that behaviors follow cause and effect seems to work, and anyone planning to do research on behavior is almost forced to start with this assumption" (pp. 5–6). This dubious claim is central to a psychology exported to the Third World.

Universalism through the Exportation of Causal Psychology

Anyone who visits psychology departments in Third World societies is immediately struck by the widespread presence of parochial Western psychology in the guise of universal psychology. Just as McDonald and Pizza Hut have been exported to the rest of the world, so has Western psychology. In this section, we point out that the psychology being exported to Third World societies is in large part causal psychology and that internationally the United States has become the dominant force in, and the main exporter of, psychology to the rest of the world. After discussing some indicators of the growth of psychology in Third World societies, we point out that the growth of mainstream cross-cultural psychology does not overcome the limitations of mainstream psychology.

Emergence of U.S. Psychology as the First World of Psychology

The exportation of causal psychology to Third World societies began on a small-scale in the latter part of the nineteenth century, soon after Wundt established a psychology laboratory in Leipzig in 1879. In that era, Germany was the leader in many areas of scholarship, and researchers from Russia, Japan, India, China, and elsewhere went to Wundt's laboratory for advanced training (Jing, 2000). One might compare the growth and exportation of causal psychology to Third World societies to a growing multinational business enterprise. Wundt's laboratory manufactured the first prototypes of a novel product: experimental psychology designed to identify causal relations. Eager entrepreneurs traveled from different parts of the world to Germany to learn how to produce this product.

The emergence of the United States as the sole superpower of psychology (Moghaddam, 1987) is in large part explained by the military and political situation after World War II. First, numerous prominent European psychologists had become uprooted because of the devastation in Europe. Some, like Freud, became refugees and did not live to see the end of the war, while many others fled to the United States. Second, in the period immediately after the war, academic institutions in Europe were left relatively weak and deprived of resources, whereas those in the United States were relatively well supported and also enriched by the flood of immigrant psychologists. Underscoring this reversal of hierarchical positions was the U.S. aid provided to Europeans for postwar reconstruction, including in the domain of psychology through the Committee on International Relations established by the American Psychological Association.

Just as the United States became the economic (and later military) superpower after World War II, so did the United States become the psychology superpower. Similarly, just as U.S. multinational corporations came to dominate the international economic market, so did U.S. psychology come to dominate at the international level (the United States has dominated psychology in a way that has not been replicated in sociology, anthropology, and other social sciences). Thus, the most important source of psychological practices and values was Germany in the nineteenth century and the United States for most of the twentieth century. The international-ization of such practices and values is reflected in trends such as growth in the numbers of laboratories and national psychology associations.

From Laboratories to National Associations

An important indicator of the spread of causal psychology is the estab-lishment of psychology laboratories around the world. By 1920, psychol-ogy laboratories had been established in academic centers in Asia, Europe, as well as in North America (Table 1). National psychology associations helped to speed up the spread of causal psychology. The American Psy-chological Association, established in 1892, served as the model for na-tional associations that sprung up in different countries around the world (Table 2), with Argentina, China, India, and Japan being part of the first wave of countries to establish associations in the late 1920s. The rapid exportation of causal psychology was also helped by the establishment in 1951 of the International Union of Psychological Science (IUPsyS), com-posed of national psychological associations. The associations of many Third World countries were early members, and the numbers of members climbed rapidly from twenty in 1951 to seventy in 2004.

TABLE 1
Year First Psychological Laboratories Were Established

Year	Country	Founder
1875	United States	William James
1879	Germany	Wilhelm Wundt
1885	Russia	Vladimir M. Bekhterev
1889	France	Henri Beaunis
1897	United Kingdom	James Sully, W. H. Rivers
1900	Japan	Yujiro Motora
1915	India	N. N. Sengupta
1917	China	Chen Daqi

Based on data from Jing, 2000; Brushlinsky, 1995; Trognon, 1987; Boring, 1957; Azuma and Imada, 1994; Sinha, 1987; and Yang, 1998.

TABLE 2
Total Numbers of National Psychological Associations in Western versus Non-Western Societies, 1900–1980

	1900	1920	1930	1940	1950	1960	1970	1980
Western Europe and North America	1	5	5	7	11	15	16	17
Non-Western	0	1	5	5	8	17	23	28

Authors' compilation based on data published by Rosenzweig (1982).

Dual Perceptions and Role of Third World Elite in International Psychology

The exportation of universalized causal psychology to Third World societies must be considered in the context of dual economies, modern and traditional economic sectors existing side by side in Third World societies, as well as dual perceptions, Westernized and traditional worldviews, also existing alongside one another (Moghaddam and Taylor, 1985). In much of Asia, Africa, and Latin America, colonial and later imperialist ties shaped local economies and social conditions, giving rise to a Westernized elite living in a relatively small modern sector and the majority of the population living in the traditional sector. In most cases, the local economy is completely dependent on a small number of raw materials, such as rubber, petroleum, minerals like cooper and zinc, and natural gas, which tie directly into the economies of Western powers. Income from the exportation of such raw materials typically benefits a small elite, who model themselves on the West, particularly in the area of education and culture. It is through this Westernized elite that causal psychology is imported to the modern sector of Third World societies.

The Westernized elite of Asia, Africa, and Latin America is in many respects more similar to Western middle-class populations than to the traditional sector of their "own" societies. This elite is more likely to be influenced by Western psychology than by local indigenous psychology, and more likely to use the services of Westernized therapists than mainstream healers. The universities and other educational institutions supported and used by this elite tend to be modeled on Western and particularly U.S. institutions, often even in terms of course titles and course contents. Even the major texts taught in countries as "radical" as the Islamic Republic of Iran tend to be American, such as Aronson's *Social Animal,* the 1999 edition of which appeared in Farsi translation in 2004 and is being used in Iranian universities.

Not only have modern-sector elites imported Western causal psychology, they also have been small-scale producers of causal psychology, as indicated by their representation in international conferences and publications. However, there is a subtle limitation to how much they have been able to influence research through their contributions, because most of their contributions have been conference presentations rather than publications in major Western journals. For example, an analysis of five meetings of the International Congress of Applied Psychology from 1982

TABLE 3
IAAP Congress Presentations and PsychLIT Entries by Geographical Region
(Adair, Coêhlo, and Luna 2002)

Geographical region	IAAP presentations (%)	PsychLIT entries (%)
West Europe	38.60	21.06
North America	29.12	60.76[a]
East Asia	9.92	2.45
East Europe	4.96	2.22
Middle East and Mediterranean	4.63	1.00
Latin America	4.59	1.33
Australia, Oceania, and Southeast Asia	4.25	2.91
South Asia	2.27	0.79
Africa	1.65	0.43
No affiliation reported	—	7.05

[a] North America values were computed for only 1990, 1994, and 1998. All other regions were computed for all five congress years.

to 1998 revealed that twenty counties contributed to over 87 percent of presentations, and eight of those top twenty countries were Japan, Israel, India, Mexico, Brazil, South Africa, Russia, and China. Together, these eight counties accounted for 14.5 percent of all presentations. However, a very different picture emerges when we look at publications. An analysis of PsychLIT for the years 1990, 1994, and 1998 revealed that the top five among these countries (Japan, Israel, Russia, India, and Brazil) accounted for only 4.7 percent of total entries, whereas U.S. authors accounted for 55 percent of all entries (Adair, Coêlho, and Luna, 2002). About 50 percent of the nation members of the IUPsyS had no first-authored papers (Table 3).

There is not only a difference between the level of contributions of First, Second, and Third World psychologists to conferences and publications but also a huge disconnect between the contents of conference presentations and publications included in PsychLIT. J. G. Adair, A. E. L. Coêlho, and J. R. Luna (2000) found zero correlation between the frequencies of topics presented at Asian international applied congresses and Asian research topics abstracted in PsycLIT. One interpretation of this situation is that editorial boards give priority to research that conforms to the Western causal tradition, and not to the kinds of Third World research topics reported at conferences.

The failure of Third World researchers to influence U.S. psychology is also indicated by the authorship of papers in U.S. journals. For example, in the period 1965–2000, 85 percent of first authors in the *Journal of Personality and Social Psychology (JPSP)*, the most frequently cited journal covering social and personality topics, were from U.S. institutions (Quiñones-

Vidal, López-García, Peñaranda-Ortega, and Tortosa-Gil, 2004). Roughly half of the 70 IUPsyS member countries' institutions did not place a single article in *JPSP* or PsychLIT in the years reviewed by Adair et al. (2002) and Quiñones-Vidal et al. (2004).

Role of "Cross-Cultural" Research in "Internationalizing" Psychology

A possible response to the criticism that mainstream psychology is "monocultural" and needs to look beyond U.S. borders is to argue that cross-cultural research is internationalizing psychology by including samples from different populations around the world. From this perspective, cross-cultural samples are broadening the base of psychological knowledge, supporting the claim that psychology is a "science of humankind." This is an important assertion that, if true, could blunt at least some of the criticisms made of mainstream causal psychology. Unfortunately, however, close scrutiny of the types of samples that are recruited in "cross-cultural" research shows that they are often not from different cultures.

Indeed, so-called cross-cultural research provides clear examples of what we have termed "double reification." On the one hand, cultural phenomena, from values to technological hardware, are being exported from the United States to Third World societies, particularly to the educational institutions of the modern sector of Third World societies. This exportation is dramatically altering the thoughts and actions of students in the modern sector. In essence, these students are taking the model, the "ideal" to be Western youth. On the other hand, research methods and paradigms exported from the United States are being "cross-culturally tested" through the participation of Westernized students in Third World societies, and the results are used to "validate" the universality of the exported psychology. This double reification feeds back into mainstream psychology as "confirmation" of its assumptions, such as the assumed universality of the "Big 5" personality traits (Moghaddam, 2005, ch. 13).

Sampling Bias in Line with Double Reification

The history of psychology in the twentieth century has witnessed a schism between sampling as discussed in psychology texts and sampling as practiced in psychological research. Again, we can turn to Kalat (2005) as representative of the standard general psychology texts used to introduce causal psychology to students. Kalat defines a population as "the entire group of individuals to be considered" and then moves on to discuss a convenient sample, "a group chosen because of its ease of study" and a representative sample, which "closely resembles the population in its percentage of males and females, Blacks and Whites, young and old, city dwellers and farmers, or whatever other characteristics are likely to affect the results" (2005, p. 41). A key question of the highest practical and theoretical importance is: When is it justified to use a convenience sample as opposed to a representative or random sample?

Kalat proposes that "in some cases almost any sample is satisfactory." These cases include research on basic sensory processes (e.g., audition, vision), as well as "the principles of learning, memory, hunger, thirst, sleep, and so forth." In these domains, Kalat argues, humans are similar enough that "an investigator can do research with almost any group—students in an introductory psychology class, for example." But in other domains where behavior varies from person to person, a representative or random sample is needed. Kalat adds that if we want to generalize about all human beings, the best strategy is to study cross-cultural samples, groups of people from two or more cultures, "preferably cultures that differ substantially" (2005, p. 41).

Kalat's approach reflects fundamental assumptions underlying Western causal psychology, such as assumptions about the domains of behavior in which humans are basically the same and other domains where they differ. Such assumptions are challenged by critics who argue that, for example, central aspects of memory are part of a normative psychology, rather than mainstream causal psychology (Moghaddam, 2002, ch.10). For example, an important aspect of memory is collective reconstruction of past events, "memory as social reconstruction" where the emphasis is on collaborative meaning making, rather than attempts by isolated individuals to reproduce the past, "memory as reproduction" where the emphasis is on how accurately a single person can recall events "as they took place."

Mainstream Violating Mainstream Tenets

Because of space limitations, in the present discussion we limit our comments to the specific assumptions (in Kalat, 2005) that:

In domains where behavior varies from person to person (and we would add, from culture to culture), representative or random (rather than convenience) samples are needed.

If our goal is to generalize findings to humankind, then samples must be from two or more samples that differ substantially.

Our assertion is that mainstream causal psychology has in practice violated this basic tenet of mainstream causal psychology. The history of psychological science reflects a trend of research participants being homogeneous in cultural characteristics even when the behavior being studied varies across individuals and across cultures. This is clearly evident in the realm of social psychology, where the focus is on social behavior such as values, attitudes, discrimination, prejudice, and other such topics that clearly vary in important ways across both individuals and cultures (Moghaddam, 1998). The vast majority of social psychological studies involve a very narrow band of participants, undergraduate students (Sears, 1986; Ponterotto, 1988). On the basis of research on middle-class, 18–22-year-olds studying in U.S. colleges, social psychologists have generalized about the social behavior of humankind.

The apparent remedy to this situation is to conduct cross-cultural research. But for the same reasons (such as economy and convenience) that most psychological research in the United States is conducted with undergraduate participants, "cross-cultural" research also typically involves undergraduate students as participants. We conducted a survey of studies published in the *Journal of Personality and Social Psychology* and the *Journal of Cross-Cultural Psychology,* respectively the flagship journals for mainstream social psychology research and mainstream cross-cultural research, for the years 1980, 1985, 2002–2004. The trends reveal an increasing use of student samples in *JCCP* and a consistent use of student samples in *JPSP* (Table 4).

The increasing reliance on student samples in so-called cross-cultural research is problematic for a number of reasons:

1. A "student culture" that is becoming more homogeneous around the world, particularly through the influence of electronic communications and mass transportation and growing study abroad programs. This seriously puts to question the assumption that students from different universities around the world really represent different "traditional cultures."

TABLE 4

Percentage of Articles Using College or School Samples in the Journal of Personality and Social Psychology (JPSP) *and the* Journal of Cross-Cultural Psychology (JCCP)

	JPSP samples				JCCP samples			
Year	College	Preschool through high school	Nonstudent	n	College	Preschool through high school	Nonstudent	n
2004[a]	77	0	24	83	87	9	13	23
2003	81	1	25	145	53	15	33	40
2002	83	3	18	155	60	20	20	35
1985	70[b]	—	17[c]	187	38	48	19	21
1980	74[b]	—	18[c]	191	35	25	45	20

[a] JPSP through October 2004; JCCP through September 2004.
[b] American undergraduate samples (Sears, 1986).
[c] Nonstudent adult samples (Sears, 1986).

2. Fundamental cultural differences between students, who are part of the modern Westernized sector in Third World societies, and local populations, the vast majority of whom are part of the traditional sector.

Thus, mainstream causal psychology has been exported to the Westernized modern sector and particularly universities of Third World societies, and students from the modern sector have been recruited to "demonstrate" the universality of this psychology. However, there are signs of a new challenge to mainstream causal psychology.

Third World Challenges to Causal Psychology

Efforts to internationalize the history of psychology should also chart the rising challenge to internationalization of mainstream psychology. First and Second World challenges are relatively well known (Crosley, 2000; Moghaddam and Harré, 1995); of more direct interest to us in this discussion is the challenge arising from the Third World. This challenge reflects serious concerns to achieve alternative, sometimes indigenous, Third World voices, in Asian (e.g., Yang, Hwang, Pederson and Diabo, 2003), Latin American (e.g., Lira, 2000), Arab (Ahmed and Gielen, 1998), and African (e.g., Serpell, 1993) contexts.

It is probably in Latin America that the challenge to universalized causal psychology has made most headway, in the form of "liberation psychology," the study of the everyday psychosocial means by which ideology is produced and reproduced and social reality is collectively constructed (Montero, 1984). Liberation psychology examines the narratives of people in everyday interaction, in relation to the wider material conditions in which these people live. Liberation psychology is action oriented, in that it is intended to change material and social conditions toward greater justice, particularly for minorities and those with less power. This politically engaged orientation is fundamentally different from the avowed disengaged and supposedly "neutral" position adopted by the mainstream psychology being exported to Latin America from Western societies.

Liberation psychology grew particularly from the mid-twentieth century out of the political context of Latin American dictatorships supported by successive U.S. administrations. Ideas now associated with action research, community psychology, critical social psychology, and political psychology merged into a psychology concerned with changing social beliefs and ideologies, particularly through local level projects involving collective citizen participation (Vásquez, 2000). "Changing minds through community projects" is one way to sum up an important aspect of liberation psychology, but the "changing" is not neutral; rather, it is directed toward greater ideological awareness.

An example of liberation psychology research is a project exploring constructions of needs in a slum neighborhood (Montero, 1994). This research project involved identifying "accepted norms" in a slum, such as lack of a reliable supply of clean water, and then intervening to achieve problematization, changes in perceptions so that what was seen to be acceptable is now seen as unacceptable. In this way, accepted norms shifted, and the new norms served as a basis for community action.

A central feature of liberation psychology is the breakout of the modern sector of Third World societies, particularly out of universities that in just about every respect copy universities in the United States, and to enter the traditional sector. Through this move, liberation psychology is able to enter urban slums and rural villages and to reach populations that tend to be far poorer, far less educated, and different in thought and action from both people in the West and the Westernized elite of the Third World. This is exactly the population that should be involved in psychological research, if and when psychological universals are to be seriously explored. Similarly, within the first and second worlds of psychology, nonstudent populations, including ethnic minorities and working-class whites, need to be far better represented in research studies. As things stand, it is mainly within the universe of middle-class students that psychological "universals" are tested.

Concluding Comment

Globalization has in large part meant Westernization, and more recently it has meant in particular the spread of American cultural phenomena to the rest of the world. The modern sectors of Third World societies are now populated by people who are in important respects Westernized, and this is particularly true for students. The schools and universities that train students in the modern sector are typically modeled after U.S. institutions, and with respect to music, films, clothing, and many other aspects of their lives, these students are very similar to students in U.S. institutions. We have argued that it is misleading to "test" the "universality" of psychological theories and findings by comparing the results of studies involving student participants in First, Second, and Third World countries. Such studies are "within culture" (the culture of modern students) and have simply served a double reification process. Internationalizing the history of psychology means that we must give attention to both the exportation of mainstream causal psychology to the Third World and the alternative movements, such as liberation psychology, that have evolved from the Third World.

REFERENCES

Adair, J. G., Coêlho, A. E. L., and Luna, J. R. (2000). Indigenous psychology in Asia: A view from abroad. Paper presented at the Symposium on Asian Contributions to Indigenous Psychology, Cross-Cultural Psychology Congress, Putusk, Poland, July.

Adair, J. G., Coêlho, A. E. L., and Luna, J. R. (2002). How international is psychology? *International Journal of Psychology, 37*, 160–170.

Ahmed, R. A., and Gielen, U. P. (Eds.) (1998). *Psychology in Arab countries.* Minufiyah, Egypt: Menoufia University Press.

Aronson, E. (1999). *The social animal* (8th ed.). New York: Freeman.

Azuma, H., and Imada, H. (1994). Origins and development of psychology in Japan: The interaction between Western science and Japanese cultural heritage. *International Journal of Psychology, 29*, 707–717.

Bartlett, F. C. (1932). *Remembering: A study in experimental and social psychology.* New York: Macmillan.

Boring, E. G. (1957). *A history of experimental psychology* (2nd ed.). New York: Appleton-Century Crofts.

Brushlinsky, A. (1995). Man as an object of investigation. *Herald of the Russian Academy of Sciences,* 65, 424–431.

Cahan, E. D., and White, S. H. (1992). Proposals for a second psychology. *American Psychologist,* 47, 224–235.

Crossley, M. L. (2000). *Introducing narrative psychology: Self, trauma and the construction of meaning.* Buckingham, UK: Open University Press.

Danziger, K., and Dzinas, K. (1997). How psychology got its variables. *Canadian Psychology,* 38, 43–48.

Gascoigne, J. (1998). *Science in the service of empire: Joseph Banks, the British State and the uses of science in the age of revolution.* Cambridge: Cambridge University Press.

Gaulin, J. C., and McBurney, D. H. (2001). *Psychology: An evolutionary approach.* Upper Saddle River, NJ: Prentice Hall.

Jing, Q. (2000). International psychology. In K. Pawlik and M. R. Rosenzwig (Eds.), *International handbook of psychology* (pp. 570–584). Thousand Oaks, CA: Sage.

Kalat, J. W. (2005). Introduction to psychology (7th ed.). Belmont, CA: Wadsworth.

Koch, S., and Leary, D. E. (Eds.) (1985). *A century of psychology as science.* New York: McGraw-Hill.

Köhler, W. (1947). *The mentality of apes.* New York: Liveright.

Lira, E. (2000). Reflections on critical psychology: The psychology of memory and forgetting. Trans. T. Sloan. In T. Sloan (Ed.), *Critical psychology: Voices for change* (pp. 82–90). New York: St. Martin's.

Moghaddam, F. M. (1987). Psychology in the three worlds: As reflected in the crisis in social psychology and the move toward indigenous Third World psychology. *American Psychologist,* 42, 912–920.

Moghaddam, F. M. (1990). Modulative and generative orientations in psychology: Implications for psychology in the Third World. *Journal of Social Issues,* 56, 21–41.

Moghaddam, F. M. (1998). *Social psychology.* New York: Freeman.

Moghaddam, F. M. (2002). *The individual and society: A cultural integration.* New York: Worth.

Moghaddam, F. M. (2005). *Great ideas in psychology: A cultural and historical introduction.* Oxford: Oneworld.

Moghaddam, F. M., and Harré, R. (1995). But is it science? Traditional and alternative approaches to the study of social behavior. *World Psychology,* 1, 47–78.

Moghaddam, F. M., and Taylor, D. M., (1985). Psychology in the developing world: An evaluation through the concepts of "dual perception" and "parallel growth." *American Psychologist,* 40, 1144–1146.

Moghaddam, F. M., and Taylor, D. M. (1986). What constitutes an "appropriate psychology" for the developing world? *International Journal of Psychology*, 24, 253–267.

Montero, M. (1984). *Ideología, alienación e identidad nacional* [Ideology, alienation and national identity]. Caracas: Ediciones Biblioteca Universidad Central.

Montero, M. (1994). Consciousness raising, conversion, and de-ideologization in community psychosocial work. *Journal of Community Psychology*, 22, 3–11.

Pandey, J. (Ed.) (2000). *Psychology in India revisited: Developments in the discipline*. New Delhi: Sage.

Ponterotto, J. G. (1988). Racial/ethnic minority research in the *Journal of Counseling Psychology*: A content analysis and methodological critique. *Journal of Counseling Psychology*, 35, 410–418.

Quiñones-Vidal, E., López-García, J. J., Peñaranda-Ortega, M., and Tortosa-Gil, F. (2004). The nature of social and personality psychology as reflected in *JPSP*, 1965–2000. *Journal of Personality and Social Psychology*, 86, 435–452.

Raine, A., Lenez, T., Bihrle, S., LaCasse, L., and Colletti, P. (2000). Reduced prefrontal gray matter volume and reduced autonomic activity in antisocial personality disorder. *Archives of General Psychiatry*, 57, 119–127.

Rosenzweig, M. R. (1982). Trends in development and status of psychology: An international perspective. *International Journal of Psychology*, 17, 117–140.

Sears, D. O. (1986). College sophomores in the laboratory: Influences of narrow data base on social psychology's view of human nature. *Journal of Personality and Social Psychology*, 51, 515–530.

Serpell, R. (1993). *The significance of schooling: Life journeys in an African society.* Cambridge: Cambridge University Press.

Sinha, D. (1987). India. In A. R. Gilgen and C. K. Gilgen (Eds.). *International handbook of psychology* (pp. 239–257). New York: Greenwood.

Spini, D., and Doise, W. (2004). Universal rights and duties as normative social representations. In N. Finkel and F. M. Moghaddam (Eds.), *The psychology of rights and duties* (pp. 21–48). Washington, DC: American Psychological Association Press.

Storey, W. K. (Ed.) (1996). *Scientific aspects of European expansion*. Aldershot, Hampshire, UK: Variorum.

Tolman, E. C. (1948). Cognitive maps in rats and men. *Psychological Review*, 55, 189–208.

Trognon, A. (1987). France. In A. R. Gilgen and C. K. Gilgen (Eds.), *International handbook of psychology* (pp. 184–207). New York: Greenwood.

Vallerand, R. J. (Ed.) (1994). *Les fondements de la psychologie sociale* [The fundamentals of social psychology]. Boucherville, Quebec, Canada: Gaëtan Morin.

Vásquez, J. J. (Ed.) (2000). *Psycología social y liberación en América Latina* [Social psychology and liberation in Latin America]. Mexico City: Universidad Autónoma Metropolitana-Iztapalapa.

Watson, J. B. (1913). Psychology as the behaviorist views it. *Psychological Review*, 20, 158–177.

Winston, A. S. (2004). Controlling the metalanguage. In A. C. Brock, J. Louw, and W. van Hoorn (Eds.), *Rediscovering the history of psychology: Essays inspired by the work of Kurt Danziger* (pp. 53–73). New York: Kluwer Academic/Plenum.

Yang, K. S., Hwang, K. K., Pederson, P. B., and Diabo, I. (Eds.) (2003). *Progress in Asian social psychology: Conceptual and empirical contributions*. Westport, CT: Praeger.

Yang, X. H. (1998). On the contribution of Cai Yuanpei as a pioneer in the history of contemporary Chinese psychology. *Psychological Science*, 21, 293–296. (Cited by Jing, 2000.)

Chapter 10

Psychology in the Eurocentric Order of the Social Sciences

Colonial Constitution, Cultural Imperialist Expansion, Postcolonial Critique

Irmingard Staeuble

Historians of Psychology had hardly started to inquire into the shaping of the discipline and profession in its Euro-American home countries when Psychology expanded rapidly outward, to Asia, Latin America, and Africa. Among historians and sociologists of science, this exciting move has not yet found the interest it deserves. The few edited books on this expansion provide hardly more than descriptive accounts of the state of Psychology around the world (e.g. Sexton and Misiak 1976; Blowers and Turtle 1987; Sexton and Hogan 1992). A notable exception is Alison Turtle's introductory chapter, which did raise essential issues to be addressed by historians and sociologists of science such as the "patterns of interaction between colony and imperialist power" and the possibility and extent of a "recognizable common form" of Psychology when its hidden world view gets "blended with or assimilated into a variety of different cultures and ideologies" (Turtle 1987, 3). An interesting attempt at assessing the advances of selected areas of Psychology in the developing world was made by Stuart Carr and John Schumaker (1996), with editors and contributors emphasizing social contexts and reflecting on the idea of a reciprocal relationship between Psychology in the "developing" and "developed" worlds. Yet the tracing of the various routes of Psychology's move to Asian, Latin American, African, and Arabic countries, of problems involved such as uneven patterns of interaction or lack of fit between Western individualism and local notions of person and world, remains largely a task for the future. This task will require the participation of scholars who work in long or recently decolonized countries, in indigenous communities, or in the diaspora. As this task gets taken up, euphemistic notions like "internationalization" and "globalization" of the discipline that are currently preferred in Western academia will likely become scutinized—for instance, in terms of their concealment of the imbalanced power structure of international knowledge production.

Historicizing the Expansion: Concepts and Contexts

This chapter is based on two premises. The first is that the conceptualization of the worldwide expansion of Psychology is inevitably linked with preconceptions of modern world history at large. Drawing on post-Eurocentric views of both modern world history and the geopolitics of knowledge (Blaut 1993; Gran 1996; Smith 1999), I argue that neither modern world history at large nor the worldwide expansion of social science disciplines can be recounted in terms of the conventional diffusionist model. According to this inadequate model, European civilization has established a superior position and remained the center from which some of its achievements spread to the "intellectual void" in other parts of the world where people desire and imitate the offers of the center. The question of an alternative conceptual frame, of course, is more difficult. Such a frame may eventually result from attempts at exploring how European modes of thought can be "renewed from and for the margins" (Chakrabarti 2000, 16).

The second premise is that an analysis of the expansion of Western Psychology can gain considerably from regarding Psychology as but one component in the constitution and expansion of the disciplinary order of the social sciences. Like the other social sciences, Psychology is part of a particular construction of social reality that is firmly rooted in Western cultural beliefs and thus tends to preclude alternative views of organizing modes of life and politics of knowledge. What needs to be reflected upon is the implication of the disciplines in both a shared cultural tradition of individualism, race/gender division, et cetera, and a geopolitics of knowledge marked by the colonizer's view of the world.

Concerning the contexts of the expansion, an important but often neglected issue pertains to the diverse colonial relations in which the expansion originated. To a greater or lesser extent, such relations involved the distortion or destruction of local knowledge systems along with local life worlds. Western authority was largely imposed on indigenous knowledges, languages, and cultures by way of missionary and secular schooling, geared to selectively creating indigenous elites that would serve colonial interests. The post–World War II period of decolonization turned the globe into a world of nation-states. Despite lasting gross inequalities, the former colonies were brought into relationship with the rival superpowers, the United States and the Soviet Union, and with international organizations, foremost the United Nations system of development organizations. The related concepts of development and modernity appealed to both "ex-masters and ex-subjects anxious to restate their inequalities in a hopeful idiom" (Geertz 1995, 137). A worldwide development initiative for the alleviation of poverty was seen as requiring a concerted intervention by the national governments of both poor and rich countries. As stated by the editors of a substantial volume, this initiative "gave rise to a veritable industry in the academic social sciences, with a complex and often ambiguous relationship in governmental, international, and private agencies actively engaged in promoting economic growth . . . and fostering beneficial social change in 'developing' regions of the world" (Cooper and Packard 1997, 1). To my regret, the role of development in the conceptual apparatus of American and European social science must be left for future investigation, including the related question of how it affected conceptualizations of Third World countries in terms of a dualistic existence of modern and traditional societal sectors (Moghaddam 1993).

The chapter focuses on Psychology as part of the disciplinary order of Western knowledge. I will first outline the organizational network of the post–World War II expansion of the social sciences, the growth of which is often taken for progress of internationalization. This includes a tentative attempt at analyzing the early period of UNESCO activities. Comparing current debates on internationalism in the international disciplinary associations, I provide some evidence for differences in the extent of reflexivity that are not flattering for Psychology. The characterization of the Euro-American make-up of the disciplinary order will then require some analysis of its emergence in the colonial geopolitics of knowledge. From the view of intertwined histories, the distortion and destruction of the knowledge systems of the colonized have been both a precondition for the establishment of the positional superiority of Western knowledge and a lasting obstacle to postcolonial attempts at establishing alternative cultures of knowledge. For my analysis, therefore, I will engage the intellectual heirs of the colonized who have for half a century voiced their collective experience and their views of the postcolonial condition.

Internationalization: Organizational History View

At the turn of the millennium, a virtual cartography of Psychology and the social sciences would have shown their presence across universities of all continents. By then the international disciplinary associations—International Union of Psychological Science (IUPsyS), International Sociological Association (ISA), International Political Science Association (IPSA), and International Economic Association (IEA)—represented 68 national disciplinary organizations of Psychology, about 45 of each Sociology and Political Science, and 56 of Economics, covering roughly one-third of the 190 independent nations. In terms of growth and localities, the expansion of organized international presence of the disciplines followed roughly the same pattern.

The international disciplinary associations were founded in the post–World War II years, between 1949 and 1951, under the auspices of UNESCO, with the rationale of fostering "peacefare" in the world. Their constitutions state similar objectives, foremost the advancement of scientific knowledge by facilitating institutional and personal contacts, convening regular world congresses, and promoting publications on an international scale. Membership in the international associations was modeled after the UN model of representation, with all nations treated equally (Platt 1998, 16). The increasing number of national associations has been analyzed in some cases of political conflict (Dumont and Louw 2001).

What does this brief sketch tell about the internationality of the disciplinary associations? Can the international expansion of the social sciences be conceived in terms of Euro-American achievements and their diffusion to the rest of the world? At the height of American behaviorist dominance, the promoters of the expansion who offered their services to policy-makers certainly believed that their disciplines were suitable to "fashion a new civilization" (Herman 1996, 306) by restructuring the cultures of the world. But this was hardly the credo of the initiators of UNESCO peacefare through education, culture, and science; nor was it to remain unshaken among the more reflective representatives of the international social science associations.

As to the credo of the initiators, the early issues of the UNESCO *International Social Science Bulletin* (1959 renamed *Journal*) provide a preliminary view of the understanding that underlay international promotion at its inception. As pointed out by the UNESCO Secretariat in 1949: "Science came relatively late into the UNESCO constitution. In the early drafts Education and Culture alone figure—Uneco not UNESCO" (Unesco Secretariat 1998, 319). The decision to give the social sciences a separate status as a department of the secretariat was taken in 1946. As a result, two departments were set up the same year, one for Culture and Humanistic Studies (comprising history, linguistics, archaeology, and ethnography), and one for the Social Sciences. The understanding of "social science" was very broad, including economics, sociology, political science, international and comparative law, psychology, public administration, statistics, anthropology, ethnology, demography, and human geography. As repeated comments in the *Journal* show, the bifurcation of the humanities and the social sciences remained a source of unease, yet it is not clear why it was not revised.

The function of UNESCO with regard to the social sciences was "to unite the social scientists of all countries in a concerted attack upon the crucial question of the age—how the peoples of the world can learn to live together in peace (Unesco Secretariat 1998, 320). Preparatory steps to concerted action consisted in the progressive organization, on an international level, of the various disciplines, beginning with Comparative Law (1949), Economics (1950), Sociology (1950), Political Science (1950), and Psychology (1951). In 1954 an International Social Science Council (ISSC) was formed as an umbrella.

How did the promotion operate? From 1952 on, UNESCO research centers were established, the first in Cologne to reconstruct the social sciences in post-Nazi Germany. A Paris center devoted to the social implications of technological change (1953) was followed in 1956 by a first research center in the postcolonial world, in Calcutta, devoted to social implications of industrialization in Southern Asia. In 1957 and 1958, two Latin American social science centers followed, of which the still existing Latin American Social Science Faculty (FLACSO) claims to have proved more successful (see website, http://www.flacso.org). Institutes for Social Studies and Research were also set up in Colombia, Iran, and Pakistan.

A veritable "educational mission" procedure was started by UNESCO in 1953 when social science officers were attached to Regional Co-Operation Offices in Cairo, New Delhi, and Havana, and to the UN Economic

Commission for Africa. In 1954, short "missions of consultants" were to report on the state of teaching to Costa Rica, Pakistan, and Greece. After a budget of assistance was established, social science teachers were sent on request to Costa Rica, Guatemala, Pakistan, Peru, Nicaragua, and Indonesia. Further technical assistance consisted in regional refresher courses for economists and sociologists in Asia and Africa.

The initial impact of UNESCO and its medium, the *International Social Science Bulletin* (first published in 1949, renamed into *International Social Science Journal* [*ISSJ*] in 1959) on communication among social science disciplines across continents seems to have been considerable. Yet in the course of both the progressive splitting into subdisciplines and the rise of international disciplinary journals it became more difficult for a generalist journal like *ISSJ* to maintain the effort of building bridges between the disciplines. Looking back at the journal's position fifty years ago, Morpurgo (1998, 309) claims it stood "as an unchallenged leader, intellectually and internationally, in all matters then within the orbit of social science, at once a meeting place for leading professionals and a source of ideas and information outward to many more." Originally bilingual, English-French, the *ISSJ* widened its linguistic scope to Spanish (1978, interrupted in 1985 and resumed in 1987), Chinese (1985), Arabic (selective from 1973, interrupted in 1981, resumed in 1988), and Russian (1992) and also published occasional translations into Greek, Turkish, and Portuguese. As compared to the international journals of the various disciplines, like *International Sociology* or the *International Journal of Psychology*, that have gradually narrowed their original multilinguistic scope to English, the *ISSJ* has remained multilingual and thus provides the internationally most widely accessible medium of social science debate. The question of whether it also remained the least Americanized medium would still have to be explored.

From the 1960s to the late 1970s, the focus of the *ISSJ* was on the poor countries of the Third World. A 1969 special issue dealing with the implementation of the social sciences in Asia, Africa, and Latin America provided reflected reports on the basis of the authors' local experience of teaching and promoting social science. For instance, two reports on sociology in Latin America (Ladden 1969; Solari 1969) described, from different views, a shift from the publicly influential philosopher and comprehensive social theorist to the new type of the professional sociologist. As to the implantation of the social sciences in Thailand, Prachoom Chomchai (1969) traced a historical shift of patterns. The first, from World War I to mid-century, was piecemeal extension around a core discipline—usually political science, law, or public administration, due to the fact that the organization of social science was mainly geared to the demands of government. The second pattern, adopted by universities founded in the 1960s, was the introduction of the "whole gamut of the social sciences . . . at one go" (385). Another historically reflected account of sociology in Asia stressed that the types of social science introduced into the colonies precluded indigenous self-awareness. "The colonizer's desire to 'know' colonial society was dictated originally by the practical requirements of governing an alien people" (Pieris 1969, 435). Ralph Pieris argues that the scholarly literature that did emanate as a by-product had an impact on the indigenous intelligentsia whose attention was drawn to certain features of Western industrial society. When they took to anthropology, they not only became "outsiders to themselves," the anthropological preoccupation with generalizing on the basis of intensive study of a single village also precluded the development of a macrosocial perspective. Such development was further precluded "because colonal rule had created a number of non-communicating 'corridors' which linked the intelligentsia of each colony to some distant intellectual center of gravity in the Occident" so that their "'underdeveloped neighbors' were of no interest" (Pieris 1969, 437). The "brain-drain" of the 1960s may thus be seen as a long-term consequence of both the indigenous intelligentsia's training to be dysfunctional in their own environment and their lack of awareness of their own situation. For Pieris, the intellectual dependence of colonial social science on Western models continued after independence, the more easily so as it was the most abstract and formalized forms of economics and sociology that had gained currency in the colonial universities. He observed that Asian scholars not only devote themselves to areas and problems of research determined in the West, they also provide the raw material for the development of "area study programs" without equal advantage to themselves. Like later Asian critics of the cloning of Western Psychology, Pieris complained that most sociologists in Asia have been "content to adopt the Western conceptual kit without serious question as to its transferability" (1969, 442).

Internationalism as Currently Discussed

At the occasion of the golden anniversaries of the international disciplinary associations of Psychology (IUPsyS), Sociology (ISA), and Political Science (IPSA), the "internationalization" of the disciplines was widely discussed. A brief comparison of millennium statements by representatives of the associations shows considerable differences as to celebratory accounts of Psychology, which emphasize the extension of membership and the move of world congresses to nearly all continents as signs of a successful internationalization, and social science accounts that give at least some consideration to the imbalance of power in international knowledge production.

The authors of the otherwise thoroughly documented *History of the International Union of Psychological Science (IUPsyS)* take the international congresses held in Tokyo (1972), Acapulco (1984), and Sydney (1988) as marks of "a genuine global expansion of international psychology" without further reflection on the notion of internationalization (Rosenzweig, Holtzman, Sabourin, and Bélanger 2000, 195). The universalistic self-understanding of the discipline seems to preclude any questions related to contextual diversity or the obvious imbalance of give and take.

In her brief history of the International Sociological Association (ISA), Jennifer Platt points out that "internationalism can take many different forms, and the appropriate models have been contested; some stress cross-national homogeneity or the irrelevance of nationality, while others emphasize the value of national diversity and the contributions which can be made from many traditions" (Platt 1998, 46). Pondering on the future of Sociology, both Craig Calhoun (2002) and Neil Smelser (2003) have tried some qualification of the revered notions of interdisciplinarity and internationalization in terms of the quality of knowledge produced. Both reflect on the relationship between Sociology and nations, pointing out that the historical emergence of the discipline was closely tied to the project of the nation-state. Internationalization, they argue, would have to overcome the lasting asymmetry of knowledge production that is still mostly done by Euro-American social scientists and Euro-American-trained ones from other parts of the world, and not the other way round. In addition, Smelser argues that current infrastructures of knowledge production inhibit the generation of comparative and international knowledge, foremost the discipline-based international organizations that "work mainly to augment the parochialization of knowledge" (Smelser 2003, 656).

In a similar vein, Mattei Dogan (2000) has observed a distorted internationalization of Political Science, stressing the uneven geographical distribution of regular teaching of the discipline, the uneven stage of discipline development, and the hegemony of European and North-American authorship in political science literature. He argues that the diffusion of political science from the core to the "new territories" bears the mark of "Euro-Americanization" in that since the 1970s 90 percent of political science literature was in English; nine-tenths of "important" authors from Europe, the United States, and Canada; and nine-tenths of citations in journals refer to European and North American authors. Stressing that the social sciences "are, by their essence, contextual" and geared to researching "social diversity" (3), he argues that many of political science concepts and theories cannot have a truly universal meaning as they do not even circulate easily within Europe if one thinks of books in German, French, or Italian. What can and should be done instead, he suggests, is a comparative tracing of key concepts and their change of meaning as they migrate between disciplines and cultural contexts.

Though such considerations are far from a euphemistic use of the notion of "internationalization," the current version of the constitution of the International Committee of the Historical Sciences (CISH/ICHS) seems to go even further. It states as objective (1) that "the ICHS is working to "de-Europeanize" itself in order to become a truly global organization and to institute a permanent dialogue between fields of knowledge and different cultures" (CISH/ICHS 2004).

Establishment of the "Superiority" and Disciplinarity of Western Science

The lasting imbalance of the power structure of international knowledge production and distribution raises questions pertaining to the establishment of the positional superiority of Western science. Among social scientists in postcolonial countries concern with this imbalance has been a pervasive theme. They have stressed the importance of economic, institutional, and organizational resources for knowledge production and diffusion in a given country. They have also identified the unilateral dependence on Western sponsoring agencies as both a systemic deterrent to discipline development and a major reason for the lack of cooperation among Third World countries. A special issue of the *International Journal of Psychology* (1995, 30) on the "Development of Psychology in Developing Countries" has provided important details on factors that facilitate or impede its progress in various Asian, Latin American, African, and Arabic countries. However, the contributors to the issue have largely failed to reflect on the hidden model underlying the comparison with Western science.

Their analysis of external impeding factors is based on the conventional model of a linear and progressive evolution of the social sciences in Euro-America and subsequent diffusion of the products from the "center" to the "peripheries." Although some authors contest the view of American Psychology as the epitome of progress, there is a lack of historical reflection on the image of Western superiority and indigenous marginality.

The impact of colonial European expansion on the shaping of the social sciences and on notions of both Western superiority and indigenous marginality has long been neglected in historical research. In an outline of this impact, Sandra Harding (1997) has argued that the problematics selected for research concerned mainly questions that expansionist Europe needed solved, like the improvement of European land and sea travel, the identification of economically useful resources, or strategies of access to indigenous labor. At the same time, there was no concern with questions relating to the consequences of European intervention, like changes of natural resources available for non-Europeans or the social, psychic, economic, and political costs of such intervention. The resulting mark of modern sciences was a "distinctive patterns of knowledge and ignorance" (Harding 1997, 55). Another of Harding's observations concerns the ways in which the consequences of modern sciences are distributed, with the benefits for the Western elites and to some extent their allies in the non-Western world, and the costs to everyone else. This distribution, she argues, remains largely masked by the accounting practices of modern sciences that keep the distribution invisible to most who benefit from it and to many who do not—for instance, by externalizing all destructive unintended consequences of science and technology. Even beyond the positivist tradition, these consequences have been attributed to (abusive) applications of science, thus keeping the notion of value-free science.

For Harding, three expansion-related features enabled Western sciences to appear universally and uniquely valid. First, as the expansion turned the world into a laboratory for emerging the European sciences, Europeans could test their hypotheses about nature's regularities over vastly larger and more diverse natural terrains than could other cultures. Second, as European scientists were taught by "native informants" about the local flora and fauna, minerals and ores, diseases and remedies, all kinds of engineering practices et cetera, they could incorporate elements of this knowledge into their own sciences. Third, "European expansion suppressed or destroyed—intentionally and unintentionally—competitive local knowledge systems" (1997, 63).

The lasting effects of this erasure of alternative knowledge systems can hardly be underrated. As stressed by Linda Tuhiwai Smith, "colonialism not only meant the imposition of Western authority over indigenous lands, indigenous modes of production and indigenous law and government, but the imposition of Western authority over all aspects of indigenous knowledges, languages and cultures" (1999, 64). The creation of new indigenous elites in colonial education fostered the acceptability of Western authority. As a result, current attempts to "indigenize" colonial academic institutions and individual disciplines are still "fraught with major struggles over what counts as knowledge, as language, as literature, as curriculum and as the role of intellectuals" (Smith 1999, 65).

The epistemological framework that contributed to the authority of Western claims to universal knowledge consisted in the substitution of "abstract for concrete, locally situated, and historical concepts of nature. For example, features of local environments became aspects of omnipresent "nature" to be explained adequately only by universally valid laws of nature" (Harding 1997, 64). The positional superiority of Western knowledge production originated in colonial contexts and got widely accepted in neocolonial contexts. It is not grounded in epistemological universalism. Genuine universalism might be imagined as negotiated universalism as it could only be the result of an all-inclusive give-and-take that might generate knowledge products that embody the whole range of social perspectives and knowledge interests articulated by groups who have as yet remained marginalized—indigenous people, feminists, migrant minorities, to mention but a few.

Colonial expansion also had an impact on the pattern of discipline formation that has long been neglected. In several respects, the disciplinary order that got established between 1850 and 1945 implied an imperial divide, on both organizational and intellectual levels, between European modernity as subject and the colonized world as object. The "colonizer's model of the world" (Blaut 1993) was first inscribed in historiography, which detached itself from its eighteenth-century comparative concern in favor of national historiographies and a macrohistorical master narrative of why Europe was able to rise to world dominance. In turn, Asia was left to an ahistorical study of Sinology, Japanology, and Indology (Osterhammel 2001). Next, disciplinary boundaries were established between, on the one hand, the study of European modernity in national economy, sociology, and political science and, on the other hand, the study of "premodern" cultures in anthropology and ethnology (Wallerstein et al. 1996;

Conrad and Randeria 2002). As to this divide, it needs to be remembered that the study of "premodern" cultures in the colonies was preceded by the marking of sites and people as "foreign" and "other," which involved practices of measuring and classifying land, of counting and categorizing populations, of managing and "civilizing" people (Dirks 1992; Appadurai 1993). It was in this process that the systems of living and the knowledge systems of the colonized have become classified, some of them submerged or driven underground, some appropriated, others represented to Western audiences and, through the eyes of the West, eventually represented back to the colonized (Smith 1999). The entangled histories of "metropolitan centers" and colonial "peripheries" were thus rendered invisible, with the consequence of narrowing the history of knowledge perspective to a mere focus on the production and distribution of Western knowedge.

As to the study of European modernity, the formation of the social sciences did not per se predetermine "a disciplinarily segmented structure" (Wagner and Wittrock 1991, 5). At least, there are pioneer examples of a comprehensive historical social science like those of Max Weber. Recent historical investigations into the formation, institutionalization, and resulting intellectual structure (identity) of the social sciences across Europe have shown that the formation of the social sciences depended on the particular links of universities to political institutions, on the kind of problematics singled out in public debate as issues for analytic concern, and on the need to provide professional training for increasing numbers of particular groups like bureaucrats, diplomats, and high school teachers. Disciplines thus do not represent "natural" kinds; rather, they are situated constructions of social reality geared to administer and control this reality.

For instance, in the state-centered societies of Continental Europe like Italy and Germany, the formative period of political science and sociology was dominated by "the debate about the formation of unified nation-states along lines of cultural identities" (Wagner and Wittrock 1991, 7) and, subsequent to nation building, by the "social question" of how to solve the problems brought about by industrialization and urbanization. As to Psychology, institutional settings such as schools, factories, prisons, and asylums provided opportunities for the systematic observation of human conduct, for sorting and hierarchizing individuals in terms of mental capacities and for designing new practices for the management of social relations (Rose 1991; Jansz and van Drunen 2004).

In the United States, the expansion of modern universities responded to public fears of social disorder and mental degeneration subsequent to millions of immigrants from Southern and Eastern Europe. Comparing the emergence of Psychology in Germany and the United States, Kurt Danziger (1979) has traced the circumstances that resulted in a philosophically embedded Psychology in Germany and a separate discipline shaped as master science of human behavior in the United States. The specific sociocultural construction of American Psychology is elucidated in two complementary studies (Danziger 1990, 1997). Danziger demonstrates how American Psychology has combined categories derived from both eighteenth-century moral philosophy and nineteenth-century biologism with twentieth-century strategies of social engineering like social selection and educational and management practices. Mediated by specific social research practices that were usually misunderstood as mere methodologies and a metalanguage of "variables," the disciplinary apparatus became increasingly opaque. The members of the community that inhabit this apparatus usually take it for granted that their work contributes to the knowledge about intelligence, behavior, or cognition, unaware of the normative implications of their classification of human conduct. Thus Psychology has become increasingly oblivious to any alternative approaches that assume a socially situated person and a dialectical process of the mutual shaping of society, culture, and the person.

As to social science, the articulation of social theories as "sciences" took a peculiar path in the United States. Academics keen to please the alliance of progressive businessmen and the new breed of "educational managers" who ran the universities used an empiricist philosophy of science and the German medical specialties' notion of "institutes." Within two generations, an American model of the social sciences was institutionalized—segmented into an abstract deductivist economics, a sociology understood as quantitative social research geared to controlling group situations, and a political science geared to advising governments at home and abroad (Manicas 1991).

By mid-twentieth century, the established disciplinary order reflected a segmented construction of social reality built on the basic distinction between what belongs inside the individual and what belongs to a social sphere entirely outside the individual. This segmentation has largely precluded reflected debate on the specific, historically interrelated notions like nation-state, civil society, citizenship, secularism, the market, the individual, and the distinction between public and private sphere. "Modernity" as comprised of such notions has been taken as a quasi-natural category and yardstick of social realities elsewhere.

This construction is Eurocentric in several respects. First, in the understanding of civilization according to which European modernity is not a civilization among others but a unique one charged with a "civilizing mission" from which result Orientalist characterizations of non-Western civilizations in ways that justify the taking possession of them (Said 1995); second, in that individuals are conceived as rationally calculating actors "according to the image of the autonomous and self-possessed political subject of right, will and agency" and collectivities (classes, ethnicities) as singularities with identities which provide the basis for political interests and actions (Rose 1999); third, in the institution of a fundamental divorce between science and philosophy/humanities. As argued by Wallerstein (1999), the resulting disciplinary culture of value-neutral expertism that provides the basis for both engineering decisions and sociopolitical choices is thus liberated or deprived from substantive debate of the socially and politically "good."

Some qualifications need to be added. Not all social knowledge that emerged in Europe needs to be characterized as Eurocentric. From the beginning of European modernity, social theory was accompanied by a critical strand aiming at the transcendence of capitalist conditions—from Rousseau to Marx to twentieth-century versions of critical theory. However, the emancipatory knowledge interests that guide critical social theory have hardly ever made an impact on the disciplinary apparatus. New generations socialized in this apparatus learn from the beginning how to think in terms of individual and group differences and how to design research in terms of variables. As a consequence of their marginalization in Western academia, critical emancipatory approaches did not get exported along with the disciplinary system. Insofar as some academics in Latin America, India, or South Africa have been receptive to critical theory, this required their special effort.

Global Expansion: Entangled in the Disciplinary Model

What does the imposition of the particular Western disciplinary construction of social reality mean for academics (and their clients) in formerly colonized countries, with religious and intellectual traditions of their own, with established practices and beliefs for dealing with everyday affairs and maintaining structured social life? What promises did Psychology, Sociology, or Political Science hold for societies as diverse as Indonesia, the Philippines, Egypt, and South Africa? How did the independent nations interact with the imperialist powers in the area of scientific development, and what changes were there in the course of half a century? These are but some of the essential questions that will hopefully be investigated by historians and sociologists of the social sciences around the world. My aim in this section is necessarily limited (cf. Staeuble 2004, 2005). Drawing on the still rare accounts from particular countries available in the West, I want to provide an at least patchy sketch of the responses to the foreign product, focusing on comments concerning the Eurocentric make-up of the product in relation to postcolonial conditions.

From an early concern with the imbalanced structure of international knowledge production that turned them into mere receivers, academics in Asia, Latin America, and Africa moved on to working with the received knowledge in order to solve major problems in their countries. In the early decades of enforced export, critiques of the foreign product resonated with the then current radical debate on society, science, and imperialism. For instance, it was stressed that the problems of Third World countries are "to a large extent an historical consequence of their colonization and exploitation by the industrialized nations of Europe and North America"; their attribution "to psychological factors within the individual members of these societies" would thus amount to an "unethical abuse of psychological concepts to cover up politico-economic realities" (Mehryar 1984, 165).

Discontent with the unsuitable "intellectual package" (Nandy 1974), as an often-used quote had it, academics turned to a critique and critical remaking of the received disciplinary knowledge. However, with a few exceptions like Ashis Nandy (1983, 1994, 1998) who pleaded for an alternative politics of psychology and wrote widely on the critique of modernity, development, and hegemony, the outlook of the critics has largely remained within the boundaries of their respective discipline. For instance, psychologists in many post-independence countries have criticized the individualistic orientation of Western micropsychology. In India, Durganand Sinha (1984, 1993, 1994) emphasized that a reorientation of Psychology toward the pressing problems of rapid social transformation would require a "macropsychology" with open links to other social sciences. Such reorientation, however, would have required a transdisciplinary scrutinizing of the interrelated notions of the "individual," "citizenship," the distinction between the public and private sphere, and the way they relate to Indian conditions. This was precluded by the dominant disciplinary orientations.

What might have been gained by exploring how the received social categories can be renewed to characterize forms of social life in India has recently been demonstrated by an imaginative representative of Subaltern studies. Dipesh Chakrabarty starts from the premise that European thought is "both indispensable and inadequate to think through the experiences of political modernity in non-Western nations" (2000, 19). He invokes Marx and Heidegger in a reading of Indian history as a contradictory dialogue between the universal narrative of capital/political modernity and some particular Indian ways of being-in-the-world. Drawing on a vast archive of Bengali literature, he shows how Bengali notions and practices of personhood, the family, and fraternity differ fundamentally from European enlightenment ones. This difference, he argues in his epilogue, need not be read in terms of a "not yet," as in concepts of an "incomplete transitions" to capitalism and modernity. Reading historical time in a non-totalizing manner would rather focus on the fragmentary and irreducibly plural nature of the "now."

Different strategies have been deployed in attempts at a critical reorientation of a received discipline, depending on the particular conditions of a country, as a brief comparison between remakings of Psychology in India and South Africa may show. In India, a remodeling of conceptual approaches to person, experience, and conduct from an Indian perspective on the human condition prevails. This perspective emphasizes a holistic spiritual worldview, a relational concept of the person, and a moral code anchored in Dharma (Misra and Gergen 1993). Abstracts of the 2002 National Congress of Yoga and Indian Psychology suggest a lively debate on philosophical traditions, but it is hardly imaginable how they can be fitted into the disciplinary apparatus of Psychology. In any case, the editor of the state-of-the arts surveys of Psychology in India that are published every ten years by the National Research Council keeps complaining that the majority of psychologists in India tend to emulate American Psychology (Pandey 1988, 2001). As observed by Sinha, they are still "finding it difficult to cast off the microscopic and individualistic orientation acquired in the West" as they are still bound by its prevailing disciplinary ethos (1993, 40).

Psychology in post-apartheid South Africa provides the impressive example of an increasing number of academics who strive for a reorientation of the received Euro-American discipline toward the particular needs of a country fraught with the triple heritage of slavery, colonialism, and apartheid. Since the inception of the alternative journal *Psychology in So-ciety (PINS)* in 1983, a strong sense of the need for both emancipatory knowledge production and the provision of appropriate social services has informed the critique of the pervasive racism in psychological research and practice (Duncan et al. 2001; Foster 2004). While a special issue of the South African *Journal of Psychology on Black Scholarship* (Duncan et al. 1997; Seedat 1997) was mainly devoted to academic racism, the impact of Black scholarship has grown, as indicated by the inclusion of chapters on Black Consciousness, Black Psychology, and African Perspectives in Psychology in a recent *Critical Psychology Reader* (Hook 2004). This suggests the possibility of a joint reorientation of Psychology that draws on the critical traditions of both Black Consciousness and Western Marxism and poststructuralism, on white and black feminism (among many, cf. Duncan et al. 2001; Hook 2004). There also is a clear recognition of the authoritar-ian grip of (Western) disciplinary organization that works as a counter-force to critical reorientations of the discipline (Henderson 2003; Macleod 2004). Still, despite similar attempts at a "liberation sociology" (Feagin 2001; Burawoy 2004), there is as yet no indication of a forming of alliances in order to challenge the received disciplinary order.

Attempts at a reorientation of Psychology or Sociology toward Hindu, African, or other perspectives may be read as a demand for knowledge that would make sense for the recipients in terms of their understanding of themselves and their world. It also may be read as a demand for em-powerment to improve collective life conditions insofar as they would seem to be reconcilable with the theoretical strands that inform "libera-tion psychology" or "liberation sociology." However, insofar as they also imply a self-conscious assertion of cultural "otherness" vis-à-vis the West, there is some danger that this may lead to constructions which essential-ize local and temporal features—for instance, in depicting spirituality, a sense of unity, and social relatedness as characteristics of a timeless Afri-can human nature. This would but mirror the cultural construction of Euro-American Psychology, minus the latter's claim to universality. To some extent, "indigenous psychologies" bear the mark of "countercolonial discourse" (Keesing 1994) that remains entangled in the colonizer's con-struction of social reality. As aptly stated by Amina Mama (1995), neither Eurocentric philosophies nor their mirror image of, for instance, Afrocen-tric philosophies will lead beyond the patterns of thought that originated in colonialism.

From a sociology of science view the notion of "indigenization" is much broader, as first elaborated by the Indian sociologist Krishna Kumar (1979). He proposed three different levels of directing social science toward the particular situation and problems of a country. On the "structural level," the institutional and organizational resources for the production and diffusion of relevant knowledge in a given country need to be assessed; on the "substantive level," the question is what relevant issues knowledge production ought to focus on; and on the "theoretical level," the concern is with conceptual frameworks that fit the sociocultural experiences, worldviews, and goals of the people addressed. As the debate on indigenous psychologies and sociologies has largely focused on the theoretical level (Sinha 1993; Mhkize 2004; Akiwowo 1999), it remained stuck in disciplinary blindfolds at the expense of any serious questioning of the hierarchy of relevance of the knowledge to be produced. In countries with limited resources, the question of relevant knowledge is vital not only because the emulation of a disciplinary system with increasing subdisciplinary specializations may leave no resources for more relevant knowledge production but also because it precludes any consideration of alternative modes of knowledge production. Why, for instance, should it not be imaginable that transdisciplinary issue-centered research as practiced at some special research centers becomes a general model for tertiary education?

Odds of Disciplinarity and Chances of Transcending It

The need for alternatives to the Eurocentric disciplinary construction of social reality that largely guides "the way we think, perceive and try to understand reality and the universe in the modern world" (Giri 1998, 380), has been voiced in many non-Western and Western places. The recent Gulbenkian Commission for Restructuring the Social Sciences (Wallerstein et al. 1996) clearly stated the increasing inadequacy of the disciplinary structure of knowledge production but in advancing an increase of transdisciplinary niches, the report lacks innovative proposals.

Where would one imagine the actors to transcend disciplinary structures? Much of the critique of both objectifying positivism and insulating disciplinarity has emerged "from the experience of people who have been studied, researched, written about, and defined by social sciences" (Smith 1999, 169)—white and black feminists, Afro-Americans, migrant minorities, and indigenous peoples. The intellectual heirs of the colonized have drawn attention to the limitations of the received Eurocentric knowledge. Aiming to think beyond dichotomies, they have introduced notions like "indigeneity," "subalternity," "ethnoscapes," and "multiple modernities" to widen the conceptual frames for dealing with entangled histories and shifting identities (Goldin 1999; Mudimbe-Boyi 2002; Randeria 2002). They have also started to unpack the seemingly coherent notions of modernity, civil society, and citizenship. As many attempts at reconceptualization have come up in thinkscapes like Subaltern Studies, Postcolonial Studies, or Developing Societies Studies, one may wonder if these niches can become the gateways for a transdisciplinary opening of the social sciences. The odds are that academics who work in these niches need not and thus are not likely to care about disciplinarity as they constitute a world apart from the value-neutral specialists that populate the academic disciplines.

Can disciplinarity be overcome from within the disciplines? For the social orientation and commitments of a discipline to change, it needs at least groups of scholars who have reasons to question the received orientation, who are articulate in voicing alternatives and able to engage allies. Changes in the social constituency of a disciplinary community can thus become important because the shaping of knowledge interests of individuals or groups depends on their social experience. Their knowledge interests in turn either make them prone to accepting taken-for-granted views or sensitize them to question certain views and practices and to seek alternative ways of approaching an issue or even a whole body of established knowledge (Samelson 1978). For instance, critical psychological approaches that take a Marxist, poststructuralist, or feminist orientation have gained some ground by organizing themselves nationally or internationally. Also, the organizations of Black, Hispanic, Asian, and Amerindian psychologists in the United States have made some impact, not only on the admittance of members of the respective group to academia but also on the shaping of new views in and of the discipline (Nagayama Hall and Okasaki 2002). Claims for a Psychology that acknowledges the diversity of cultural selves are surely claims for its opening toward a view of humans as both socioculturally shaped and self-defining beings. Still, issues of cultural selves and identities may not provide the most suitable anchors for the overdue decolonization of minds and patterns of knowledge.

Critical alternatives to the social orientation of a discipline that are able to challenge the disciplinary order itself would have to be able to build alliances with critics both from other disciplines and from sectors of the public in a joint concern with a just world. If "the world as we know it" (Wallerstein 1999) has come to an end, we are still left with a world in which major social decisions will be taken. Lest these be grounded in mere technocratic or ideological concerns, substantive intellectual debate is required. As observed by historians committed to post-Eurocentric perspectives, the situation is difficult because "what are gone are not only concepts for organizing the world, but also concepts that served to give coherence to projects of emancipation" (Dirlik et al. 2000, 7). How can the current configuration of the world be conceptualized? How can one account for the perseverance of dichotomous thinking? What images of a just world are held by people, and what are their commonalities?

As I hope to have shown, there is no lack of substantial criticism of the Euro-Americanization of international knowledge production. This implies a rethinking of the categories of "modernity" and "modernization" that have set the terms in which countries not shaped by capitalism, industrialism, and science "are these days perceived, discussed, analyzed, and judged, both by the world at large and by their own populations" (Geertz 1995, 140). Critiques of modernity, disciplinarity, and the politics of knowledge need to be grounded in historical analysis as the present configurations of domination are largely reconfigurations of forces that have been shaping the world for long. Yet recognition of the persisting hierarchies of disciplines, regions, and peoples does not mean to conceive of the globalization of capital as an inescapable process worked by forces beyond human decisions. It is full of contradictions which, if recognized, may "provide the spaces from which to think alternatives to the present" (Dirlik et al. 2000, 3).

REFERENCES

Akiwowo, Akinsola. 1999. Indigenous Sociologies: Extending the Scope of the Argument. *International Sociology* 14(2): 115–138.
Appadurai, Arjun. 1993. Number in the Colonial Imagination. In *Orientalism and the Postcolonial Predicament: Perspectives on South Asia*, ed. Carol A. Breckenridge and Peter van der Veer. Philadelphia: University of Pennsylvania Press.
Blaut, J. M. 1993. *The Colonizer's Model of the World: Geographical Diffusionism and Eurocentric History.* New York: Guilford.
Blowers, Geoffrey H., and Alison M. Turtle, eds. 1987. *Psychology Moving East: The Status of Western Psychology in Asia and Oceania.* Sydney: Sydney University Press.

Burawoy, Michael. 2004. Public Sociology: South African Dilemmas in a Global Context. *Society in Transition* 35(1): 11–26.

Calhoun, Craig. 2002. The Future of Sociology: Interdisciplinarity and Internationalization. Presentation to the University of Minnesota Sociology Department at its Centennial Celebration, March 29–30.

Carr, Stuart C., and John F. Schumaker, eds. 1996. *Psychology and the Developing World.* Westport, CT: Praeger.

Chakrabarty, Dipesh. 2000. *Provincializing Europe: Postcolonial Thought and Historical Difference.* Princeton, NJ: Princeton University Press.

Chomchai, Prachoom. 1969. Implantation and Acclimatization of the Social Sciences in Thailand. *International Social Science Journal* 21(3): 383–392.

CISH/ICHS (Comité international des sciences historiques / International Committee of Historical Sciences). *2004 Presentation: Constitution Objectives.* Available at: http://www.cish.org/GB/Presentation/Objectifs.htm. Retrieved November 2004.

Conrad, Sebastian, and Shalini Randeria, Hg. 2002. *Jenseits des Eurozentrismus: Postkoloniale Perspektiven in den Geschichts- und Kulturwissenschaften.* Frankfurt: Campus.

Cooper, Frederick, and Randall Packard, eds. 1997. *International Development and the Social Sciences: Essays on the History and Politics of Knowledge.* Berkeley: University of California Press.

Danziger, Kurt. 1979. The Social Origins of Modern Psychology. In *Psychology in Social Context,* ed. Alfred R. Buss. New York: Irvington.

Danziger, Kurt. 1990. *Constructing the Subject: Historical Origins of Psychological Research.* Cambridge: Cambridge University Press.

Danziger, Kurt. 1997. *Naming the Mind: How Psychology Found Its Language.* London: Sage.

Dirks, Nicholas B., ed. 1992. *Colonialism and Culture.* Ann Arbor: University of Michigan Press.

Dirlik, Arif, Vinai Bahl, and Peter Gran, eds. 2000. *History after the Three Worlds: Post-Eurocentric Historiographies.* Lanham: Rowman and Littlefield.

Dogan, Mattei. 2000. Distorted Internationalization. Roundtable on Political Science Concepts, Quebec. http://www2.Hawaii.edu/~fredr/dogan.htm. Retrieved November 2004.

Dumont, Kitty, and Johan Louw. 2001. The International Union of Psychological Science and the Politics of Membership: Psychological Associations in South Africa and the German Democratic Republic. *History of Psychology* 4(4): 388–404.

Duncan, Norman, Mohamed Seedat, Ashley van Niekerk, Cheryl de la Rey, Pumla Goboda-Madikizela, Leickness C. Simbayi, and Arwin Bhana. 1997. Black Scholarship: Doing Something Active and Positive about Academic Racism. *South African Journal of Psychology* 27(4): 201–205.

Duncan, Norman, Ashley van Niekerk, Cheryl de la Rey, and Mohamed Seedat, eds. 2001. *"Race," racism, knowledge production and psychology in South Africa.* New York: Nova Science.

Feagin, Joe R. 2001. *Liberation Sociology.* Boulder, CO: Westview.

Foster, Donald. 2004. Liberation Psychology. In *Critical Psychology.* Ed. Derek Hook. Lansdowne: University of Cape Town Press.

Geertz, Clifford. 1995. *After the Fact: Two Countries, Four Decades, One Anthropologist.* Cambridge: Harvard University Press.

Giri, Ananta K. 1998. Transcending Disciplinary Boundaries. *Critique of Anthropology* 18(4): 379–404.

Goldin, Liliana R., ed. 1999. *Identities on the Move: Transnational Processes in North America and the Caribbean Basin.* Austin: University of Texas Press.

Gran, Peter. 1996. *Beyond Eurocentrism: A New View of Modern World History.* New York: Syracuse University Press.

Harding, Sandra. 1997. Is Modern Science an Ethnoscience? Rethinking Epistemological Assumptions. In *Postcolonial African Philosophy: A Critical Reader,* ed. Emmanuel Chukwudi Eze. Oxford: Blackwell.

Henderson, Jill. 2003. (De)Constructing the Future of Professional Psychcology in South Africa. Paper presented to the 10th Biennual Conference of the International Society for Theoretical Psychology, June 22–27, Istanbul.

Herman, Ellen. 1996. *The Romance of American Psychology: Political Culture in the Age of Experts.* Berkeley: University of California Press.

Hook, Derek, ed. 2004. *Critical Psychology.* Cape Town: University of Cape Town Press.

Jansz, Jeroen, and Peter van Drunen, eds. 2004. *A Social History of Psychology.* Oxford: Blackwell.

Keesing, Roger M. 1994. Colonial and counter-colonial discourse in Melanesia. *Critique of Anthropology* 14(1): 41–58.

Kumar, Krishna. 1979. Indigenization and Transnational Cooperation in the Social Sciences. In *Bonds without Knowledge: Exploration in Transcultural Interactions,* ed. K. Kumar (pp. 103–119). Honolulu: University Press of Hawaii.

Ladden, Jean. 1969. The role of the sociologist and the growth of sociology in Latin America. *International Social Science Journal* 21(3): 428–432.

Macleod, Catriona. 2004. Writing into action: The critical research endeavour. In *Critical Psychology,* ed. Derek Hook. Cape Town: University of Cape Town Press.

Mama, Amina. 1995. *Beyond the Masks: Race, Gender and Subjectivity.* London: Routledge.

Manicas, Peter T. 1991. The Social Science Disciplines: The American Model. In *Discourses on Society: The Shaping of the Social Science Disciplines,* ed. Peter Wagner, Björn Wittrock, and Richard Whitley. Dordrecht: Kluwer Academic.

Mehryar, Amir H. 1984. The Role of Psychology in National Development: Wishful Thinking and Reality. *International Journal of Psychology* 19: 159–167.

Mhkize, Nhlanhla. 2004. Psychology: An African Perspective. In *Critical Psychology,* ed. Derek Hook (pp. 24–52). Cape Town: University of Cape Town Press.

Misra, Giriswar, and Kenneth J. Gergen (1993). On the Place of Culture in Psychological Science. *International Journal of Psychology* 28(2): 225–243.

Moghaddam, Fathali M. (1993). Traditional and Modern Psychologies in Competing Cultural Systems: Lessons from Iran 1978–1981. In *Indigenous Psychologies: Research and Experience in Cultural Context,* ed. Uichol Kim and John W. Berry. London: Sage.

Morpurgo, Paul von. 1998. A half-century of the *International Social Science Journal. International Social Science Journal* 157: 309–318.

Mudimbe-Boyi, Elizabeth, ed. 2002. *Beyond Dichotomies: Histories, Identities, Cultures, and the Challenge of Globalization.* Albany: State University of New York Press.

Nagayama Hall, Gordon C., and Sumie Okazaki, eds. 2002. *Asian American Psychology: The Science of Lives in Context.* Washington, DC: American Psychological Association.

Nandy, Ashis. 1974. The Non-paradigmatic Crisis of Indian Psychology: Reflections on a Recipient Culture of Science. *Indian Journal of Psychology* 49: 1–20.

Nandy, Ashis. 1983. Towards an Alternative Politics of Psychology. *International Social Science Journal* 35(2): 323–338.

Nandy, Ashis. 1994. Culture, Voice and Development: A Primer for the Unsuspecting. *Thesis Eleven* 39: 1–18.

Nandy, Ashis. 1998. *Exiled at Home. Comprising "At the Edge of Psychology," "The Intimate Enemy," "Creating a Nationality."* New Delhi: Oxford University Press.

Osterhammel, Jürgen. 2001. *Geschichtswissenschaft jenseits des Nationalstaats: Studien zu Beziehungsgeschichte und Zivilisationsvergleich.* Göttingen: Vandenhoeck and Ruprecht.

Pandey, J., ed. 1988. *Psychology in India: The State-of-the-Art* (3 vols.) New Delhi: Sage.

Pandey, J., ed. 2001. *Psychology in India Revisited: Developments in the Discipline* (3 vols.) New Delhi: Sage.

Pieris, Ralph. 1969. The Implantation of Sociology in Asia. *International Social Science Journal* 21(3): 433–444.

Platt, Jennifer. 1998. *A Brief History of the ISA: 1948–1997.* Montreal: International Sociological Association.

Randeria, Shalini. 2002. Entangled Histories of Uneven Modernities: Civil Society, Caste Solidarities and Legal Pluralism in Post-Colonial India. In *Unraveling Ties: From Social Cohesion to New Practices of Connectedness,* ed. Yehuda Elkana, Ivan Krastev, Elisio Macamo, and Shalini Randeria. Frankfurt: Campus.

Rose, Nikolas. 1991. Experts of the Soul. *Psychologie und Geschichte* 3(1/2): 91–99.

Rose, Nikolas. 1999. *Powers of Freedom: Reframing Political Thought.* Cambridge: Cambridge University Press.

Rosenzweig, Mark R., Wayne H. Holtzman, Michel Sabourin, and David Bélanger, eds. 2000. *History of the International Union of Psychological Science (IUPsyS)*. Hove, East Sussex, United Kingdom: Psychology Press.

Said, Edward W. 1995. *Orientalism: Western Conceptions of the Orient*. London: Penguin.

Samelson, Franz. 1978. From "Race Psychology" to "Studies in Prejudice": Some Observations on the Thematic Reversal in Social Psychology. *Journal of the History of the Behavioral Sciences* 14: 265–278.

Seedat, Mohamed. 1997. The quest for a liberatory psychology. *South African Journal of Psychology* 27(4): 261–270.

Sexton, Virginia Staudt, and John D. Hogan, eds. 1992. *International Psychology: Views from around the World*. Lincoln: University of Nebraska Press.

Sexton, Virginia Staudt, and Henryk Misiak, eds. 1976. *Psychology around the World*. Monterey, CA: Brooks/Cole.

Sinha, Durganand. 1984. Psychology in the Context of Third World Development. *International Journal of Psychology* 19: 17–29.

Sinha, Durganand. 1993. Indigenization of Psychology in India and Its Relevance. In *Indigenous Psychologies: Research and Experience in Cultural Context*, ed. Uichol Kim and John W. Berry. London: Sage.

Sinha, Durganand. 1994. Origins and Development of Psychology in India: Outgrowing the Alien Framework. *International Journal of Psychology* 29(6): 695–705.

Smelser, Neil J. 2003. On Comparative Analysis: Interdisciplinarity and Internationalization in Sociology. *International Sociology* 18(4): 643–657.

Smith, Linda Tuhiwai. 1999. *Decolonizing Methodologies: Research and Indigenous Peoples*. Dunedin: University of Otago Press.

Solari, Aldo E. (1969). Social Crisis as an Obstacle to the Institutionalization of Sociology in Latin America. *International Social Science Journal* 21(3): 445–456.

Staeuble, Irmingard. 2004. De-centering Western Perspectives: Psychology and the Disciplinary Order in the First and Third World. In *Rediscovering the History of Psychology: Essays Inspired by the Work of Kurt Danziger*, ed. Adrian Brock, Johann Louw, and Willem van Hoorn. New York: Kluwer.

Staeuble, Irmingard. 2005. The International Expansion of Psychology: Cultural Imperialism or Chances for Alternative Cultures of Knowledge. In *Contemporary Theorizing in Psychology: Global Perspectives*, ed. Aydan Gulerce, Arnd Hofmeister, John Kaye, Guy Saunders, and Irmingard Staeuble. Concord: Captus University Publications.

Turtle, Alison M. 1987. A Silk Road for Psychology. In *Psychology Moving East: The Status of Western Psychology in Asia and Oceania*, ed. Geoffrey H. Blowers and Alison M. Turtle. Sydney: Sydney University Press.

Unesco Secretariat. 1998. UNESCO and the Social Sciences. *International Social Science Journal* 157: 319–320. Originally published 1949.

Wagner, Peter, and Björn Wittrock. 1991. Analyzing Social Science: On the Possibility of a Sociology of the Social Sciences. In *Discourses on Society: The Shaping of the Social Science Disciplines,* ed. Peter Wagner, Björn Wittrock, and Richard Whitley. Dordrecht: Kluwer.

Wallerstein, Immanuel. 1999. *The End of the World as We Know It: Social Science for the Twenty-First Century.* Minneapolis: University of Minnesota Press.

Wallerstein, Immanuel, Calestous Juma, Evelyn Fox Keller, Jurgen Kocka, Domenique Lecourt, V. Y. Mudkimbe, Kinide Miushakoji, Ilya Prigonine, Peter J. Taylor, and Michel-Rolph Trouillot. 1996. *Open the Social Sciences: Report of the Gulbenkian Commission for Restructuring the Social Sciences.* Stanford: Stanford University Press.

Chapter 11

Universalism and Indigenization in the History of Modern Psychology

Kurt Danziger

Problem of Coherence in the History of Modern Psychology

No historical study, whether of psychology or of something else, ever consists simply of a jumble of unrelated facts. Some thematic unity always ties the facts together. They may all have something to do with a particular person, for example, or a school of thought, or perhaps some form of psychological practice. Without such a unifying principle one would not be able to specify what any assembly of historical facts was the history *of.*

Where do these thematic unities come from? Unlike nuggets of historical information lying around in dusty archives, waiting to be collected, the thematic unities of historical discourse have to be constructed by the historian. Not that they are ever constructed arbitrarily. For the most part, historians follow in the footsteps of their predecessors and adopt unifying principles that have become uncontroversial by tradition. To be plausible, such principles must also appear to correspond to "natural" unities in the world whose history is being explored. Individual persons who have been active as psychologists, for example, constitute such natural unities. One can write their biographies or an account of their contributions without having to think twice about the propriety of one's choice of unifying theme.

But not all themes are so straightforward. Most unities have fuzzy borders, and this requires decisions about what to include and what to exclude. These decisions inevitably affect the definition of what one's history is about. The further back we go in time the more intractable these decisions become (Smith, 1988).

However, in the modern period, during which psychology became a discipline practiced by professionals who saw themselves as scientists and employed technical procedures they regarded as scientific, psychology has had a solid institutional basis in the form of laboratories, clinics, scientific journals, accreditation procedures, regularly organized conferences, professional associations, and so on. Although the forms of these institutions have varied quite a lot from one country to another, they have sufficient generic similarity to provide at least one plausible justification for treating the history of modern psychology as a unitary topic.

Surprisingly, histories of modern psychology have seldom emphasized the institutional sources of such unity as the topic possesses. To do so would have suggested that the factors which constitute psychology as one discipline were essentially external to the content of psychological knowledge. What most histories of modern psychology prefer to suggest, however, is that the existence of the discipline depends on some intrinsic coherence of its subject matter. This is because such histories have usually been marketed as aids in the professional socialization of aspirant members of the discipline. The assumption of intrinsic coherence of subject matter is an important unifying force counteracting dangerous centrifugal tendencies within the professional community.

When a particular assembly of historical information is presented under one set of covers as the history of modern psychology, there is a clear implication that everything in this assembly belongs together as a reflection of a complex but ultimately unitary and distinct part of the natural world. However, there are two sets of facts that are both undeniable and awkward for this approach. First, there is the evident heterogeneity of the subject matter of "psychology"; second, there is the lack of unity associated with the territorial dispersion of the subject.

At different times different places have been prominent in the accumulation of psychological knowledge, and the nature of that knowledge has sometimes differed profoundly from place to place.

How has the historiography of psychology dealt with these kinds of diversity? The short answer is that it has dealt with them by privileging certain aspects of the historical picture at the expense of others. As regards heterogeneity of subject matter, the classical example of this move is provided by E. G. Boring's *A History of Experimental Psychology* (1950), where the traditional experimental parts of the discipline are at the center of attention and everything else becomes a matter of relatively peripheral interest. It has been suggested that this bias was connected to the author's involvement in intradisciplinary politics where he represented the interests of the experimentalists (O'Donnell, 1979). More generally, historians' own affiliation with a particular part of the discipline might well lead them to assign a central, unifying role to that part, even substituting the history of that part for the history of the field as a whole.

This certainly applies to the way in which national diversity is handled in standard accounts of the history of modern psychology. Such accounts usually present modern psychology as originating in Europe in the late nineteenth century, then going from strength to strength in the United States, and possibly undergoing some growth in the rest of the world in the latter part of the twentieth century. This account is more remarkable for what it leaves out than for what it puts in. Its tendency is to depict the international circulation of psychological knowledge in terms of quantity and geography. There is explosive growth in one place, the United States, slow growth in some parts of the world, and extraordinary ups and downs in others, notably Europe and parts of East Asia. As long as progress is equated with growth, there is certainly progress, even if most of the overall growth was contributed by one country. That makes it easy to equate the progress of modern psychology with its progress in the United States and to present an essentially linear historical trajectory.

One problem with this linear scheme is that the discipline did not develop from a single seed sprouting in one specific location. One would have to go not only to Wundt's laboratory in Leipzig but also to Galton's anthropometric laboratory in London, to Charcot's clinic in Paris, to the Bureau of Salesmanship Research at the Carnegie Institute of Technology in Pittsburgh, and to many other places if one really wanted to trace the roots of modern psychology. Different versions of modern psychology appeared at more or less the same time in a number of countries. Nor did these versions undergo a progressive fusion. On the contrary, during the three decades between 1915 and 1945 the gap between different national psychologies did not narrow, it widened.

It is certainly true that international exchange has been a feature of modern psychology from the beginning. As soon as the first psychological laboratories appeared scholars from other countries began to visit them. Some came for relatively brief periods, others stayed for years and obtained doctorates at the end. Textbooks of the new science were translated into other languages, experimental apparatus was copied in other countries, and soon World Congresses of Psychology were being scheduled at regular intervals.

But at the same time the discipline exhibited a profound localism in that virtually all significant contributions were deeply marked by the cultural context of their place of origin and were therefore not easily transplanted. Before World War II there had been very marked differences in the kind of psychological knowledge that predominated in the major national sites for its production. These differences were referred to in terms of distinctions among "schools" of psychology, the language of "schools" being a way of fudging the fact that there was fundamental disagreement about the subject matter of psychology and the appropriate way of studying it. All of these schools had unmistakable local roots, and their attempts at proselytizing were often unsuccessful. The relative predominance of these schools varied from country to country, and their exportability varied considerably. Germany was the place where *Ganzheitspsychologie* (holistic psychology) flourished, of which Gestalt Psychology proved to be the only exportable version. Behaviorism was an American phenomenon that was then not taken seriously anywhere else. British psychology was recognized for its strong tradition of mental testing and the kind of faculty psychology that it supported, but though this was exportable to North America and the Commonwealth it was either rejected or changed beyond recognition elsewhere. Differences of national style operated not merely on the level of theories and concepts but also on the level of research practice. The paradigmatic psychological investigation looked quite different as one traveled from one national school to another.

Yet all schools of psychology made explicit or implicit claims to universal validity. What they all agreed on was that there was one underlying psychological reality and that there were right and wrong ways to come to grips with it. They simply differed about which way was right and which was wrong. Somewhat ironically, the prewar school of psychology that had the strongest claim to be truly international, namely psychoanalysis, quite commonly found itself on the wrong side of the discipline's boundaries.

Intellectual Geography of Center and Periphery

After World War II, these differences became far less pronounced or disappeared altogether, to be replaced by a neo-behaviorist synthesis of U.S. origin that prescribed how empirical psychological research was to carried out, how research questions were to be formulated, and what kinds of data were scientifically relevant. The leading position of the United States in terms of quantitative measures of knowledge production had already been established earlier, but by about 1940 this lead was overwhelming. The social resources that supported psychological research and practice were of a different order of magnitude in America and in the rest of the world. Combined with American economic and political expansionism, this led to a pattern of international exchange of psychological knowledge that was very different from what had existed earlier in the century. Instead of a somewhat limited traffic among a number of more or less autonomous centers, we now find a great deal of unimpeded traffic from one center to many other places that form a kind of periphery around this one true center.

During the last half of the twentieth century, the international flow of scientific psychological knowledge ballooned, mediated by regular international conferences, mass circulation of journals and marketing of textbooks, foreign teaching and research missions by established figures, graduate training of large numbers of foreign students, research collaboration across frontiers and oceans, and many relatively informal contacts. That there was a lot of traffic, a great deal of traveling, and a huge flow of information is beyond question. But most of this flow was not so much an exchange among more or less equal local centers but essentially a one-way flow from one national source to a number of national recipients. In the West the source was of course the United States, and the recipients were found at various places in the rest of the world that were not in the Soviet sphere of influence. There was some other traffic as well, but it was dwarfed by this major effect. In other words, the flow of psychological knowledge was essentially asymmetrical. (This applied to the Soviet sphere as well, though in psychology the amount of activity was minute compared to the West.) In each case, there was a geographical center and a periphery, and the flow of information was mostly from the center to the periphery and not back. In the West, if psychologists outside the United States remained poorly informed about developments there, they were at risk of suffering some loss of professional status, whereas American psychologists habitually ignored work done elsewhere with complete impunity.

This state of affairs was at its most extreme in the decades after the end of World War II. (Germany formed a partial exception because the legacy of its recent past imposed a certain delay before it too fell into line.) The consequence was an unprecedented degree of international homogenization in what counted as scientific psychological knowledge.

The fact that the discipline seemed to have a recognizable geographical center imposed a particular structure on its historiography (Danziger, 1991). American textbooks on the history of psychology could ignore virtually everything outside the United States and still claim, with some degree of plausibility, that they were presenting not a history of American psychology but a history of modern psychology as such. Other nationally based histories would have to accept the status of merely local histories.

Moreover, the scheme of center and periphery was metaphorically applied to the internal structure of the discipline. Certain areas of the discipline, usually involving particular methodological commitments, were designated as "basic" or "core" areas and others as areas of "application." In the core areas experimental research was to discover universal principles of psychological functioning, while in the peripheral areas less rigorous procedures might suffice to study local manifestations of these principles. The basic principles were always conceived of as asocial and ahistorical, and their investigation was typically pursued in a decontextualized manner. Examples of such principles are the so-called laws of learning or the principles of cognition. There is supposed to be nothing intrinsically social about these laws and principles; they are thought to apply to individual organisms and individual minds, irrespective of the social content of either learning or cognition. It is assumed at the outset that the laws of learning and the principles of cognition are the same everywhere and at all times. They have the same kind of universality as the laws and principles of chemistry. However, just as in chemistry, local conditions can affect the results of their operation. In psychology, these local conditions are generally social in nature.

So we get a dualistic model: on the one hand, basic processes that are regarded as inherent features of individual organisms and individual minds; on the other hand, local social conditions that affect the specific manifestations of these processes. The core of psychological science is constituted by the investigation of universally valid basic processes; the study of human psychology in social and historical context, however, is regarded as peripheral to this core endeavour, less important because its results are not universally generalizable.

There was always a very marked parallelism between core and periphery on the level of geography and on the level of disciplinary content. Those at the geographical periphery usually did not have the resources to mount major investigations of basic processes. That kind of thing generally remained the prerogative of those at the geographical center. Those at the geographical periphery typically had to content themselves with being at the scientific periphery as well. If they claimed universal validity for their findings, they could expect these claims to be ignored. But more often they did not make such claims; accepting the leadership of a far away center, they accorded their own work a purely peripheral significance in terms of the discipline as a whole. They would take over the conceptual categories and the methodological imperatives of the center and try their best to apply them under local conditions that differed profoundly from those that prevailed at the center. They were subject to the limitations imposed by what has sometimes been called a "borrowed consciousness" (Easton, 1991).

Nowhere has this been more evident than in colonial, quasi-colonial, and postcolonial parts of the world. The export of modern psychological knowledge to these areas had begun on a small scale after World War I and occasionally even earlier. In the latter part of the century this export gradually gained momentum and also changed in content. The dominant position of American exports, already a fact of life in Western Europe, became even more marked in most of the rest of the world. A flood of graduate students from Asia, Latin America, and the British Commonwealth received their professional training in the United States and quite often returned to their home countries to teach and practice what they had learned in academic or nonacademic contexts. The prestigious journals of the discipline were published and edited in America, and ambitious overseas scholars would aim to publish there, while the reverse process was almost unheard of. Funds for research in developing countries dispensed by American agencies were frequently the only viable sources of research support in those countries. Because of this extreme asymmetry of resources, the standard of what constituted good scientific psychological research and practice continued to be provided by American exemplars. It was taken for granted that the conceptual categories and the research practices that had evolved historically within American psychology would provide access to those universally valid generalizations that were the goal of psychology as a natural science.

But this one-way transfer of psychological knowledge from a dominant center to a scattered periphery has not always gone smoothly. Localized doubts about the appropriateness of American notions of psychological science were often voiced, and in certain cases these doubts congealed into articulate attempts at opposition that sometimes took on the character of a movement. A relatively early example was provided by a movement in the 1960s and 1970s to differentiate a "European" from an "American" social psychology (Moscovici, 1972).

Later on, resistance to the forces of homogenization emerged with some intensity in several developing countries. The movement acquired a name, "indigenous psychology," which in this context does not mean the "folk psychology" of ordinary people but a self-conscious attempt to develop variants of modern professional psychology that are more attuned to conditions in developing nations than the psychology taught at Western academic institutions. The first stirrings of such a movement followed the period of decolonization after World War II, gradually achieving some global visibility within the discipline in the 1980s (Moghaddam, 1987; Kim and Berry, 1993; Sinha, 1997; Yang, 1997).

Although part of the program of modern indigenous psychology may involve a greater openness to local pre-modern traditions, both scholarly and folk, the movement of indigenization itself is unambiguously a phenomenon of modern psychology. A critique of current Western psychological doctrines and practices forms the starting point of proposed reforms, the advocates of the reforms have been trained and professionally certified by Western academic institutions, and most public discourse about indigenous psychology is conducted via regular professional channels (Allwood and Berry, in press). In some cases indigenization involves relatively superficial changes to received disciplinary practices. Hitherto unrecognized variables of personality and social psychology may be added to those investigated in the West, or research may be directed at previously neglected or overlooked problems and problem areas. But in other cases the changes entailed by indigenization are more profound, leading to a fundamental restructuring of psychological research methods (Smith, 1999) and to a replacement of traditional psychological categories and concepts by apparently incommensurable alternatives (Enriquez, 1987, 1993; Nsamenang, 1992, 1995).

Historical Echoes of Indigenization

From the more recent literature on indigenization, one gets the impression that this is rather a new phenomenon in the history of modern psychology. It is true that the identification and labeling of the phenomenon is new, and this indicates a degree of reflexivity that is characteristic of this most recent form of indigenization. But the process now described as "indigenization" is one that has been a feature of modern psychology from its earliest days. What became the universalistic science of psychology had its roots in distinctly local traditions of science and philosophy in nineteenth-century Europe. British evolutionary biology, French psychiatry, and German experimental physiology each gave rise to different ways of conceptualizing and investigating human subjectivity scientifically (Danziger, 1990), and the export of each of these forms was always accompanied by considerable modification of the original. This process had some elements in common with what is now referred to as indigenization, but when one turns from the circulation of psychological knowledge within Europe to the export of this knowledge to the United States one encounters indigenization on a massive scale.

Comparing the late-nineteenth and early-twentieth-century export of experimental psychology from Germany to the United States with the late-twentieth-century export of psychology from the United States to the ex-colonial world is instructive. In both cases the transfer of knowledge was unidirectional, from an academically more prestigious source to the periphery of the academic world. Also in both cases advanced students were the major carriers of this transfer. (Textbooks played some role in the earlier case but not as much as later, partly because of language problems and partly because textbook publishers had not yet become a significant economic force.) Then as now the flow of psychology students was part of a much broader flow that covered virtually all academic subjects. The University of Göttingen, for example, enrolled over a thousand American students between the end of the eighteenth and the beginning of the twentieth century (Sokal, 1981, p. 2)—an impressive total relative to student numbers in that period. There were published guides for the use of American students, who by the mid-nineteenth century had established a quasi-official colony with its own rules, regulations, and rituals (Sokal, 1981, p. 2). In psychology the flow of American students started almost as soon as Wilhelm Wundt had established the first designated experimental psychology laboratory at Leipzig University in 1879. Among the Wundt students who subsequently had a foundational role in the establishment of experimental psychology in the United States were James McKeen Cattell, Edward B. Titchener, Hugo Münsterberg, Frank Angell, Walter Dill Scott, Edward W. Scripture, and Lightner Wittmer (Tinker, 1980). These all completed doctorates at Leipzig, but there were many, often somewhat older men, who spent time at Leipzig and elsewhere in Germany without bothering with the formality of a doctorate. Stanley Hall, William James, and James Mark Baldwin are well-known examples.

After these men returned to the United States, they founded laboratories modeled after Wundt's and filled with apparatus that was either imported from Germany or copied from German models. Inspired by the journal that Wundt had begun to publish in 1880, *The American Journal of Psychology* made its appearance in 1887, followed by others a few years later. In the pages of these journals there were reports on experimental investigations whose problems and methods were very similar to their German models. The number of psychological laboratories in the United States expanded very rapidly, and many of Wundt's students quickly began training the next generation of experimentalists who dominated the field in the early twentieth century.

But in spite of the massive early influence of German experimental psychology American psychology soon took a very different turn and developed along lines that were actually antithetical to the vision of scientific psychology that had motivated the work of men like Wundt (Rieber, 2001). By the 1920s many American psychologists had come to regard the kind of experimentalism that had been imported from Germany as a model of how not to do psychology, and soon the figure of Wundt, the once highly respected forefather, had come to represent the negative alternative for a discipline that was desperately trying to establish its scientific credentials in America. After a relatively brief period of academic colonialism American psychology had become well and truly indigenized.

It is only to be expected that when a science is transplanted from one part of the world to another there will be some shift of priorities, some change in the topics that receive the most attention, some adaptive modification of the techniques considered most appropriate. Some would consider even this to constitute indigenization. But I doubt that we need a special category to describe such everyday events that raise no fundamental issues for the historiography of science. However, the transformation of the discipline of psychology in the course of its trans-Atlantic migration does seem to raise such issues. In the first place, this was a transformation that changed the very object which the science was set up to investigate.

Experimental psychology had been invented in Germany as a systematic investigation of individual consciousness with the help of standard pieces of physical apparatus. Soon different views emerged regarding the most appropriate categories for conceptualizing the life of individual consciousness, but throughout all these debates there was tacit agreement on the object to be investigated, which remained the individual conscious mind. Consequently, there was also basic agreement that the data of experimental psychology had to be based on self-report, though this did not exclude arguments about the boundaries of what constituted scientifically admissible self-report.

Neither the original scientific object of modern psychology nor its preferred method of data gathering long survived the transatlantic migration. Certainly, there were valiant attempts to reproduce something like the German psychology of consciousness in the early American laboratories. But this is not what provided the fuel for the rocket-like advance of the new science in America. That depended on the opening up of altogether different fields for the play of psychological expertise, fields like child study, education, clinical psychology, ergonomics, personnel selection, and more generally, the scientific study of individual differences. Interestingly, some of these fields were pioneered by the very people who had set off to sit at the feet of the German masters a few years earlier. And it was not long before some of the most prominent figures in American psychology began to raise doubts, not only about the value of defining the primary object investigated by psychology in terms of consciousness but also about the value of data gathering based on self-report (Cattell, 1904; James, 1904). Shortly before World War I this gradual process of indigenization had given rise to the more radical form of a movement, a movement which called itself "behaviorism."

The discipline of psychology that emerged from this movement was based on a negation of most of the features that had defined the discipline in its earlier Central European incarnation. Overt behavior replaced the inner consciousness as the primary object of psychological investigation; psychology became "the psychology of the other one," as one early behaviorist put it (Meyer, 1921), and "responses" whose form and meaning were determined by the investigator, not the subject, became the sole source of legitimate psychological data.

Closely related to these changes were changes in the knowledge interests of the discipline. In its first incarnation experimental psychology had been intended as a way of shedding light on epistemological questions by empirical means: the a priori nature of space perception, for example, or the translation of physical energy into sensory experience. Wundt, its most prominent figure, was a prolific contributor to the philosophical literature of his day and made no secret of his strong opposition to the idea of psychology as a practical rather than a philosophical science (Wundt, 1909). Yet, with only one or two exceptions, his American students showed no sign of sharing his philosophical interests and proceeded to engage themselves in various practical projects once they had established themselves back home. Cattell, who had actually become Wundt's official assistant during his stay in Germany, soon became a purveyor of instruments for measuring individual differences to which he gave the name by which they have been known ever since, "mental tests." Many of Wundt's other American students drifted into practical applications of psychology that were not exactly what he had had in mind for the new science. Witmer founded the first psychological clinic; Judd went into educational psychology; Scripture studied speech disorders, and so on.

This is not to say that similar tendencies did not exist among some of Wundt's German students. Ernst Meumann, for example, another of his assistants, ended up as an educational psychologist with a strong practical orientation and duly earned his mentor's disapproval. But the spread of applied psychology encountered many obstacles in Germany and only succeeded under the Nazis in the specific area of military psychology (Geuter, 1992). As late as 1929 the German Psychological Society published a protest against the tendency to reduce the number of academic positions in psychology in favor of philosophy. But it defended psychology in terms of its philosophical, not its practical, value: "The reciprocal influence between psychology and philosophy has become steadily stronger, especially in relation to phenomenology, epistemology, and the theory of values" (Bühler et al., 1930). By then, there was little overlap between the content of the discipline of psychology in Germany and the United States.

Toward a Polycentric History

By the end of World War II, the world system of a seriously fractionated discipline had collapsed, to be replaced by a system in which there were still local differences but in which one local variant constituted the unchallengeable center of the discipline. Everything else constituted a kind of periphery, as described in the second section of this chapter. That state of affairs provided a convincing legitimation for a historiography of modern psychology that focused on the history of American psychology and treated everything else in terms of its relationship to this central narrative.

The history of modern psychology seems to be marked by recurring tensions between the discipline's claims to the universality of its knowledge and the sometimes profound differences between the kinds of knowledge produced at different local sites. Insofar as psychology is regarded as delivering knowledge about the universal nature of human individuals, the places where this knowledge is gathered can have no intrinsic significance for the knowledge itself. However, insofar as psychology is regarded as a social project producing locally grounded knowledge, the characteristics of the sites for the production of that knowledge become quite important. Locally grounded knowledge is likely to vary in kind where the differences among sites of knowledge production are profound. But if such differences are regarded as irrelevant to the universal nature of psychological knowledge, which is everywhere the same, then it becomes very easy to identify one socially limited kind of knowledge with what is truly universal.

If this error is to be avoided, then the sites at which psychological knowledge is produced must be taken much more seriously, not simply as geographical locations but as sites of cultural and socioeconomic diversity. But recognition of the relationship between the results of psychological knowledge production and the local context for that production represents only a first step. If we go no further, we end up with a multiplicity of local histories that are usually of no more than parochial interest. Such romanticizing of the local only constitutes one side of the coin; universalist triumphalism represents the other side. Both need to be replaced by a focus on the interlinking of local influences, the changing interrelationships among centers, that have constituted the world history of the subject in the modern period. The real challenge for the historian is to do justice to the fact that, from the beginning, modern psychology was dependent both on diverse local sites for its cultivation and on organized international exchange of psychological knowledge, practice, and scholarship.

International relationships have always played a prominent role in the shaping of modern psychology, a situation reflected by the historiography of psychology only insofar as it adopts a global perspective. But the tradition of presenting disciplinary history in terms of "contributions" to a singular subject has led to a neglect of the changing relationships between local centers for the scientific production of psychological knowledge. What such a "polycentric" history reveals is a world of contested psychological objects and practices, successful and unsuccessful impositions and resistances, selective adaptations, and an incorporation of local values to which universal validity is often attributed. The term "indigenization" provides a convenient label for this complex set of relationships.

Indigenization in the wake of the international transfer of psychological knowledge has happened throughout the history of modern psychology. It has led to significant changes in psychological concepts and theories, in the choice and the formulation of psychological problems, and in the methods applied to the solution of those problems. Sometimes it has had a spectacularly successful outcome, as in the German-American case, and sometimes the outcome has been uncertain, as is the case currently in many developing countries. A historiography that is adequate to the course of these events must necessarily adopt a viewpoint that is polycentric. It must work with categories that seek to capture the interrelations among centers, rather than the characteristics of centers considered in isolation. Intellectual migration is perhaps the most obvious of these categories, not only in reference to persons, but, more significantly, in reference to concepts and practices. What happened to psychological concepts, theories, and procedures when attempts were made to transplant them? Why did some of these prove to be much better travelers than others? How did traveling change them, sometimes beyond recognition? Who found them useful and why? There are stories of successful transfer to be told here, but also stories of misunderstanding, mistranslation, total incomprehension, and downright hostility that are often more illuminating.

In general, a polycentric understanding of the history of the discipline favors a contextualist historiography. As long as there was an equation of one locally generated truth with the truth as such, the question of the social roots of that truth was not likely to be asked. But with the end of privilege, both on the geographical and the conceptual level, the intelligibility of alternative accounts rests on seeing them in terms of their social context. For a polycentric historiography the question of how to characterize social context therefore becomes crucial. Historians with a background in psychology face a particular danger here, because of the discipline's long-established tendency either to ignore the social context of human action altogether or, more recently, to represent it in terms of poorly analyzed and often misapplied categories, such as "culture" and "ecology." There is a certain irony in psychology's awakening to the importance of cultural differences just as traditional cultural differences are being eroded at an unprecedented rate and cultural hybridization and interpenetration has become the norm (Hermans and Kempen, 1998). I accept that references to cultural differences can have a useful role as a kind of shorthand for complex factors whose full analysis requires separate treatment, the reification of cultures in terms of geographically based and essentialist entities no longer has a place in serious social science (Kuper, 1999).

The tendency to conceptualize social context solely in terms of "culture" almost invariably goes hand in hand with a tendency to overlook the importance of power relationships. This may be acceptable within mainstream psychology, but it does not provide a good basis for historical work, especially in an international context. It is understandable that an interpretation of international relations in terms of cultural differences rather than inequalities of power and resources should appeal to those at the privileged center (both geographically and intellectually). But an adequate historical account would also have to reflect the voices from the periphery that interpret many aspects of the asymmetrical transfer of psychological knowledge in terms of "cultural imperialism" or "intellectual colonialism" (Ho, 1988; Oommen, 1991), and who chafe under the "exoticizing" of non-Western psychologies and the "orientalism" that has long disfigured the representation of colonized and previously colonized people by Western social science (Misra, 1996; Bhatia, 2002).

Another dubious but powerful convention of the traditional historiography of psychology is its marked disciplinary focus. The history of modern psychology is commonly identified with the history of the discipline of psychology, where the boundaries of the discipline are defined by academic and professional organizational structures, not by the subject matter. Whether some topic is regarded as forming part of the history of modern psychology depends on its reception by academic departments and professional associations. But this, too, is subject to local and temporal variation. Common examples of topics with a variable status are psychoanalysis, graphology, parapsychology, and much of social psychology. However, instead of being taken for granted, organizationally and administratively enforced boundaries become a major focus of inquiry for a polycentric historiography. The locally variable reasons for the erection of such boundaries and their historical effects constitute important features of variant developments in different parts of the world. Clearly, when the historical construction of disciplinary boundaries becomes an object of inquiry, the perspective of a purely intradisciplinary history has to be abandoned (Staeuble, 2004).

A polycentric historiography of psychology would have to explore the historical dependence of the categories and procedures of scientific psychology on culturally embedded beliefs and on local forms of institutionalized practice (Danziger, 1997). This is likely to reinforce existing trends in the direction of a less autocratic, more self-reflective, form of disciplinary practice. But localization is only one side of the historical process. The other side involves the interaction of centers and the consequent emergence of common understandings, as well as renewed differentiation. In the past, certain locally generated categories of psychological discourse were often regarded as the only true descriptions of the universal attributes of a timeless "human nature." Insofar as they were built into the ahistorical methodology of so-called cross-cultural psychology they were immune to empirical refutation. A different approach to the history of psychology, however, offers the possibility of another perspective on the question of the universality of psychological phenomena. Instead of taking such universality for granted, one could treat it as one possible outcome of specific historical conditions that are open to investigation. "Trans-social meanings emerge not as a result of methodological tricks, but of a real historical process" (Stompka, 1990, p. 52).

The turn away from a unifocal linear history to a socially contextualized polycentric history is not a matter of merely antiquarian interest. It entails an enhanced link between historical reflection and current practice that is likely to reduce the high level of ethnocentrism that disfigures so much of what passes for core psychology. By encouraging a genuine historicizing of psychological knowledge it would open up the categories and practices of the discipline to hitherto unthinkable possibilities (Shweder, 2000). Who knows, one day we might even end up with a history of modern psychology that actually contributes to the further development of psychological knowledge.

REFERENCES

Allwood, C. M. and Berry, J. W. (in press). Origins and development of indigenous psychologies: An international analysis. *International Journal of Psychology.*

Bhatia, S. (2002). Orientalism in Euro-American and Indian psychology: Historical representations of "natives" in colonial and postcolonial contexts. *History of Psychology,* 5, 376–398.

Boring, E. G. (1950). *A history of experimental psychology* (2nd ed.). New York: Appleton-Century-Crofts.

Bühler, K. et al. (1930). Kundgebung der deutschen Gesellschaft für Psychologie

[Proceedings of the German Society of Psychology]. In H. Volkelt (Ed.), *Bericht über der XI. Kongress für experimentelle Psychologie in Wien 1929* [Report on the 22th Congress of Experimental Psychology in Vienna 1929] (pp. vii–x). Jena: Fischer.

Cattell, J. McK. (1904). The conceptions and methods of psychology. *Popular Science Monthly, 66*, 176–186.

Danziger, K. (1990). *Constructing the subject: Historical origins of psychological research*. New York: Cambridge University Press.

Danziger, K. (1991). Introduction: Special issue on new developments in the history of psychology. *History of the Human Sciences, 4*, 327–333.

Danziger, K. (1997). *Naming the mind: How psychology found its language*. London: Sage.

Easton, D. (1991). The division, integration and transfer of knowledge. In D. Easton and C. S. Schelling (Eds.), *Divided knowledge: Across disciplines, across cultures* (pp. 7–36). Newbury Park, CA: Sage.

Enriquez, V. G. (1987). Decolonizing the Filipino psyche: Impetus for the development of psychology in the Philippines. In G. H. Blowers and A. Turtle (Eds.), *Psychology moving East* (pp. 365–287). Boulder, CO: Westview.

Enriquez, V. G. (1993). Developing a Filipino psychology. In U. Kim and J. W. Berry (Eds.), *Indigenous psychologies: Research and experience in cultural context* (pp. 152–169). Newbury Park, CA: Sage.

Geuter, U. (1992). *The professionalization of psychology in Nazi Germany*. New York: Cambridge University Press.

Hermans, J. M., and Kempen, H. J. G. (1998). Moving cultures: The perilous problems of cultural dichotomies in a globalizing society. *American Psychologist, 53*, 1111–1120.

Ho, D. Y. F. (1988). Asian psychology: A dialogue on indigenization and beyond. In A. C. Paranjpe, D. Y. F. Ho and R. W. Rieber (Eds.), *Asian contributions to psychology* (pp. 53–77). New York: Praeger.

James. W. (1904). Does consciousness exist? *Journal of Philosophy, 1*, 497–491.

Kim, U., and Berry, J. W. (1993). *Indigenous psychologies: Research and experience in cultural context*. Newbury Park: Sage.

Kuper, A. (1999). *Culture: The anthropologists' account*. Cambridge, Mass.: Harvard University Press.

Meyer, M. F. (1921). *Psychology of the other-one: An introductory text-book of psychology*. Columbia, Mo.: Missouri Book Co.

Misra, G. (1996). Toward indigenous Indian psychology. *American Psychologist, 51*, 497–499.

Moghaddam, F. M. (1987). Psychology in the Three Worlds: As reflected by the crisis in social psychology and the move toward indigenous third-world psychology. *American Psychologist, 42*, 912–920.

Moscovici, S. (1972). Society and theory in social psychology. In J. Israel and H.

Tajfel (Eds.), *The context of social psychology: A critical assessment* (pp. 17–68). London: Academic Press.

Nsamenang, A. B. (1992). *Human development in cultural context: A third world perspective.* Newbury Park, CA: Sage.

Nsamenang, A. B. (1995). Factors influencing the development of psychology in sub-Saharan Africa. *International Journal of Psychology,* 30, 729–739.

O'Donnell, J. M. (1979). The crisis of experimentation in the 1920's: E. G. Boring and his uses of history. *American Psychologist,* 34, 289–295.

Oommen, T. K. (1991). Internationalization of sociology: A view from developing countries. *Current Sociology,* 39, 67–84.

Rieber, R.W. (2001). Wundt and the Americans: From flirtation to abandonment. In R. W. Rieber and D. K. Robinson (Eds.), *Wilhelm Wundt in history* (pp. 145–160). New York: Kluwer Academic.

Shweder, R. A. (2000). The psychology of practice and the practice of the three psychologies. *Asian Journal of Social Psychology,* 3, 207–222.

Sinha, D. (1997). Indigenizing psychology. In J. W. Berry, H. Poortinga, and J. Panday (Eds.), *Handbook of cross-cultural psychology,* vol. 1 (pp. 129–170). Boston: Allyn and Bacon.

Smith, L. T. (1999). *Decolonizing methodologies: Research and indigenous peoples.* London: Zed Books.

Smith, R. (1988). Does the history of psychology have a subject? *History of the Human Sciences,* 1, 147–177.

Sokal, M. M. (1981). *An education in psychology: James McKeen Cattell's letters from Germany and England, 1880–1888.* Cambridge, MA: MIT Press.

Staeuble, I. (2004). De-centering Western perspectives: Psychology and the disciplinary order in the first and third world. In A. C. Brock, J. Louw, and W. van Hoorn (Eds.), *Rediscovering the history of psychology: Essays inspired by the work of Kurt Danziger* (pp. 183–205). New York: Kluwer.

Stompka, P. (1990). Conceptual frameworks in comparative inquiry: Divergent or convergent? In M. Albrow and E. King (Eds.), *Globalization, knowledge and society* (pp. 47–58). London: Sage.

Tinker, M. A. (1980). Wundt's doctorate students and their theses. In W. G. Bringmann and R. D. Tweney (Eds.), *Wundt studies* (pp. 269–279). Toronto: Hogrefe.

Wundt, W. (1909). Über reine und angewandte Psychologie [On pure and applied psychology]. *Psychologische Studien,* 5, 1–47.

Yang, K-S. (1997). Indigenizing Westernized Chinese psychology. In M. H. Bond (Ed.), *Working at the interface of cultures: Eighteen lives in social science* (pp. 62–76). London: Routledge.

Postscript

Adrian C. Brock

In the introduction to this book, I suggested that it would be misguided to justify an international history of psychology in terms of "inclusion," however well-meaning the intentions might be. No one can hope to cover everything that has ever happened in the history of psychology at all times and in all places. Selection will inevitably occur. My quarrel is not with selection itself but with the kind of selections that have been made.

In a well-known article on the future of the history of psychology, Kurt Danziger wrote:

> Psychologists in East and South Asia, in Africa and Latin America, are raising questions about their own traditions and their relationship to the theory and practice of psychology. . . . The more they do this, the more dissatisfied they become with the parochialism of a historiography of psychology anchored in North American and European perspectives. (1994, p. 477)

What is particularly interesting here is not that such a development has occurred but what the consequences of this development might be:

> This leads to questions that are alien to traditional histories of the discipline, including questions about psychology and cultural imperialism, for example, or the link between psychology and the historical project of modernism. . . . These developments have also led to the emergence of new concepts that that are of great interest to the disciplinary historian. The concept of "indigenization," for example, refers to the process by which imported psychological notions and practices become assimilated and changed by the local context. (p. 477)

The important point is that this development can enrich the field. It enables us to see aspects of psychology that the traditional focus on Western Europe and North America has led us to overlook. We can gain a better understanding of psychology as a result and apply this new understanding to more familiar issues and debates.

Cultural Imperialism

This is not a topic that is traditionally discussed in work on the history of psychology, but it can hardly be avoided in an international account of the field. As noted in the introduction, there have been some major changes in the relationship between European and American psychology over the years. There is an interesting story of how European social psychologists issued what amounted to a "declaration of independence" from American social psychology in the early 1970s. They argued that American social psychology was not just American in the sense that it was produced in the United States. It was also a reflection of American values and concerns. Europeans, therefore, needed to develop their own approach (Moghaddam, 1987). These changes should be seen in their historical context. The years after World War II were the height of American influence in psychology and this "declaration of independence" in the early 1970s represents a decline in that influence.

If we look outside Western Europe and North America, the situation becomes even more extreme. Some examples of cultural imperialism in this book include France with respect to Argentina (Taiana), Britain with respect to India (Paranjpe), the United States with respect to Turkey (Gulerce), and even Japan with respect to China (Blowers).[1] Countries outside Europe and North America have traditionally been "importers" of psychology. Although there are particular patterns of dependency, the biggest exporter of psychology has been, and continues to be, the United States.

There would be no problem here if the knowledge being imported was "culture free," but anyone who looks at the situation of psychology in many third world countries is unlikely to come to that conclusion. There is often a lack of "fit" between psychology and the local culture. This divergence can manifest itself in the kind of topics that are investigated. Many of the topics that are investigated by first world researchers are of little interest or relevance to psychologists in the third world. The problem may run deeper, however. The local population may not even think in psychological terms. Louw shows that this is the case in the more tradi-tional sectors of South African society. Blowers points out that Chinese did not even have a word for "psychology" when the discipline arrived and translated it as something like "heart-spirit-study." Also, anyone who is bilingual will be aware that the psychological concepts of each language are not exactly the same. This is true of European languages like German, Spanish, and French. The problem is even more extreme when one looks at Asian or African languages. Danziger (1997) mentions the difficulty of finding mutually intelligible themes for joint study by himself and a repre-sentative of an indigenous psychology in Indonesia. In this situation, it is easy to see how alien Western psychology is.

Modernity

Just to complicate the situation even further, many third world societies have a modern, Westernized sector where psychology can be found and a traditional sector where there is little or no psychology in the Western sense of the term. Most, if not all, cultures have views on what it is to be human but in traditional societies, the authority for these views is likely to be found in religion rather than science. This point applies not just to beliefs but to practices as well. Thus several countries have "indigenous healers" who have a similar role to psychologists in the modern sector. In some countries, there have been clashes between the two.

Moghaddam and Lee discuss this situation in some detail, but it is also mentioned by Louw with respect to South Africa and by Gulerce with respect to Turkey. Psychologists always belong to the modern sector. That goes with the territory. All of the contributors to this book, regardless of where they come from, received part of their education in Western Europe or North America.

Sometimes countries will embark on a modernization program, and psychology will suddenly appear. The situation after the revolution in Cuba is a case in point. In fact, we do not need to go outside Western Europe to see that. Psychology came to Ireland around the same time as it came to Cuba. The first psychology department in the country was estab-lished at Trinity College in 1964. My own department was established in 1967. The reason for this late arrival of psychology is that Ireland was a very traditional country up to that point. Agriculture formed the back-bone of its economy, and the church wielded enormous power. In 1958, a new government embarked on an extensive program of modernization and lo and behold: psychology appeared.

This link between psychology and modernity explains why most of the significant developments in the early history of psychology occurred in Britain, France, and Germany and not, for example, Spain, Italy, or Greece. Britain, France, and Germany became modern societies at an early stage and so it is not as easy to see this link as it is when countries suddenly adopt a program of modernization or in places where modern and traditional sectors exist side by side. Presumably, the exorcists who were in great demand in seventeenth-century Europe performed a similar role to that of the "indigenous healers" of today.

Indigenization and Universalism

A common response to the lack of "fit" between psychology and the surrounding society in many countries has been to call for the indigenization of psychology. Indigenization refers to the process by which psychological knowledge and practices are assimilated into a new society.

Indigenization is one of the most important issues in the field of international psychology. However, apart from one or two exceptions, historians of psychology have been notable from the debates mainly by their absence. This is unfortunate because the debates themselves often lack a historical perspective. This point is made by Louw when he criticizes attempts to describe Western psychology as "Eurocentric" or "Westocentric." Cultures are in a constant state of change. What is alien to a culture today may not be alien tomorrow, especially if cultural imperialism continues to do its work.

The "received view" in American psychology is that psychology is a universal science which is, or ought to be, the same all over the world. When one of the contributors to this volume, Moghaddam (1987), published an article in the *American Psychologist* in which he outlined the moves toward indigenization in Europe and the third world, the response was almost predictable. It was immediately followed by a "Comment" by Matarazzo (1987) titled, "There is only one psychology, no specialities but many applications." Two years later, the same view was being expressed in another "Comment" by Kunkel (1989) titled, "How many psychologies are there?"

Presumably, the "one" psychology that these authors endorse happens to be the same psychology that currently exists in the United States. Let us imagine for one moment that these authors are wrong and that the psychology that they endorse happens to be a distinctively "American" approach to the subject. It would then become an ethnocentric view that could unwittingly promote cultural imperialism around the world. Many American psychologists might be surprised to learn that this is how many of their counterparts in Europe and the third world view the situation.

The back issues of the *American Psychologist* contain several examples of foreign psychologists claiming that American psychology is peculiarly "American" and not a universal science. Thus in an article titled "American Psychology," one German psychologist wrote: "American psychology can be said to be truly American" (Brandt, 1970, p. 1003). A few years later a Chilean psychologist wrote of his experience under the Allende government: "A problem that was specific to psychologists . . . was the cultural homogeneity of their training or, to put it more bluntly, the unanalyzed 'Americanness' of their science. Much of the theoretical background and the totality of their professional creed were not only culturally derivative but also culturally dependent" (Zuñiga, 1975, p. 105).

Why is it that foreign psychologists can see this dimension of American psychology when American psychologists cannot? The answer lies not in some kind of anti-American conspiracy but in the "taken-for-granted" aspects of culture. If we are raised in a particular culture, it is shared by all the people around us and appears "normal" and "natural." This is especially true if we continue to live in that culture and, more importantly, if we have never experienced anything else. It is only when we go outside that culture and look at cultures that are different from our own, that we can see that it is specific to a particular place. Pointing this out has been a feature of anthropology over the years.[2]

There is, of course, nothing unique about Americans in this regard, though the general lack of knowledge of other countries and cultures that was discussed in the introduction plays a contributing role. American psychology is singled out for discussion only because of its size and its influence around the world. No other country "exports" its psychology to the same degree.

History can also help to shed some light on this situation. In this volume, Danziger points out that the psychology that appeared in the United States at the end of the nineteenth century was not the psychology that existed in Europe at the time. It was modified to suit the local conditions. For example, Wundt was totally opposed to the idea that psychology should be an "applied" science, claiming that psychology needed to be more advanced before its findings could be applied (Wundt, 1909). This view was unlikely to find much support in the United States. American psychologists had to rely on private funding to a greater degree than their counterparts in Europe and could not afford the luxury of a psychology without any practical relevance.

This move toward practical application affected not just the kind of topics that were investigated but also the theoretical basis of the subject. In a famous part of his "behaviorist manifesto," John B. Watson (1913) wrote: "If psychology would follow the plan I suggest, the educator, the physician, the jurist and the business man could utilize our data in a practical way. . . . One of the earliest conditions which made me dissatisfied with psychology was the feeling that there was no realm of application for the principles that were being worked out in content terms" (p. 168). Thus Watson was offering his colleagues an approach to psychology that was more likely to result in private funding and support. Danziger provides other examples in his chapter, but the important point that he makes is that American psychologists were the original pioneers in the indigenization of psychology, even if their modern descendents are no longer aware of that fact.

It is this peculiarly "American" aspect of American psychology that led to the situation in the 1930s where, unlike their counterparts in mathematics and the natural sciences, the German psychologists who emigrated to the United States encountered a psychology that was very different from their own. This situation is amusingly described in a well-known article titled "The Gestalt Psychologists in Behaviorist America" (Sokal, 1984).

The cultural specificity of psychology is there for all to see, and yet it has generally gone unnoticed. As Danziger points out, it has often been disguised under the notion of "schools." Thus if we take a typical "Theories of Personality" text, it can be seen that all the behaviorists were Americans with Anglo-Saxon names, all the psychoanalytic theorists had German-sounding names, and the hereditarian trait theorists were educated in London. In spite of this, their views on psychology are typically presented as decontextualized "theories" that have no relationship to a particular time or place.

Danziger provides us with a sophisticated account of this situation. He does not see local differences in psychology as something that is inevitable. These, too, have varied historically. For example, at a time when it was common for Americans to study in Europe or to travel to Europe to find out what European psychologists were doing, there were relatively few differences between psychology in Europe and in North America. However, as contact between psychologists on the two continents became less frequent in the years leading up to World War II, their psychologies began to diverge. Similarly, it seems reasonable to suppose that more international contact in the future will lead to a lessening of the differences. However, it is not always clear if this lessening of difference is the product of a genuine universalism or of cultural imperialism.

This point is made by Moghaddam and Lee with their concept of "double reification." I am not sure that I like the choice of terminology, but the idea behind it is an interesting one. We have already seen how there is often a lack of "fit" between imported Western psychology in a particular country and the society around it. It has also been noted that psychology tends to exist in the more modern, Westernized sectors of society. It can even exist in a kind of "colonial enclave," as Blowers (1987) once portrayed English-language psychology in Hong Kong.

Moghaddam and Lee warn against seeing the psychology in these countries as evidence that psychology is universal. As one recent guide to globalization puts it:

> Whether you walk the streets of Nairobi, Beijing or Buenos Aires, globalization has introduced a level of commercial culture which is eerily homogenous. The glittering, air-conditioned shopping malls are interchangeable; the fast food restaurants sell the same high carbohydrate foods with minor concessions to local tastes. Young people drink the same soft drinks, smoke the same cigarettes, wear identical branded clothing and shoes, play the same computer games, watch the same Hollywood films and listen to the same Western pop music. (Ellwood, 2001, p. 53)

It would therefore be unsurprising if these young people were to study the same kind of psychology as well. This does not mean, however, that this psychology is any more "universal" than the baseball caps that they wear.

Of all the authors in this book, Ardila is probably the most universalist. He takes issue with the view that behavior analysis and therapy are "American" approaches to psychology and points to their existence in several countries around the world. What is particularly interesting about his account is the particular countries to which they have been successfully exported. These countries include Latin America, an area that the United

States has traditionally regarded as part of its sphere of influence. They also include English-speaking countries like the United Kingdom, South Africa, and Australia, whose shared language and related cultures make them more amenable to American ideas.

In contrast, these approaches were rejected by the members of the former Soviet bloc on ideological grounds, and the French can always be relied on to put a spanner in the works where American culture is concerned. The French language and culture were once major forces in the world, and to some extent still are, but many French people have never got over the fact that the English language and American culture have taken their place.

Although Ardila sees these countries as "problem cases" where behavior analysis and behavior therapy have been misunderstood, their rejection can also be explained in social and cultural terms. It might be useful to think about whether an approach to psychology would have been adopted so widely if it had been developed in Turkey, India, or Brazil. These countries, unlike the United States, have not spread their culture around the world.

All of the authors address the topic of indigenization to varying degrees. Even Taiana's notion of a "cultural filter" has much in common with these ideas. I believe that the topics of indigenization and universalism would be one of the main issues of a genuinely international history of psychology. With the exception of the authors in this book, such issues are rarely discussed. This is unfortunate since they can help us see psychology in a different light.

These issues have much in common with what historians of psychology call a "contextualist" approach. It has become common in recent years to explain why a particular type of psychology emerged in a particular place at a particular time with reference to the social context. It is, for example, easy to see why "crowd psychology" emerged in France at the end of the nineteenth century (Ginekken, 1992) or why "race psychology" emerged in Germany during the Nazi period (Geuter, 1992). Studies of indigenization or the lack thereof can provide us with a more sophisticated approach to contextualism. Sometimes an approach to psychology will be related to the social context; sometimes it can be better explained by reference to the social context elsewhere. This is particularly true of colonial and quasi-colonial situations. These provide a social context of a kind, but it has to be qualified in important ways.

Disciplinarity

The issue of disciplinarity is discussed mainly by Staeuble in this book, but I believe it warrants a section on its own. Staeuble takes issue with the third world psychologists who have called for the indigenization of the field, arguing that the spread of "psychology" around the world is itself a form of cultural imperialism. It may be worth a reminder of the point that Blowers made about the Chinese not having an equivalent word. This is likely to have been the case in other languages as well.

Staeuble takes issue with what she calls a "diffusionist" approach to the history of psychology. We have now thankfully passed the point where it is acceptable to say that Columbus "discovered" the Americas. We are prepared to acknowledge that the millions of Native Americans who were already living there discovered them first. It is also no longer acceptable to say that these Native Americans were without civilization until Europeans arrived. If anything, the European conquistadores helped destroy the civilizations that were already there.

Why should we view the expansion of psychology around the world as any different? It is not expanding into a cultural vacuum but to places that already have cultural views of their own. In order for psychology to expand to these places, the traditional views must disappear. We might regard these views as "unscientific," but this is suspiciously like the terms "primitive" and "savages" that the colonizers used. In both cases, the Western view is seen as inherently superior to the local view.

According to Staeuble, what are variously called the behavioral, social, or human sciences—psychology, sociology, economics, political science, and so on—are not "natural kinds"; that is, they do not correspond to pre-existing divisions within nature but are social conventions that are tied to a particular time and place. It should not be forgotten that these subjects are historically recent even in Western civilization. Thus it is not easy to categorize the work of seventeenth-century figures like Thomas Hobbes and John Locke. They wrote on topics that would now be regarded as physics, political theory, psychology, education, philosophy, and much more.

To someone who sees individual human beings as embedded in society, culture, and history, it makes no sense to study the "abstract individual" apart from these things. There is evidence to suggest that even this idea arose in Western civilization at a particular time and is by no means something that all cultures share (e.g., Macpherson, 1962). Staeuble quotes a prominent Indian psychologist, Durganand Sinha, as saying that his colleagues find "it difficult to cast off the microscopic and individualist orientation acquired in the West."

Staeuble's views are very different from those of Sinha and other third world psychologists who have argued for a more indigenous approach. In an interesting sideswipe at the literature on "indigenous psychologies" (Heelas and Lock, 1981), Staeuble argues that the very notion of an indigenous psychology bears the mark of what she calls "countercolonial discourse." This is discourse in opposition to the colonizer but expressed in the colonizer's terms. There is no reason to suppose that all cultures have "psychology" or anything remotely like it.

Staeuble's arguments have practical consequences. She suggests that the current division of labor in the behavioral/social/human sciences may be inappropriate for the third world not only on cultural grounds but also on practical grounds. It is expensive to replicate the entire range of these sciences with their own university departments, conferences, textbooks, journals, and the like. This is particularly true of societies where only a handful of each type of specialist exists. In this situation, it would make much more sense to adopt an interdisciplinary approach.

I do not expect that all psychologists will welcome these views, given that psychology is a part of their social identity and they have a vested interest in promoting its growth. However, I would recommend that all readers pay special attention to what I regard as one of the most interesting, original, and intellectually challenging chapters in the book.

Psychologization

Connected to the issue of disciplinarity is the topic of "psychologization" since it shows that psychological explanations are by no means universal. It might be appropriate to provide an explanation of this concept first.

In everyday situations, psychological explanations are given, but they are not the only kind of explanations that can be used. Some years ago when I was living in Canada, the government workers went on strike for better pay. One of the government's responses was to offer free counseling to the strikers so that they could deal with their "problems." Many of the strikers were horrified. They saw their problems as economic, not psychological. Indeed, more cynical observers might suggest that it was cheaper for the government to provide free counseling services than to give its workers the pay increase that they wanted.

These kind of issues rarely come to the fore in Western societies since we live in a highly psychologized culture. This is not the case in other parts of the world. Gulerce points out that the majority of the Turkish population do not think in psychological terms. This point is taken up in greater detail by Louw, who points out that people from the more traditional sectors of South African society who testified before the Truth and Reconciliation Commission tended to interpret their problems in physical or spiritual ways. It was the facilitators who encouraged them to interpret these problems in psychological ways, using labels like "trauma" that the people themselves did not use. As Louw points out, this situation is a reflection of the situation discussed earlier where in many third world countries, modern and traditional sectors exist side by side. Also, just as different countries have different levels of status and power, it is the modern sector that is the more influential of the two. It is usually the members of this sector who have most of the wealth and power. Thus the situation that Louw describes is a kind of "internal" colonization of the traditional sector by its modern counterpart.

Some readers may be wondering what all the fuss is about. Surely we all know what "trauma" is. In fact, the term itself is historically recent. Like many common psychological terms ("stress" is another example), it originally had a purely physical meaning. A trauma referred to a physical wound. During the nineteenth century, it was used metaphorically to refer to a "psychological wound." The metaphor has became so popular that its physical origins have largely been forgotten.

Post-Traumatic Stress Disorder (PTSD) is even more recent still. It appeared on the *Diagnostic and Statistical Manual of Mental Disorders* (known as the "Bible" of psychiatry) for the first time in 1980 and was linked to a political campaign in the 1970s to provide compensation for Vietnam War veterans (Hacking, 1995; Young, 1997; Leys, 2000). A similar process is under way with recent attempts to promote "Gulf War Syndrome."

"Psychologization" continues unabated in Western societies, but it is more difficult to recognize since these societies are already highly psychologized. It is much easier to see this phenomenon in traditional societies like the one that Louw describes where the people do not use psychological explanations at all. Blowers (1987) makes a similar point in relation to traditional Chinese society where people favor physical or spiritual explanations rather than psychological ones.

It is also very likely that a similar situation existed in Europe when what we now regard as "psychological disorders" had physical treatments, such as bloodletting, or spiritual treatments like exorcism. However, the shift to psychological explanation occurred a long time ago, though it was an essential prerequisite for the birth of psychology as we know it today. Work of the kind that Louw provides is invaluable in that it can show these changes occurring in contemporary situations.

"Of What Is History of Psychology a History?"

The title of this section, "Of what is history of psychology a history?" is taken from an article by Graham Richards (1987) on what the proper subject of history of psychology should be. This article was supplemented by further discussion from Roger Smith (1988) in an article titled "Does the History of Psychology Have a Subject?"

These authors were particularly concerned with the boundaries of the history of psychology. One of the standard texts of the 1960s and 1970s was Robert Watson's *The Great Psychologists from Aristotle to Freud* (Watson, 1963). To what extent can Aristotle be regarded as a "psychologist"? The point has already been made in the section on "disciplinarity" that such labels cannot even be applied to seventeenth-century figures like Hobbes and Locke, who certainly wrote on psychological topics in the broadest sense of the term but who can hardly be regarded as members of a discipline or a profession that did not exist. Applying such labels to distant historical figures may have the advantage of providing psychology with distinguished ancestors (and they do not come any more distinguished than Aristotle), but it seems to involve a "presentism" of the worst kind: that is, a projection of the views of the present onto the past. One of the advantages of studying the views of historical figures is that they are very different from our own. If we assume that their views were similar to ours, those differences will be missed.

Thus these authors suggest that the history of psychology should be concerned with the discipline and profession called "psychology" that emerged in Europe in the second half of the nineteenth century. This does not mean, however, that events prior to the second half of the nineteenth century can be ignored. Many philosophers and scientists from earlier periods had a profound influence on the course that psychology took, and so their work must be studied as well. The important point, however, is that their work should always be studied in relation to the discipline and profession called "psychology" that emerged in Europe in the second half of the nineteenth century. In a sense, it forms part of the "pre-history" of psychology rather than the history of psychology itself.

I read these works soon after they appeared and was broadly in agreement with them. It was only after reading some of the work on the history of psychology in the third world that I became aware of the fact that some third world psychologists would regard these views as "Eurocentric." Typical of this view would be Paranjpe who goes into great detail about "psychology" in India before scientific or modern psychology was introduced under British colonial rule. I put the word in quotation marks because there is some dispute as to whether it can be called "psychology" at all. If we are reluctant to call Aristotle a "psychologist," then surely we should do the same with Buddha, Confucius, and the authors of the Upanishads.

Paranjpe, of course, is an advocate of a more indigenous psychology in India, and his attempt to incorporate ancient Sanskrit texts into the history of psychology is a part of that broader aim. He also points out that, under British colonialism, Western views were always seen as superior to Indian views. From his point of view, the arguments of Richards and Smith would lead to a focus on Western psychology, with his own culture being ignored. Moreover, if Indian psychology begins to adopt indigenous practices, such as Yoga, then these will become a part of the history—or at least the pre-history—of psychology as well.

To this already complicated situation, we must add the ideas of Staeuble, who suggests that such views bear the mark of "countercolonial discourse"—that is, anticolonialism expressed in the colonizer's terms. However, this view raises the issue of what the alternative might be and whether it would have any practical value in the real world.

I do not pretend to know all the answers to these questions. Words are socially defined, and much depends on the labels that people apply to the things that they encounter in their lives. There is scope for disagreement on such matters, especially when different social agendas are involved. My point is simply that an international history of psychology cannot just help bring new issues to the fore. It can reinvigorate old debates.

Final Word

I could not hope to discuss every aspect of every chapter here. That would require a separate book, and it would not be a particularly interesting book. Instead, I have focused on issues that I find interesting, knowing full well that a different commentator might have chosen other themes. I also do not agree with all of the views of the authors, and I would not expect them to agree with mine. That is all part of the fractiousness of academic life. In spite of this, we are all united in the belief that internationalizing the history of psychology would be a worthwhile thing to do. In our increasingly globalized world, parochialism is no longer a serious choice.

NOTES

1. It would be tiresome to include the words, "this volume" every time an author's work is discussed. If no specific reference for an author is given, the reference is to the relevant chapter in this book.

2. See also my discussion of this subject in the introduction.

REFERENCES

Blowers, G. H. (1987). To know the heart: Psychology in Hong Kong. In G. H. Blowers and A. M. Turtle (Eds.), *Psychology moving East: The status of Western psychology in Asia and Oceania* (pp. 139–161). Sydney: Sydney University Press.

Brandt, L. W. (1970). American psychology. *American Psychologist, 25*, 1091–1093.

Danziger, K. (1994). Does the history of psychology have a future? *Theory and Psychology, 4*, 467–484.

Danziger, K. (1997). *Naming the mind: How psychology found its language.* London: Sage.

Ellwood, W. (2001). *The non-nonsense guide to globalization.* Oxford: New Internationalist.

Geuter, U. (1992). *The professionalization of psychology in Nazi Germany.* New York: Cambridge University Press.

Ginneken, J. van (1992). *Crowds, psychology and politics, 1871–1899.* New York: Cambridge University Press.

Hacking, I. (1995). *Rewriting the soul: Multiple personality and the sciences of memory.* Princeton, NJ: Princeton University Press.

Heelas, P., and Lock, A. (Eds.) (1981). *Indigenous psychologies.* London: Academic Press.

Kunkel, J. H. (1989). How many psychologies are there? *American Psychologist, 44*, 573–574.

Leys, R. (2000). *Trauma: A genealogy.* Chicago: University of Chicago Press.

Macpherson, C. B. (1962). *The political theory of possessive individualism: Hobbes to Locke.* Oxford: Oxford University Press.

Matarazzo, J. D. (1987). There is only one psychology, no specialities but many applications. *American Psychologist,* 42, 893–903.

Moghaddam, F. H. (1987). Psychology in the three worlds: As reflected by the crisis in social psychology and the move toward indigenous Third World psychology. *American Psychologist,* 42, 893–903.

Richards, G. (1987). Of what is history of psychology a history? *British Journal for the History of Science,* 20, 201–211.

Smith, R. (1988). Does the history of psychology have a subject? *History of the Human Sciences,* 1, 147–177.

Sokal, M. (1984). The Gestalt psychologists in behaviorist America. *American Historical Review,* 89, 1240–1262.

Watson, J. B. (1913). Psychology as the behaviorist views it. *Psychological Review,* 20, 158–177.

Watson, R. I. (1963). *The great psychologists from Aristotle to Freud.* Philadelphia: Lippincott.

Wundt, W. (1909). Über reine und angewandte Psychologie [On pure and applied psychology]. *Psychologische Studien,* 5, 1–47.

Young, A. (1997). *The harmony of illusions: Inventing post-traumatic stress disorder.* Princeton, NJ: Princeton University Press.

Zuñiga, R. B. (1975). The experimenting society and social reform. *American Psychologist,* 30, 99–115.

Contributors

Ruben Ardila received his Ph.D. in experimental psychology from the University of Nebraska-Lincoln and is currently Professor of Psychology at the National University of Colombia. He has published 28 books and over 250 articles in journals from several countries. He has served on the executive committee of the International Union of Psychological Science (IUPsyS) and is a former president of the Interamerican Society of Psychology (SIP).

Geoffrey Blowers is Lecturer in the Department of Psychology and Associate Dean of the Faculty of Social Sciences at the University of Hong Kong. He is co-editor with Alison Turtle of *Psychology Moving East: The Status of Western Psychology in Asia and Oceania* (1987) and co-author with Kieron O'Connor of *Personal Construct Psychology in the Clinical Context* (1996), and he has published papers on the reception of psychology and psychoanalysis in China and Japan.

Adrian C. Brock is Lecturer in Psychology at University College Dublin. He holds an M.Phil. in history and philosophy of science from the University of Cambridge and a Ph.D. in psychology from York University, Toronto. He has published widely on the history of psychology and is the co-editor (with Johann Louw and Willem van Hoorn) of *Rediscovering the History of Psychology: Essays Inspired by the Work of Kurt Danziger* (2004).

Kurt Danziger is Professor Emeritus of Psychology at York University, Toronto, and Honorary Professor of Psychology at the University of Cape Town. He has lived and lectured on psychology in five different continents during his career. His many publications on the history of psychology include *Constructing the Subject* (1990) and *Naming the Mind* (1997). He is currently writing a book on the history of the concept of "memory."

Aydan Gulerce completed her graduate degrees in clinical psychology at the University of Denver and the City University of New York. She is Professor at the Bogazici University in Istanbul, Turkey, where she has been teaching since 1987. Her research interests include transdisciplinarity, (meta)theorizing subjectivity and social transformations, critical psychologies, sociohistorical and cultural psychologies, everyday cognitions of psychological health and development, discourse analysis, psychoanalysis as social practice, familial dynamics and discourse in Turkish society.

John D. Hogan is Professor of Psychology at St. John's University, New York. He received his Ph.D. from Ohio State University in developmental psychology in 1970. His primary scholarly interests are in the history of psychology, international psychology, and developmental psychology, and he has written articles and chapters in each of these areas. He has also served as historian for several academic and professional organizations and is currently the Chair of the Psychology Section of the New York Academy of Sciences.

Naomi Lee is completing a Ph.D. in psychology at Georgetown University. Her research interests include narrative psychology and discursive representations among minority and majority groups. She is multilingual and has conducted field research among diverse groups in North America and Latin America.

Johann Louw is Professor of Psychology at the University of Cape Town. He holds a Ph.D. from the University of Amsterdam and has been working on aspects of the social history of psychology for many years. He is a co-editor (with Adrian Brock and Willem van Hoorn) of *Rediscovering the History of Psychology* (2004), on the work of Kurt Danziger.

Fathali M. Moghaddam is Professor of Psychology at Georgetown University. His most recent books are *Great Ideas in Psychology* (2005), *The Psychology of Rights and Duties* (2004, co-edited with N. Finkel), *Understanding Terrorism* (2004, co-edited with A. J. Marsella), *The Self and Others* (2003, co-edited with R. Harré), and *The Individual and Society* (2002).

Anand C. Paranjpe is Professor Emeritus of Psychology and Humanities at Simon Fraser University, Burnaby, Canada. He obtained his Ph.D. from the University of Poona, India, did postdoctoral work at Harvard University, and has taught at Simon Fraser University since 1967. His main research interests are theoretical psychology and psychological concepts from the intellectual and spiritual traditions of India. His books include *Theoretical Psychology: The Meeting of East and West* (1984), and *Self and Identity in Modern Psychology and Indian Thought* (1998).

Irmingard Staeuble is Professor of Psychology at the Free University Berlin. She holds a Ph.D. in philosophy from the Free University Berlin and has for several years taught in the History Department of U.C.L.A. and in the Philosophy Department of the University of Sydney. She has written articles and chapters on the social history of psychology and the social sciences. She looks forward to her retirement to read and write on aspects of postcolonial social and intellectual history.

Cecilia Taiana holds a Ph.D. in psychology from Carleton University, where she is an Assistant Professor in the School of Social Work. Her scholarly interests are focused in the region of Latin America, in particular Argentina. She has published on issues related to the psychological trauma caused by war and torture. Currently, she is mapping the transatlantic migration and emergence of psychological discourses in Argentina in the first half of the twentieth century and the role of Lacanian psychoanalysis in the last Argentinean dictatorship (1976–1983).

Thomas P. Vaccaro is a doctoral candidate at St. John's University, New York. He has an M.A. degree in psychology from St. John's University and a Cand. Mag. degree from the University of Oslo. He is currently an intern at the Albert Ellis Institute. His published work includes articles on the history of psychology and international psychology.

Index

254 *Index*